Photos, Video and Music with Windows Vista for SENIORS

Studio Visual Steps

Photos, Video and Music with Windows Vista for SENIORS

Learn how to use the Windows Vista tools for digital photos, home videos, music and entertainment

www.visualsteps.com

This book has been written by Yvette Huijsman and Henk Mol
using the Visual Steps™ method.
Translated by Yvette Huijsman and Chris Hollingsworth.
Edited by Marleen Vermeij and Ria Beentjes.
Copyright 2008 by Visual Steps B.V.
Cover design by Studio Willemien Haagsma bNO

First printing: February 2008
ISBN 978 90 5905 065 5

Would you like more information?
www.visualsteps.com

Do you have questions or suggestions?
E-mail: info@visualsteps.com

Website for this book:
www.visualsteps.com/photovista
Here you can register your book.

Register your book
We will keep you aware of any important changes that are necessary to you as a user of the book. You can also take advantage of our periodic newsletter informing you of our product releases, company news, tips & tricks, special offers, etcetera.
www.visualsteps.com/photovista

Table of Contents

Appendices

Foreword

There are a number of tools available in *Windows Vista* that can help you get the most out of your photo, video and music collection. This book provides an introduction to the programs that are bundled with *Vista*. If you are a *Vista* user, this means the programs have already been installed on your computer, so you can get started right away!

Do you like music? With *Vista* you have various options to save, organize and play your music collection. Or would you rather learn something about video editing, photo management or photo editing? These subjects are described extensively in this book.

You can work through this book at your own pace. Our indispensable step by step method emphasizes learning by doing. Each procedure is carefully laid out in small steps with clear instructions and many screenshots. You do not need to fear that you will get lost in any way.

We hope you have fun learning to work with the multimedia programs available in *Windows Vista*!

The Studio Visual Steps Team

P.S.
Your comments and suggestions are most welcome.
Our e-mail address is mail@visualsteps.com

Introduction to Visual Steps™

The Visual Steps handbooks and manuals are the best instructional materials available for learning how to work with computers. Nowhere else can you find better support for getting to know the computer, the Internet, *Windows* and related software programs.

Characteristics of a Visual Steps book:

- **Comprehensible contents**
  Addresses the needs of the beginner or intermediate computer user by a manual written in simple, straightforward language.
- **Clear structure**
  Precise, easy to follow instructions. The material is broken down into smaller segments to allow easy absorption.
- **Screenshots of every step**
  Quickly compare what you see on your screen with the screenshots in the book. Pointers and tips guide you when new windows are opened so you always know what to do next.
- **Get started right away**
  All you have to do is turn on your computer, place the book next to your keyboard, and begin at once.
- **Format**
  The text is formatted to allow easy readability.

In short, I believe these manuals will be excellent guides for you.

dr. H. van der Meij

Faculty of Applied Education, Department of Instruction Technology, University of Twente, the Netherlands

What You Will Need

In order to work through this book, you will need a few things on your computer:

First of all, you need to make sure you have the US version of **Windows Vista** already installed on your computer. You can find out which version of *Windows* you have by turning on your computer and watching what happens in the opening screen.

Windows Vista is available in various editions.
- *Windows Vista Home Basic* *
- *Windows Vista Home Premium*
- *Windows Vista Ultimate*

* Not all programs described in this book are available in Vista Home Basic.

The following programs are described in this book:

- ▶ Windows Media Player — *Windows Media Player 11*
- Windows Movie Maker — *Windows Movie Maker 6*
- Windows Photo Gallery — *Windows Photo Gallery*
- Paint — *Paint*
- Windows DVD Maker — *Windows DVD Maker* *
- Windows Media Center — *Windows Media Center* *

* Not available in Vista Home Basic.

Network and Internet
View network status and tasks

A functioning **Internet connection** is needed for working with certain features in *Windows Media Player* and *Windows Media Center*.

The items pictured here will come in handy. However, if you do not have them, just proceed on to the next section.

Printer

Audio CD

Writable CD and DVD

How to Use This Book

This book utilizes the Visual Steps™-method. It is simple and easy: place the book in your work area so that you can easily see the pages and your computer screen together. A book rest next to your keyboard may be useful. Read the section of your choosing. Each task is carefully explained and a screenshot illustrates each step you need to take. By actually using the program that is described and by working in small steps, your become more confident and your competence steadily improves.

In this Visual Steps™ book you will see various icons. This is what they mean:

Techniques
These icons indicate an action to be carried out:

☞ The mouse icon means you should do something with the mouse.

⌨ The keyboard icon means you should type something on the keyboard.

☞ The hand icon means you should do something else, for example insert a CD-ROM in the computer. It is also used to remind you of something you have learned before.

Extra help is given when we want to alert you about a particular topic.

Help
These icons indicate that extra help is available:

⇨ The arrow icon warns you about something.

✖ The bandage icon will help you if something has gone wrong.

✓ The check mark is used with the exercises. These exercises directly reinforce what you have learned in the chapter you just read.

👣1 Have you forgotten how to do something? The number next to the footsteps tells you where to look it up in **Appendix B How Do I Do That Again?**

In separate boxes you will find tips or additional, background information.

Extra information
Information boxes are denoted by these icons:

 The book icon indicates that background information is available for you to read at your convenience. It is not necessary for any specific task.

 The light bulb icon indicates an extra tip for using the program.

The Reading Order

This book is set up in such a way that you do not necessarily need to work through the book from beginning to end. Work through the chapters at your own pace and in the order you want, depending on your interests.

The CD-ROM in This Book

This book contains a CD-ROM with practice files. In **Appendix A Copying the practice files to your computer**, you can read how to copy the practice files to your computer.

The Screenshots

The screenshots in this book were made on a computer running *Windows Vista Ultimate*. The screenshots may appear slightly different from what you see on your screen. This will depend on which edition of *Vista* you are using and your individual settings. These differences will not prevent you from performing any necessary action. It will be noted in the book when a difference may occur.

How to Continue After This Book?

When you have finished this book, you have familiarized yourself with the *Vista* programs available for working with photos, video and music. Would you like to learn more about photo editing? There are excellent user-friendly photo editing programs available that offer many more options than *Windows Photo Gallery* and *Paint.*

On the website **www.visualsteps.com/digital/book** you can find more information about another book in our *Windows for SENIORS* series: **Digital Photo Editing for SENIORS**. This book is bundled with a CD-ROM containing the full version of the digital photo editing program *ArcSoft PhotoStudio 5.5*.
On the website **www.visualsteps.com** you will find extensive information on other available titles. For every title listed, there is a complete table of contents and a chapter excerpt (PDF files) for you to preview. All Visual Steps books have been written using the same step by step method. If you like this method, do not hesitate to try another Visual Steps book.
If you have a question about a book, or need some additional information, you can send an e-mail to **mail@visualsteps.com.**

Test Your Knowledge

When you have completed this book, you can test your knowledge by taking one of the free tests available on the website **www.ccforseniors.com**
These multiple choice tests will show you how much you know about the computer, *Windows* and related programs.
If you pass the test, you are eligible to receive a Free Computer Certificate by e-mail.
There are **no costs** involved in taking part in these tests. The test website is a free service provided to subscribers of the free Visual Steps newsletter.

Newsletter

All Visual Steps books follow the same methodology: each new concept is carefully explained in small steps and richly illustrated with screenshots.

A listing of all available books can be found on **www.visualsteps.com**
Visit our website and subscribe to the **free Visual Steps Newsletter** sent by e-mail.

The Visual Steps Newsletter provides periodic information about:
- the latest titles and previously released books;
- special offers, free guides;
- news about recent updates that may apply to a Visual Steps book.

Our Newsletter subscribers have access to free information booklets, handy tips and guides which are listed on the webpages **www.visualsteps.com/info_downloads** and the tips on **www.visualsteps.com/tips**

For Teachers

This book is designed as a self-study guide. It is also well suited for use in a group or a classroom setting. A free teacher's manual (PDF file) is available.
The teacher's manual and other additional materials regarding this book can be found on our website: **www.visualsteps.com/photovista**

1. Playing a CD

In the last few decades the computer has slowly evolved into an Internet and entertainment center. With the *Vista* program *Windows Media Player* you have an extensive CD player at your disposal. It has the same functionality as the CD player in your stereo system, plus several other useful features.

In this chapter you will learn how to play a CD, how to quickly go to the next or previous track, how to make the CD repeat and how to play tracks in random order.

When your computer is connected to the Internet, *Windows Media Player* can retrieve information about the tracks of the CD you are playing. Then the titles of the tracks and the CD cover are displayed. Different graphic *visualizations* that move to the sound of the music are another way to visualize the music you play.

For musical connoisseurs *Windows Media Player* is equipped with a *graphic equalizer*. You can use it to change certain frequencies in your music according to your own taste.

In this chapter you will learn how to:

- open *Windows Media Player*;
- adjust the settings of the program;
- play an audio CD;
- go to another track;
- play the tracks in random order;
- set up automatic replay;
- find track and CD information on the Internet;
- choose visualizations and change audio settings.

⇨ **Please note:**

To be able to work through this chapter you need an audio CD. The examples provided in this chapter were made using a CD featuring *Elvis Costello* and *Burt Bacharach*:

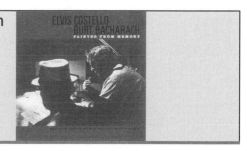

If you prefer, you can select a CD from your own audio library to use with this chapter.

1.1 Setting Up Windows Media Player

Windows Media Player is a *Vista* multimedia application with several different features. In this chapter you will learn how to play music from an audio CD.
This is how you open *Windows Media Player*:

☞ **Turn on your computer**

☞ **If necessary, turn on the monitor**

☞ **If necessary, enter the password for your user account**

👆 **Click**

👆 **Click** ▶ All Programs

You see *Windows Media Player* somewhere in your programs list:

👆 **Click**
  ▶ Windows Media Player

When you start *Windows Media Player* for the first time, you will need to configure some initial settings for the program. You can use the default settings.

⇨ **Please note:**

If you started *Windows Media Player* before, you will not see the next window. Then you can proceed to the next step.

Click the option
  ○ Express Settings (Recommen

Click [Finish]

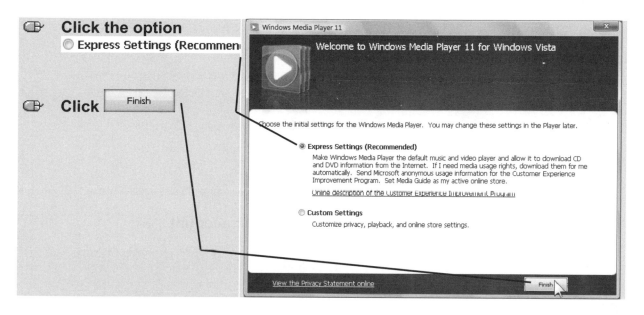

As soon as you have chosen the settings, *Windows Media Player* starts to look for music files on your computer.

After a few moments you see
the songs that were found:

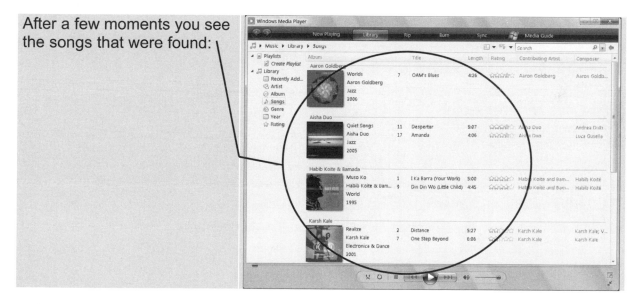

⇨ **Please note:**

You may see different songs in your *Windows Media Player* window than you see in this example.

You are going to change some default settings. If you have used *Windows Media Player* before, please check if the settings on your computer are the same:

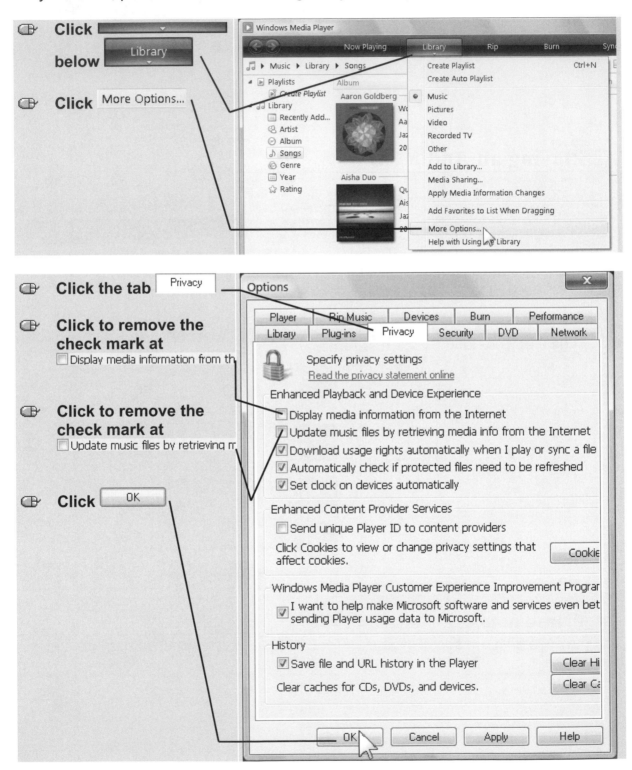

Click ⬛⬛⬛⬛ ▼ below | Library |

Click | More Options... |

Click the tab | Privacy |

Click to remove the check mark at
☐ Display media information from th

Click to remove the check mark at
☐ Update music files by retrieving m

Click | OK |

Click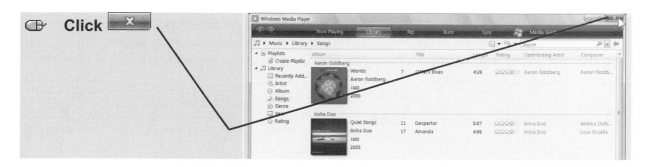

1.2 Playing an Audio CD

In the previous section you made *Windows Media Player* the default player for most audio files. When you insert an audio CD in your CD/DVD player, *Windows* will use *Media Player* to play it.

➡ **Please note:**

To be able to work through the rest of this chapter, you need an audio CD. The CD used in this example is:	

By default, *Windows* plays audio CDs using *Windows Media Player*. See what happens when you insert an audio CD in your computer:

☞ **Insert an audio CD from your own collection in the CD or DVD drive of your computer**

☞ **Close the drawer carefully**

In most cases the window below will appear. *Windows* recognizes the CD you placed in the CD/DVD player as an audio CD. To prevent this window from appearing again, you make sure that all audio CDs are played in *Media Player* as soon as you insert them in the CD/DVD player:

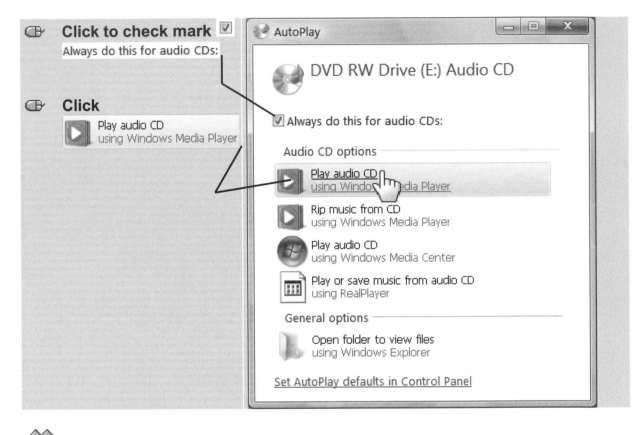

HELP! Nothing happens after inserting the CD.

If an audio CD will not play after you have inserted it, there may be protection mechanisms that disable playback on a computer. In that case, try a different CD.

✖ HELP! I do not see that window.

If the *Windows Media Player* window opens directly, then *Windows Media Player* has already been set as the default player for audio CDs.

✖ HELP! Another program is opened.

Does another program start after you insert an audio CD? Then this program has been set as the default player for your audio CDs. Refer to the Tip at the end of this chapter to see how you can make *Windows Media Player* the default player.

The *Windows Media Player* window is opened and the CD starts playing.
The songs on a CD are called *tracks*. This word will also be used in this book.

The first track is played: ——

You may see shapes moving. These moving graphics are called *visualizations*:

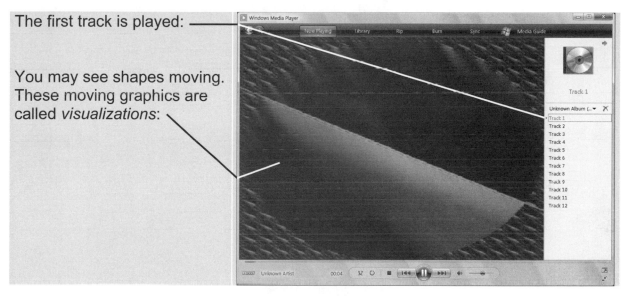

✖ HELP! The volume is too loud or too soft.

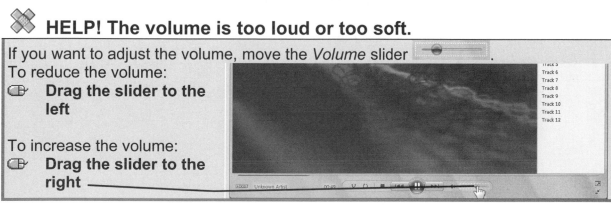

If you want to adjust the volume, move the *Volume* slider ⬤.
To reduce the volume:
☞ **Drag the slider to the left**

To increase the volume:
☞ **Drag the slider to the right** ——

💡 Tip

Quickly mute the volume?

To mute the volume, click 🔊.

To restore the volume, click 🔇.

Just like on your regular CD or DVD player, there is a button you can use to go to the next track:

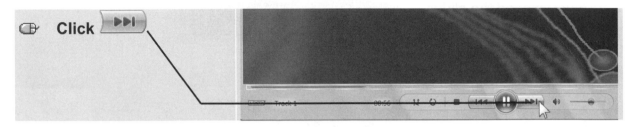

Click ▶▶|

You can return to the previous track like this:

Track 2 is played: ——

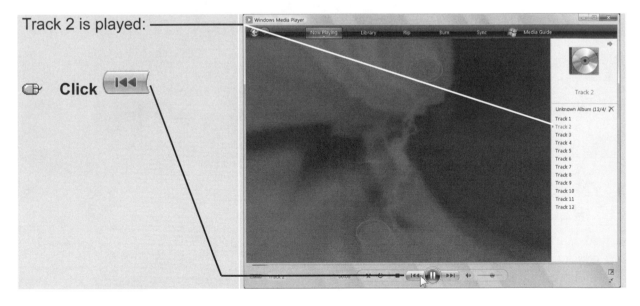

Click |◀◀

◌ **Tip**

Quickly find a certain part of a track
While the track is played, you see a slider ▬▬▬ move from the left to the right below the visualization window. You can use this slider to find a certain part of a track.

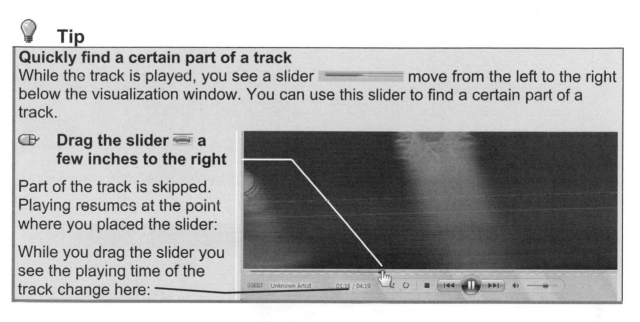

☞ **Drag the slider ▭ a few inches to the right**

Part of the track is skipped. Playing resumes at the point where you placed the slider:

While you drag the slider you see the playing time of the track change here: ─────

You can also pause playing the audio CD:

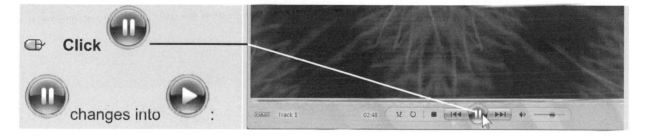

☞ **Click** ⏸ ───── changes into ▶ :

1.3 Playing the Tracks in Random Order

Windows Media Player contains a feature you already know from your regular CD player: the ability to play tracks in random order. This is also known as *shuffle*. In *Windows Media Player* you can turn *shuffle* on like this:

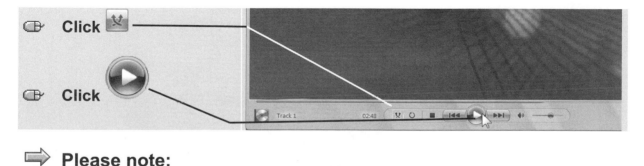

☞ **Click** 🔀 ─────

☞ **Click** ▶

⇨ **Please note:**

It is not possible to play a DVD in random order.

The music continues at track 1. When you skip to the next track now, a random track will be chosen. Give it a try:

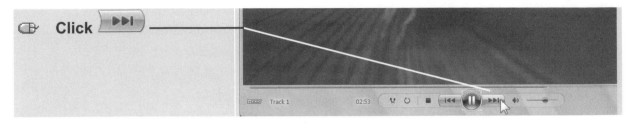

1.4 Repeating

You can also make the tracks repeat:

The tracks are now played in random order. As soon as the CD has finished, it is played again.

⇨ **Please note:**

It is not possible to repeat playing a DVD.

To repeat the tracks in the normal order, just turn shuffle off:

You can also turn the repeat function off:

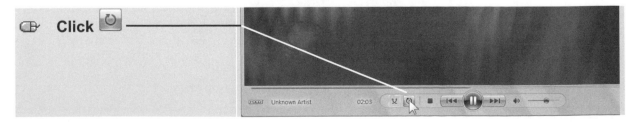

Now the CD is played in the correct order. When the last track has finished, *Windows Media Player* will stop playing the CD.
You can stop playing this audio CD yourself like this:

Click ■ ——

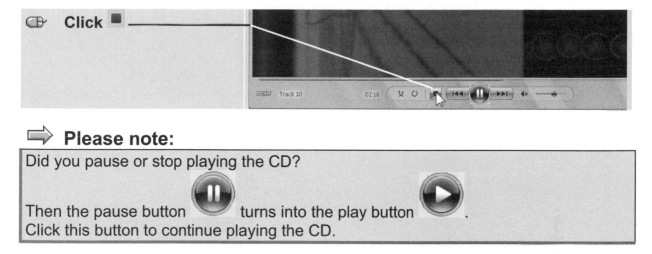

⇨ **Please note:**

Did you pause or stop playing the CD?

Then the pause button turns into the play button .
Click this button to continue playing the CD.

1.5 Downloading Media Information from the Internet

If an Internet connection is available while you play your CD, *Windows Media Player* can search for information about the CD. As soon as the information is found, the correct track titles and the CD cover are displayed.

⇨ **Please note:**

To be able to work through this section you need an Internet connection. If you do not have an Internet connection, you can skip to the next section.

First there are some settings to change:

Click

below

Click More Options...

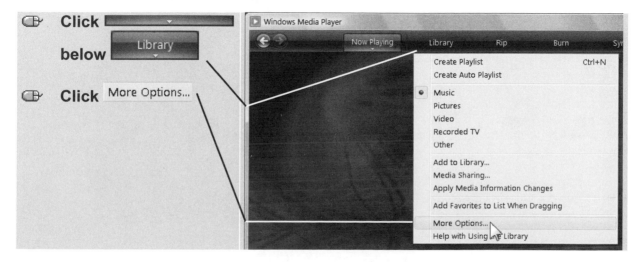

☞ **Click the tab** | Privacy |

☞ **Click to place a check
mark by**
☑ Display media information from th

☞ **Click to place a check
mark by**
☑ Update music files by retrieving m

☞ **Click** | OK |

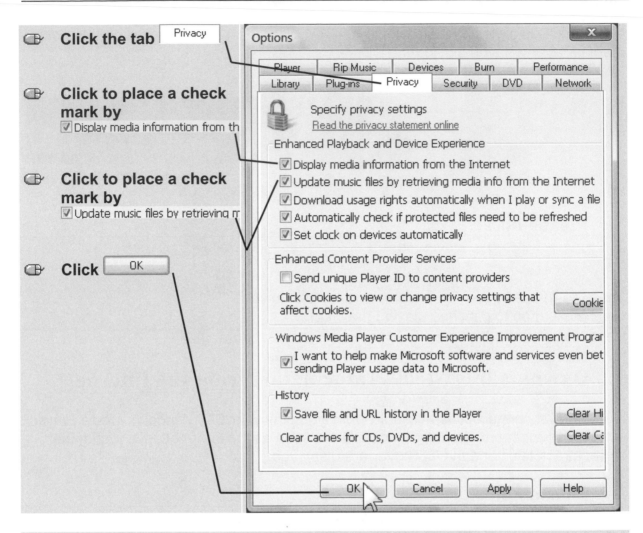

☞ **If necessary, connect to the Internet**

Windows Media Player
downloads information about
the CD:
You see the titles of the
tracks in the *List Pane*:

☞ **Click**

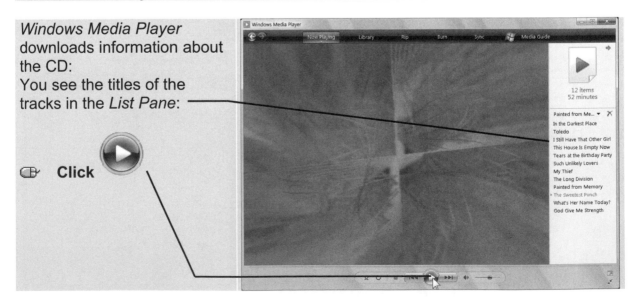

When the CD is played you also see the CD cover:

You will see the CD cover of your selected CD on your PC.

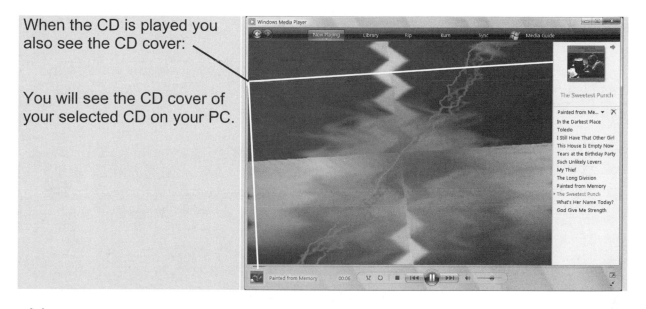

⊗ HELP! I do not see a track list or CD cover.

Not every CD can be found on the Internet. For some CDs the track list or cover may not be displayed. Try another CD if this happens.

In the next chapters of this book you will see that the track information is very useful when you play and organize tracks on your computer.

☞ If necessary, disconnect from the Internet

The information about this CD is also stored in the *Library*. This means that when you play the CD in the future, the track information is displayed immediately. In chapter 3 you will be introduced to the *Library*.

⇨ Please note:

Media information is downloaded automatically
According to the default settings of *Media Player*, the media information is downloaded automatically when you insert a CD in the CD player if there is an Internet connection. Using the settings you changed at the beginning of this chapter, it is not done automatically.

1.6 Quickly Changing Tracks

In the *List Pane* on the right side of the *Windows Media Player* window you see the track list of the CD. When you double-click a track, *Windows Media Player* 'jumps' to this track:

Double-click the fourth track for example

Windows Media Player now continues playing track 4 of the CD.

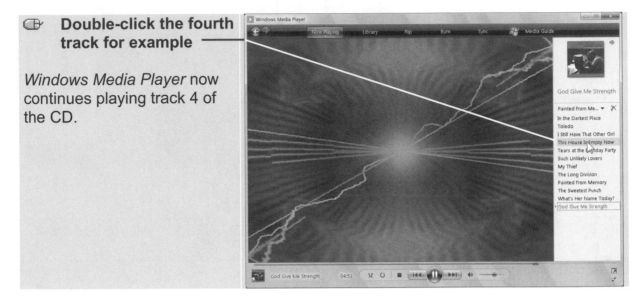

1.7 Visualizations

The moving patterns in the *Windows Media Player* window are called *visualizations*. There are many visualizations to choose from. You can do that like this:

Click [▾] below Now Playing

Click Visualizations

Click Bars and Waves

Click Fire Storm

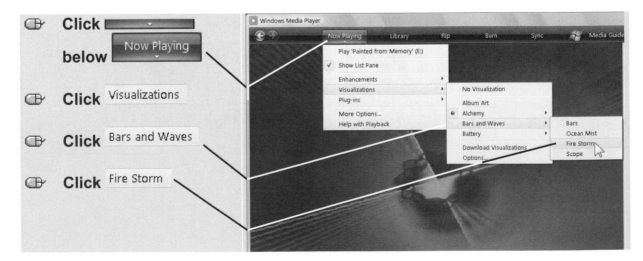

You see that the new visualization moves to the sound of the music:

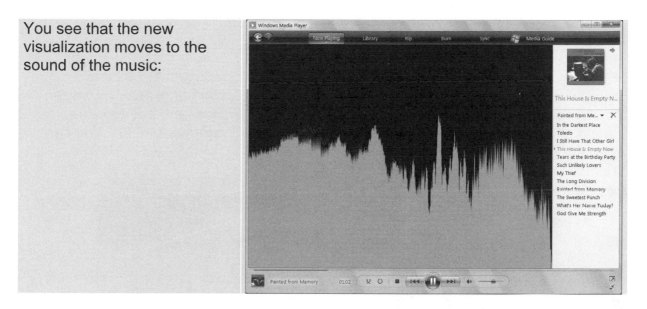

If you do not want a moving visualization, you can just view the CD cover instead.

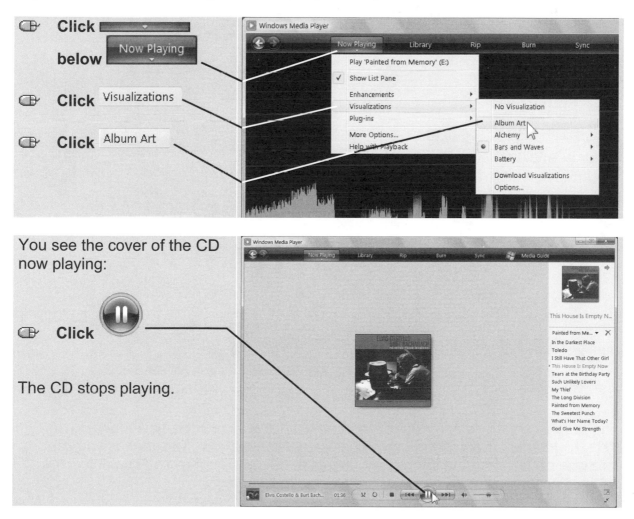

Click ⬇ below **Now Playing**

Click Visualizations

Click Album Art

You see the cover of the CD now playing:

Click ⏸

The CD stops playing.

1.8 The Graphic Equalizer

Windows Media Player is a very complete program for playing music. Just like a good stereo sound system, *Windows Media Player* is equipped with a *graphic equalizer*. You can use the graphic equalizer to adjust the way high, low and mid tones are played. It contains a wide variety of presets, for different genres of music. You can open the graphic equalizer like this:

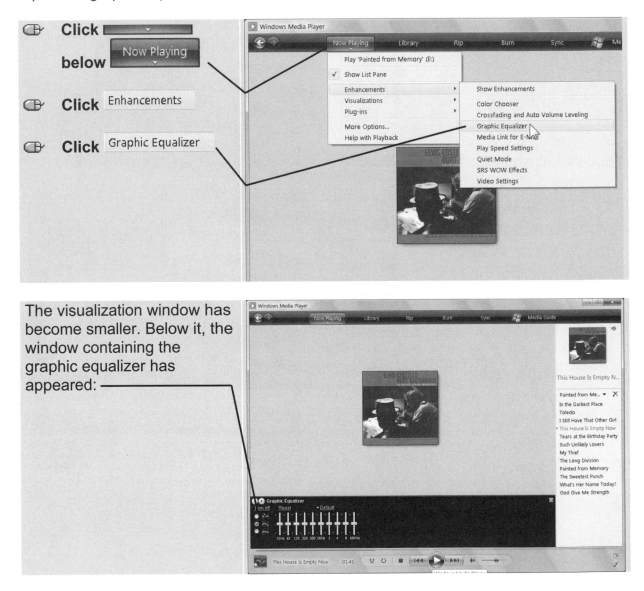

The graphic equalizer consists of ten bands, ranging from 31Hz (low tones) to 16 KHz (high tones). Each band can be adjusted using a slider. This means you can increase or decrease the intensity of certain frequency ranges. You can adjust the settings according to the genre of music you are listening to.

You can try one of the presets first:

👆 **Click ▼ beside** `Default`

👆 **Click** `Classical`

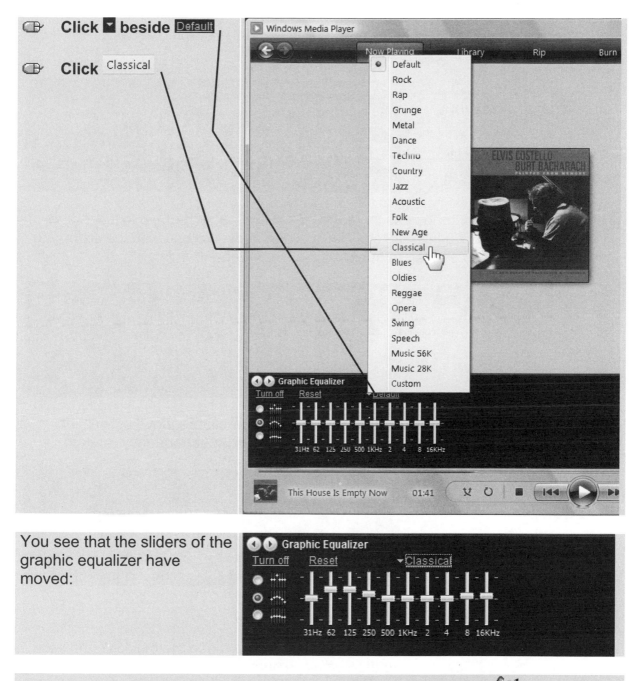

You see that the sliders of the graphic equalizer have moved:

☞ **Continue playing the CD to hear the effect of this change** 🎧¹

Sometimes the changes are very subtle. It is possible that you do not hear the difference very clearly. The next section will show you how to adjust the settings of the graphic equalizer manually.

1.9 Setting the Graphic Equalizer Manually

You can adjust the settings of each individual slider of the graphic equalizer in *Media Player*. You do that by dragging the sliders up and down:

☞ **Drag the slider ⊡ at 31Hz all the way up**

You see that the other sliders move up a bit as well:

The intensity of the low tones has increased. At the same time, the mid tones and high tones have shifted a little bit too. These sliders moved along with the slider you dragged. You can also choose to move each slider independently:

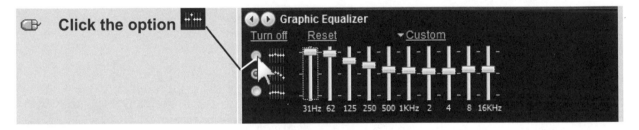

☞ **Click the option**

Now you can move each slider without having the other sliders move as well. For example, you can decrease the intensity of the three highest frequency ranges:

☞ **Drag the sliders at 4, 8 and 16KHz all the way down**

The other sliders did not move.

The increased low tones and the decreased high tones make the music sound very muffled. You can quickly return to the default setting:

☞ **Click Reset**

Now the sliders are lined up again.

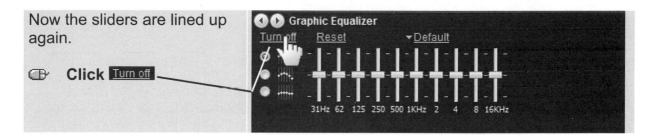

☞ **Click** Turn off

You can close the graphic equalizer window:

☞ **Click** ⊠

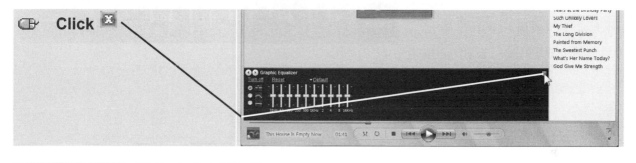

☞ **Stop playing the CD** 𝓁𝓅²

☞ **Remove the CD from the CD/DVD player**

In this chapter you have learned how to play audio CDs in *Windows Media Player*. In the next section you find some exercises you can use to repeat the tasks covered in this chapter.

1.10 Exercises

The following exercises help you to practice what you have learned in this chapter. Have you forgotten how to do something? Use the number beside the footsteps to look it up in the appendix *How Do I Do That Again?*

Exercise: Playing a CD

Windows Media Player offers you the same features as a modern stereo system, with extra possibilities for graphics.

☑ Insert an audio CD in your CD/DVD player.

☑ Stop playing the CD. $\ell\ell^2$

☑ Play the third track. $\ell\ell^1$

☑ Play the tracks in random order. $\ell\ell^{43}$

☑ Go to the next track. $\ell\ell^{44}$

☑ Change the visualization. $\ell\ell^{45}$

☑ Open the graphic equalizer and turn it on. $\ell\ell^{46}$

☑ Select the preset genre *Rock*. $\ell\ell^{47}$

☑ Return to the default settings. $\ell\ell^{48}$

☑ Close the graphic equalizer. $\ell\ell^{49}$

☑ Turn off playing the tracks in random order. $\ell\ell^{43}$

☑ Remove the audio CD from your CD/DVD player.

☑ Close *Windows Media Player*. $\ell\ell^3$

1.11 Background Information

Glossary	
Mute	(Temporarily) turn off the volume.
Equalizer	Slider to change certain frequency ranges in music.
Library	The location in *Windows Media Player* that lists all of the music, videos, and pictures on your computer.
Shuffle	Play tracks in random order.
Track	An individual song or other discrete piece of audio content.
Visualization	A graphical display that constantly changes in response to the audio signal in *Windows Media Player*.

Source: Windows Help and Support

What is digital music?
Digital music is music that has been converted to the only language a computer can understand: ones and zeroes. The ones and zeroes can be decoded in a computer program like *Windows Media Player*, enabling you to listen to the music.

Digital music is as old as the CD, the Compact Disc. With the introduction of the CD format, analog music (from LPs) was stored digitally for the first time. The CD player in your stereo system is capable of converting this digital data (the large amount of ones and zeroes) into music.

The digital files on a CD are not suitable for use on your computer or the Internet. That is because the files are very large. A four minute track takes up about 40 MB of disk space. For a typical music CD you need about 600 MB of space.

File types

Windows Media Player can work with many file types. The different file types can be identified by their *extension*, the letter/number combination preceded by a (.) that follows the file name. These are the most important file types for *Windows Media Player*:

- *MP3*. This is the most widely used file type for music. The abbreviation *MP3* stands for *MPEG Audio Layer-3*. MPEG is a way to compress video and audio files. Compressing decreases the file size, making it easier to send files over the Internet. MP3 is the most popular way to compress audio files: the files become a lot smaller while the quality remains good. When music is exchanged on the Internet, most of the time MP3 files are used.

- *WMA*. This abbreviation stands for *Windows Media Audio*. This file type is developed by *Microsoft* as an alternative for the MP3 file type. WMA compresses audio files a lot, while the quality remains good.
  The special thing about this file type is that WMA files can be protected. This way copyright holders can prevent music from being copied.
  WMA is less popular than MP3.

- *WAV*. This is the file type used most on computers. For example, the system sounds you hear when you turn on your computer or receive an e-mail have this format. Usually, WAV files are only used for short sound fragments because these files become very large very quickly.

- *MIDI*. This abbreviation stands for *Musical Instrument Digital Interface*. These sound files themselves do not sound very good, but they contain information that can be used to control a sound card.

- *CDA*. This abbreviation stands for *CD Audio*. These are the audio files you find on an audio CD. They can be played in regular CD players, like the CD player in your car or your home stereo system. CDA files have excellent quality.

- *ASF*. Short for *Advanced Streaming Format*. This is a format for *streaming audio* and *streaming video* developed by *Microsoft*. These are audio and video files that can be played on the Internet while you are downloading them. These files are not stored on the hard disk of your computer.

1.12 Tips

💡 Tip

A different player

It is possible that your audio and video files are not played in *Windows Media Player*. Another player, like *Real Player* opens instead. If you want to change this setting and make *Windows Media Player* your default player, follow these steps:

☞ **Open the *Control Panel* 👣⁴**

👉 **Click**

Play CDs or other media automaticall

👉 **Click ▾ beside**

💿 Audio CD

👉 **Click**

▶ Play audio CD using Windows Media Player

👉 **Click** Save

☞ **Close the *Control Panel* 👣³**

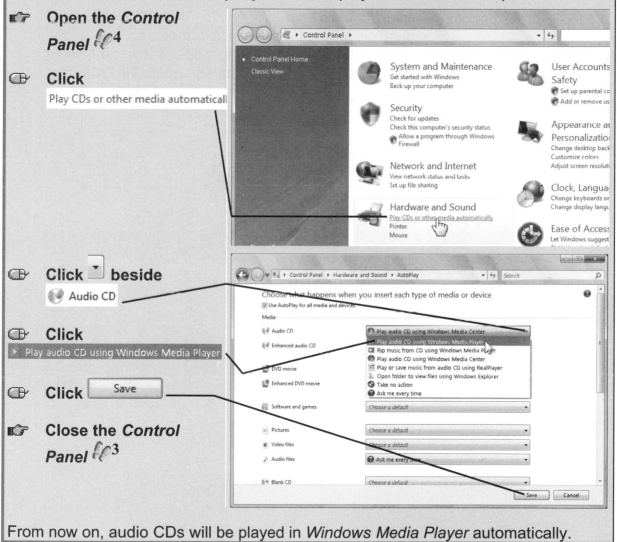

From now on, audio CDs will be played in *Windows Media Player* automatically.

Notes

Write down your notes here.

2. Ripping a CD

You have probably heard the word 'ripping' before. It means converting the tracks on an audio CD to files that can be used on a computer.

In *Windows Media Player* you can create *MP3* or *WMA* files from the tracks on an audio CD. These files take up less space than the regular audio files on your CD. You can play these files on your computer as well as an MP3 player. An MP3 player is a small portable device for playing MP3 files. In addition, you can use these files to create a compilation CD with your favorite tracks.

In *Windows Media Player* you can determine the audio quality you want to use to rip the tracks. You can also change the file name of the ripped files so that they are easier to find and organize at a later time.

Ripping a CD and saving the tracks to the hard disk of your computer for your own use, is a convenient way to safeguard your CD collection. However, sharing these files with other music lovers is not allowed.

In this chapter you learn how to:

- prepare to rip a CD;
- adjust the audio quality;
- change the file names of the ripped tracks;
- rip CDs;
- find and play the ripped tracks;
- organize tracks.

⇨ Please note:

To be able to work through this chapter you need two audio CDs. In the examples, the CDs of Elvis Costello & Burt Bacharach and Neil Diamond are used.

If you prefer, you can use CDs from your own collection.

2.1 Preparing to Rip a CD

Windows Media Player makes it very easy to copy the tracks of a CD to the hard disk of your computer. This process is also called *ripping.* When the tracks are stored on the hard disk of your computer, you no longer need to insert the audio CD to play your favorite music.

☞ **Open *Windows Media Player*** *𝓁℘⁵*

First you are going to check if the automatic rip feature has been turned off. This enables you to adjust the settings before you start to rip a CD:

Click ▭   **below** ▭ Library

Click More Options...

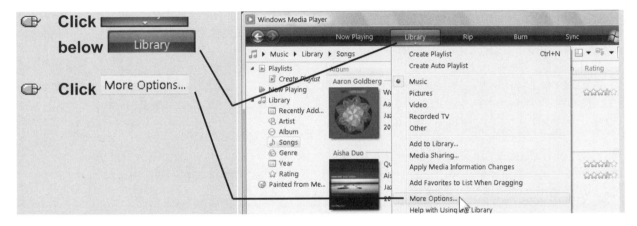

Click the tab Rip Music

Is the option Rip CD when inserted check marked ☑?

Then click Rip CD when inserted

The box changes into ☐:

Click OK

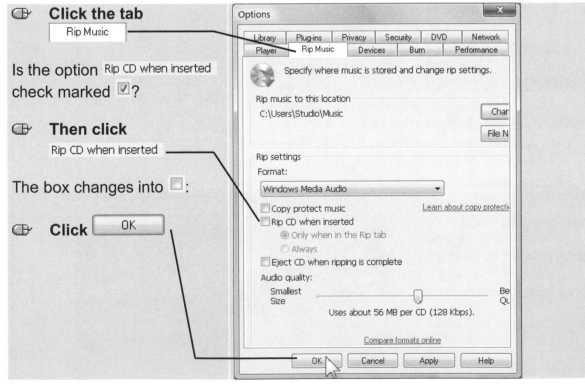

☞ **Insert a CD from your own collection in the CD/DVD player**

The CD starts playing automatically.

☞ **Stop playing the CD** *ℰℓ²*

There is a special tab for ripping CDs in the *Windows Media Player* window:

Click   Rip

The tab *Rip* opens.

You see that every track on
the CD is check marked:

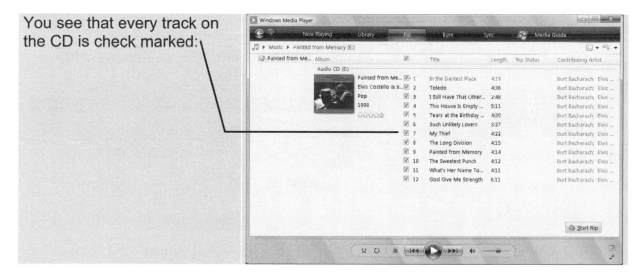

Before you start copying the tracks, you choose the file format and audio quality.

2.2 Adjusting the Audio Quality

By default, *Windows Media Player* rips tracks to the *Windows Media Audio (WMA)* format. This is the format developed by *Microsoft* itself. You can also rip the tracks in the more popular MP3 format. You can do that like this:

Next you can choose the *audio quality*. The quality of ripped MP3 files is measured by the *bit rate* (speed) that was used to rip the CD. When you choose a higher bit rate, the quality of the MP3 files will improve.

Please note that the size of MP3 files increases when a higher bit rate is used. At a low bit rate of 128 kbps, the ripped tracks of a CD take up about 56 MB of space. At the highest bit rate of 320 kbps you need 144 MB of space on the hard disk of your computer for the same tracks.

You choose the highest bit rate of 320 kbps. You can adjust the bit rate like this:

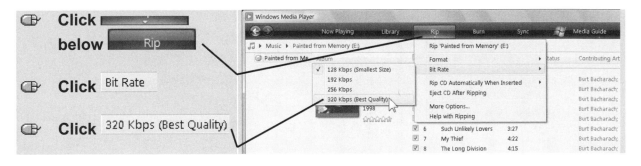

💡 Tip

Bit rate
When you rip a track just to listen to it on your computer, a low bit rate of 128 kbps is sufficient. The quality of computer speakers is usually not good enough to be able to hear the difference between the original CD track and a ripped track.

When you plan to copy the tracks to an audio CD that can also be played on your regular home stereo system, it is better to choose a bit rate of at least 192 kbps or higher. At higher bit rates the quality of the MP3 files comes closer to the quality of the original files on the audio CD.

2.3 Adjusting the File Names of Ripped Tracks

When you plan to rip a lot of CDs, it is a good idea to set a fixed file naming convention. That will make it easier to find and organize your files later. This is how you can adjust the file name:

☞ **Click** 
below ▊ Rip

☞ **Click** More Options...

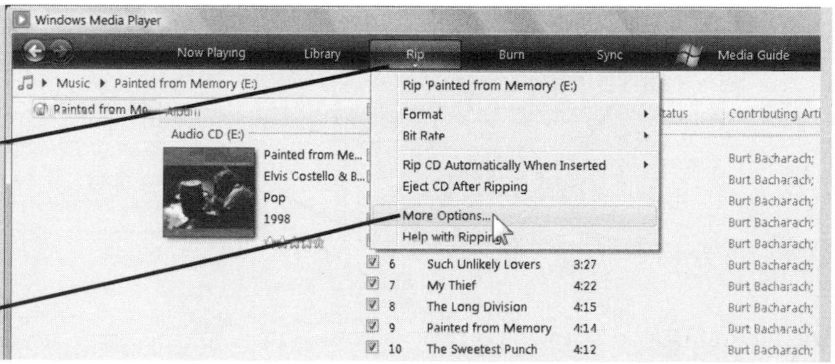

☞ **Click** File N

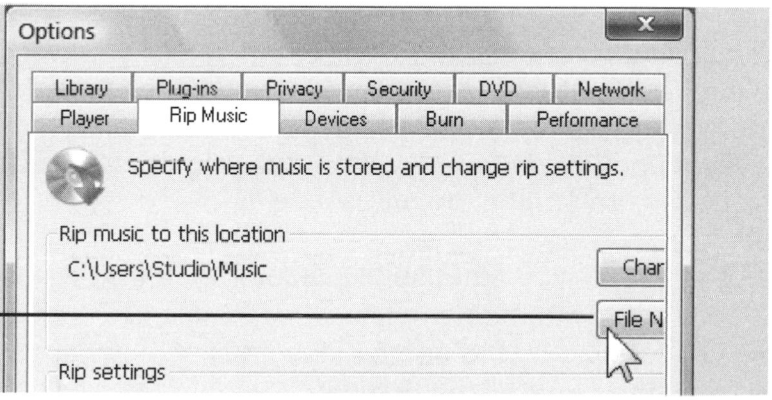

In this window you can select which details to include in the file names of the copied tracks.

Windows Media Player suggests that you include the track number and the song title in the file names:

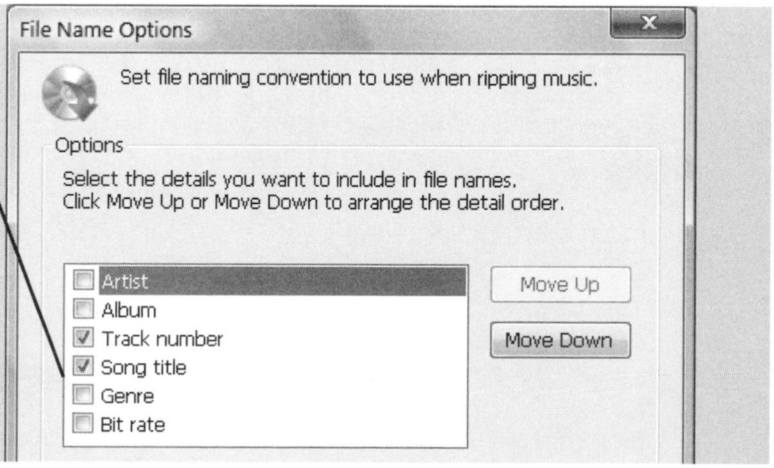

The names of the artist and the album, as well as the track number, are automatically imported in *Windows Media Player*. In other programs that may not happen automatically. That is why it is a good idea to add these details to the file name:

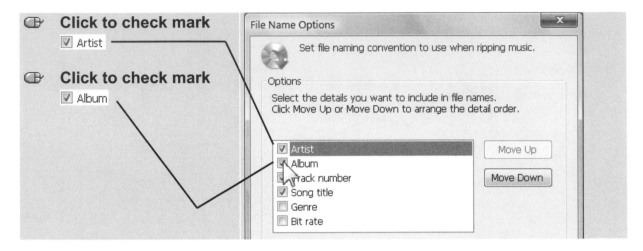

You can also change the order of the details you want to include in the file name. Keep in mind that the tracks are sorted by the first element of their file name. By default, tracks can be sorted by artist, album and track number in *Windows Media Player* and in *Windows Explorer*. Starting the file name with the song title then gives you an extra sorting option.

For example, you can use this order for the file names:
- you start with the song title
- you follow it by the name of the artist
- then the name of the original CD where the track comes from
- and finally the track number on the original CD

To move *Song title* to the top of the list:

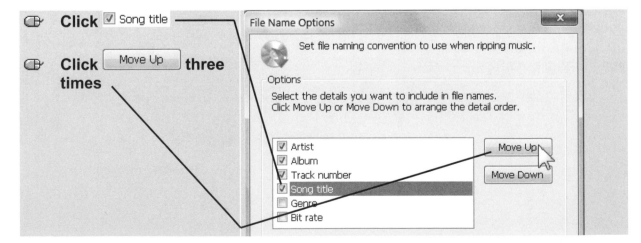

You can also change the separator that is placed between the various details in the file name. In this example, select the dash:

The *Song title* is on top of the list:

→ **Click** next to

Separator: _____

→ **Click** - (Dash)

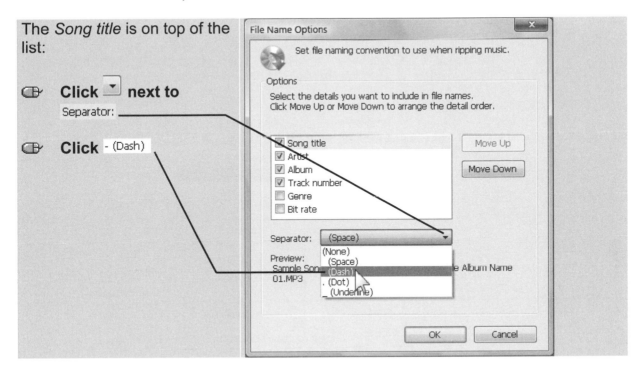

You have now finished setting the file name.

→ **Click** OK

You can also close the
Options window:

☞ **Click** [OK]

Options

| Library | Plug-ins | Privacy | Security | DVD | Network |
| Player | Rip Music | Devices | Burn | Performance |

Specify where music is stored and change rip settings.

Rip music to this location

C:\Users\Studio\Music   Char

File N

Rip settings

Format:

MP3

☐ Copy protect music   Learn about copy protecti

☐ Rip CD when inserted
   ○ Only when in the Rip tab
   ○ Always
☐ Eject CD when ripping is complete

Audio quality:

Smallest   Be
Size   Qu
         Uses about 144 MB per CD (320 Kbps)

Compare formats online

[OK]   [Cancel]   [Apply]   [Help]

2.4 Ripping a CD

Now that you have finished adjusting the settings, you can start ripping the CD:

☞ **Click** [Start Rip]

Windows Media Player

| Now Playing | Library | Rip | Burn | Sync | Media Guide |

Music ▶ Painted from Memory (E:)

Painted from Me...

Album	☑	Title	Length	Rip Status	Contributing Artist
Audio CD (E:)					
Painted from Me... ☑ 1		In the Darkest Place	4:19		Burt Bacharach; Elvis ...
Elvis Costello & B... ☑ 2		Toledo	4:36		Burt Bacharach; Elvis ...
Pop ☑ 3		I Still Have That Other...	2:48		Burt Bacharach; Elvis ...
1998 ☑ 4		This House Is Empty ...	5:11		Burt Bacharach; Elvis ...
☑ 5		Tears at the Birthday ...	4:39		Burt Bacharach; Elvis ...
☑ 6		Such Unlikely Lovers	3:27		Burt Bacharach; Elvis ...
☑ 7		My Thief	4:22		Burt Bacharach; Elvis ...
☑ 8		The Long Division	4:15		Burt Bacharach; Elvis ...
☑ 9		Painted from Memory	4:14		Burt Bacharach; Elvis ...
☑ 10		The Sweetest Punch	4:12		Burt Bacharach; Elvis ...
☑ 11		What's Her Name To...	4:11		Burt Bacharach; Elvis ...
☑ 12		God Give Me Strength	6:11		Burt Bacharach; Elvis ...

Start Rip

In the `Rip Status` column you see the progress of the ripping process for each track `Ripping (50%)`:

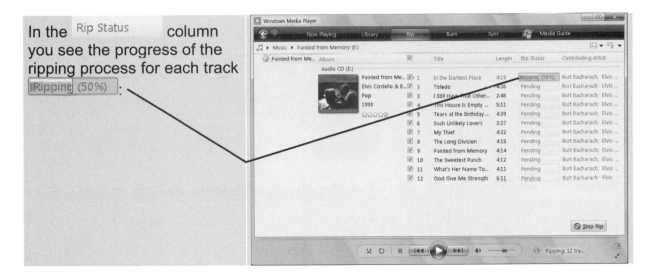

💡 Tip

Stop ripping

You can stop ripping the CD at any time by clicking ⊘ Stop Rip.

You see the message `Ripped to lib...` next to each ripped track:

As soon as the last track has been ripped, the 🌐 Start Rip button appears again:

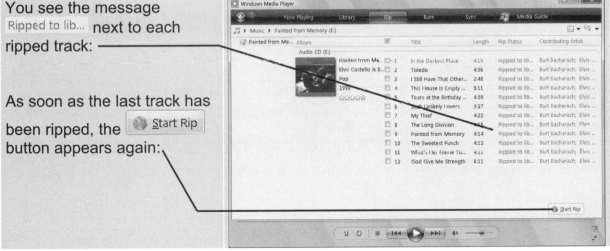

☞ **Remove the CD from the CD/DVD player**

2.5 Ripping Another CD

Now that all the rip settings are correct, ripping another CD is a piece of cake.

☞   **If necessary, connect to the Internet**

☞   **Insert another CD in the CD/DVD player**

The CD starts playing
automatically again.

When you are connected to
the Internet and the details of
this CD are found, they are
displayed automatically:

☞   **Click** ■

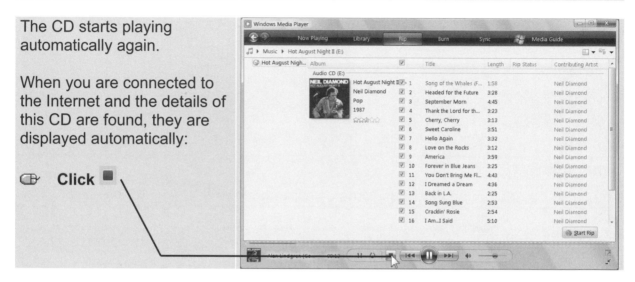

⇨   **Please note:**

Listening to your CD while you rip it does not harm the ripping process. However,
ripping will start at the track that is currently being played. It may be more convenient
to stop the playing of the CD first before ripping.

The track names are neatly listed. Now you can rip the tracks of this CD as well.

✖ HELP! The CD information is not displayed.

Sometimes it takes a few minutes before the album information is displayed in
Windows Media Player. It is also possible that you see the CD cover in the bottom
left corner of the window, but not yet next to the track list. When you stop and restart
playing the CD, that image will usually appear next to the track list.

If you still do not see the CD information, the information may not yet have been
added to the *Windows Media* database. This happens frequently with new
commercial CDs. Also a CD containing a custom mix may lack individual track
information. You may want to try another CD in this case.

☞   **If necessary, disconnect from the Internet**

💡 Tip

> If you do not want to rip every track on the CD, just click to uncheck the tracks you do not want, for example ☐ 6   Sweet Caroline .

🖰 **Click** [🌐 Start Rip]

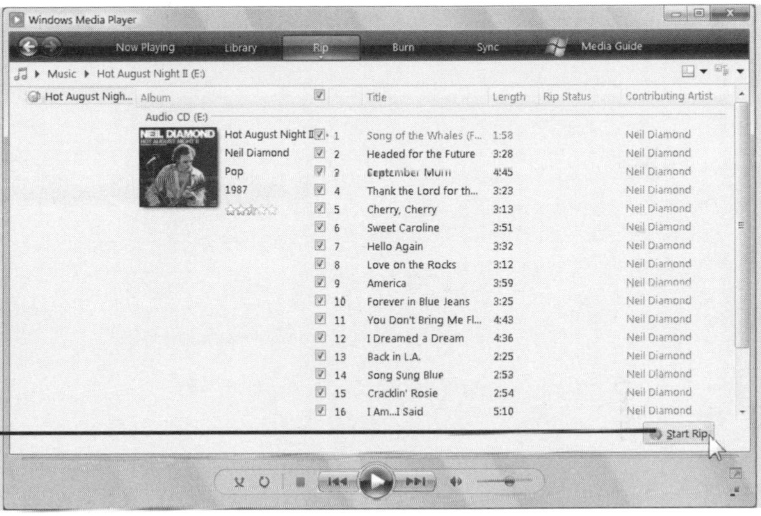

As soon as the ripping has finished, the tracks are unchecked ☐ and the message Ripped to lib... appears after each track:

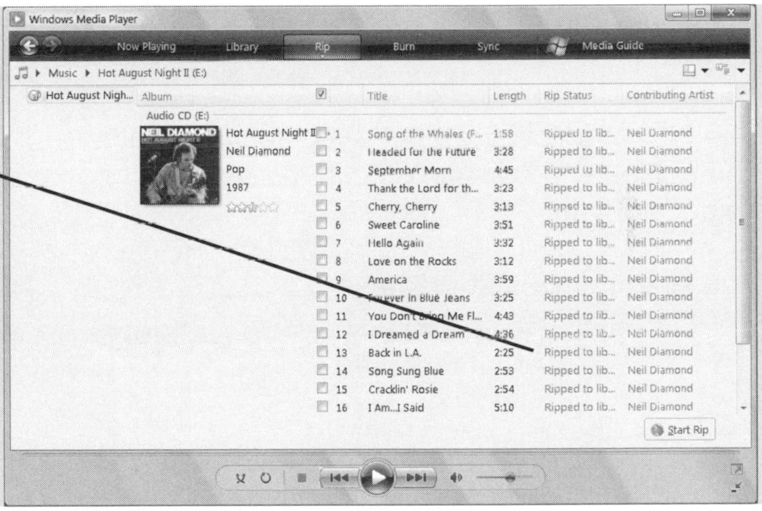

In the next section you are going to see where the ripped tracks have been saved on your computer.

☞ **Remove the CD from the CD/DVD player**

☞ **Close *Media Player* 🐾³**

2.6 Finding the Ripped Tracks on the Hard Disk

The tracks of both audio CDs have been copied to the folder *Music* on the hard disk of your computer. You can verify that:

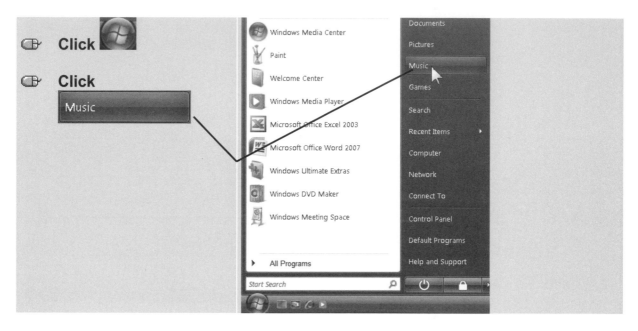

Click

Click

Music

The *Music* folder is opened. You see the contents of this folder in the file list. The contents may be displayed differently on your computer. This depends on the settings of your PC.

You see that two folders have been created. These folders have the names of the artists of the ripped audio CDs.
Open the first folder:

Double-click

Elvis Costello & Burt Bacharach

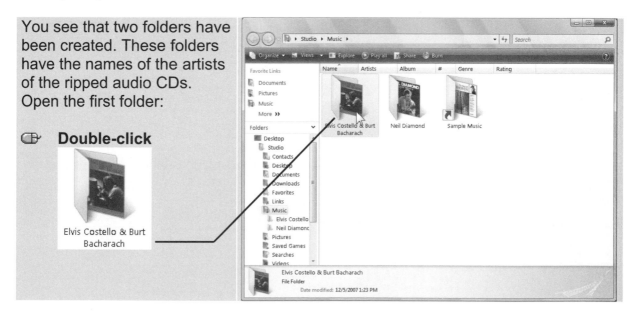

On your computer this folder is named after the artist of the CD you ripped.

This folder contains a new folder with the title of the audio CD. When you rip several CDs of the same artist, each CD has its own folder here. Open this folder now:

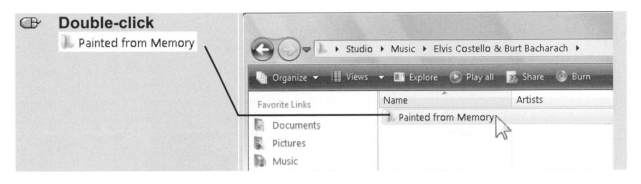

Double-click Painted from Memory

HELP! The window looks a lot different.

Depending on the settings of your computer, the albums may be displayed differently. You can customize the *view* settings to see the file details like this:

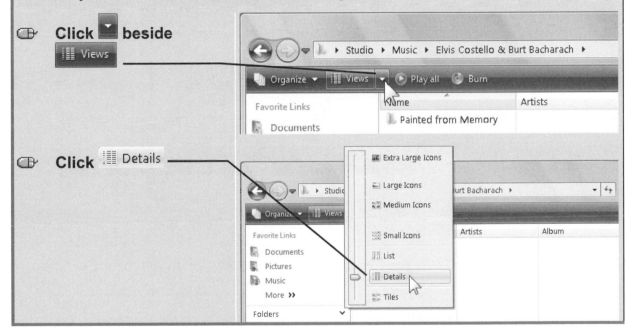

Click ▾ beside **Views**

Click Details

You see the ripped tracks. The file names have the format you have defined earlier:

⇨ **Please note:**

You also see the artists, album and track number in separate columns. Since these columns are not displayed in every view, it is advisable to incorporate these details in the filename of each track.

💡 **Tip**

Displaying the full track name

When you double-click the border between the column headers Name and Artists, the column Name is enlarged to show the full track name.

☞ **Place the mouse pointer between** Name **and** Artists

The mouse pointer changes into ⇔:

☞ **Double-click the border**

Now you see the full name:

By dragging the arrow ⇔ to the left or to the right instead of double-clicking it, you can make the column narrower or wider yourself.

You can play any track listed in this folder directly in *Windows Media Player*. You do that like this:

☞ **Click** ▶ Play all

Windows Media Player opens and the first track starts playing.

☞ **Stop playing the track** 🐾²

☞ **Close** *Windows Media Player* 🐾³

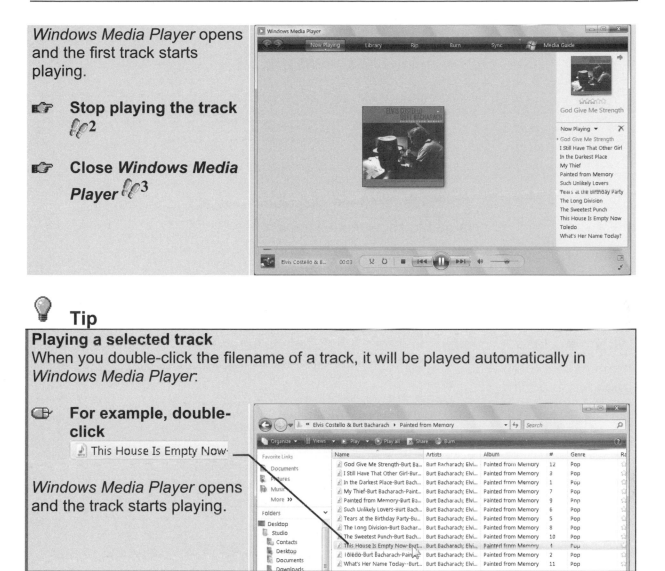

💡 **Tip**

Playing a selected track

When you double-click the filename of a track, it will be played automatically in *Windows Media Player*:

👆 **For example, double-click**

🎵 This House Is Empty Now

Windows Media Player opens and the track starts playing.

2.7 Sorting Tracks

You may have noticed that the tracks are no longer played in the track order of your CD. The tracks are now sorted alphabetically based on the track names in the column *Name*. To sort the tracks by their track numbers:

👆 **Click** #

The tracks are now sorted by their track numbers:

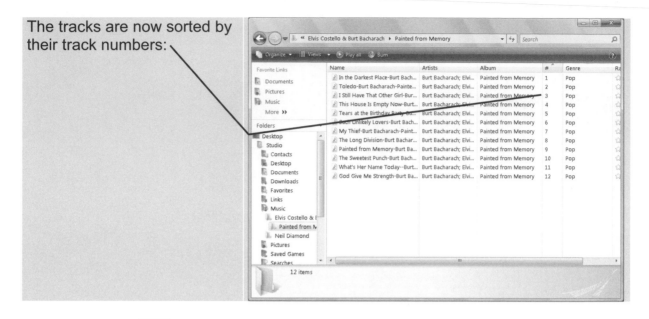

When you click ▢# again, the tracks are displayed in reversed track number order (from high to low). When you click ▢Name, the tracks are sorted alphabetically by track name again.

☞ **Click** ▢X

In the next chapter you learn about various new and unique features of the *Library*.

2.8 Exercises

The following exercises help you to practice what you have learned in this chapter. Have you forgotten how to do something? Use the number beside the footsteps to look it up in the appendix *How Do I Do That Again?*

Exercise: Ripping a CD

When you rip a CD you can store the tracks in your *Library* and use them to create your own CDs.

✔   Insert an audio CD in your CD/DVD player.

✔   Stop playing the CD. $\ell\ell^2$

✔   Go to the tab Rip. $\ell\ell^{50}$

✔   Check if the format is set to MP3. $\ell\ell^{51}$

✔   Set the bit rate to 128 kbps. $\ell\ell^{52}$

✔   Uncheck the first three songs so they will not be ripped. $\ell\ell^{53}$

✔   Rip the CD. $\ell\ell^{54}$

✔   Go to the *Library*. $\ell\ell^{8}$

✔   Remove the audio CD from your CD/DVD player.

✔   Close *Windows Media Player.* $\ell\ell^{3}$

2.9 Background Information

Glossary

Audio	Sound.
Bit rate	The number of bits transferred per unit of time, typically expressed in bits per second.
Compressing	To reduce the size of a file so that it takes up less storage space.
File format	The structure or organization of data in a file. The file format is usually indicated by the file name extension. The file format decides which program can be used to open the file.
MP3	File format used to compress audio, allowing a relatively high sound quality.
Ripping	Copying digital media content from an audio CD. Content may be converted to a different format during the ripping process.

Source: Windows Help and Support

What is file compression?
The introduction of MP3 made it possible to compress an audio file so much that the file size is strongly reduced.

When an audio file is compressed to MP3, many frequencies are removed from the music. This is sound that is outside the hearing range of most people. Frequencies that are so similar to one another that most people cannot detect any difference, are omitted.

The file size is reduced even further by a special compression program. A track that takes up 40 MB of storage space on the CD, will only take up 4 MB in the MP3 file format.

Bit rate and quality loss

When tracks are converted to MP3, certain frequencies are removed from the music before the file size is decreased. Once this has been done it cannot be reversed. It is not possible to revert back to the original format that was on the audio CD.

When you write an audio CD using MP3 tracks, you will permanently lose data information. This means there is quality loss. That is why MP3 is also called a *lossy* compression method.

The lower the bit rate used to rip a CD, the lower the sound quality of the MP3 file will be. An average listener will not hear a lot of difference between a 192 kbps MP3 file and the same track on an original CD. But sound technicians and real 'audiophiles' will surely hear the difference. They prefer a conversion to digital music without quality loss. For that purpose several *lossless* compression methods like FLAC and SHN have been developed. Using these methods the size of an audio file is reduced without information being lost. The audio files created like this, are a lot bigger than MP3 files.

In *Windows Media Player* you can choose the audio format *Windows Media Audio Lossless* when you rip a CD. Keep in mind that this file format results in large files of up to 200 to 400 MB for each CD!

WMA

Windows Media Audio (WMA) is *Microsoft's* answer to MP3. The general idea behind MP3 and WMA is the same. WMA is however a proprietary technology, forming a part of the *Windows Media* framework. WMA is a lossy audio codec based on the study of psychoacoustics. Audio signals which are deemed to be imperceptible to the human ear may be discarded during the compression process. This results in a loss of audio quality in regular WMA files.

Microsoft claims that a WMA file encoded at 64 kbps is better than an MP3 file encoded at 128 kbps. But the WMA file is two times smaller than an MP3 file. Tests have shown that the differences in sound quality between these two file types are almost impossible to distinguish.

Variable bit rate
Aside from MP3 and WMA you can also rip CDs using the format *WMA with variable bit rate* in *Windows Media Player*. This means the amount of compression is continuously adapted to the sound fragment. Variable Bit Rate (VBR) allows a higher bit rate (and therefore more storage space) to be allocated to the more complex segments of media files while less space is allocated to less complex segments.

Variable compression also results in different file sizes. One three minute track may result in a 3 MB file, while another track results in a 5 MB file.

The variable bit rate is not exclusive for *Windows Media Audio*. The *LAME* encoder is an MP3 encoder that also uses a variable bit rate. Even the more demanding *audiophile* has become enthusiastic about the high quality produced when using LAME. The MP3 files created using this encoder cannot be distinguished from the original CD by 99% of the population.

Illegal?
Are MP3 and WMA illegal? No, MP3 and WMA are simply varying methods to compress audio files. It is more important what you do with the MP3 or WMA files!

For example, when you exchange MP3 files with other users on the Internet, the copyright of the artist is violated. His music is passed around, while he is not getting paid for it. That is illegal.

The same thing happens when you copy a CD and sell or give that copy to someone else. This is also discouraged. The artist does not receive the royalties he would have received when one of his CDs was sold in a store.

2.10 Tips

Tip

Adjusting the file location of ripped tracks
By default, *Windows Media Player* creates a folder for the ripped tracks in the *Music* folder. But you can save the files somewhere else if you want to. For example in a separate folder or (if available) on a different hard disk:

☞ **Open the *Options* window** ℓℓ6
👆 **Click the tab** │ Rip Music │

Here you see the location of the ripped files
C:\Users\Studio Visual Steps\Music :

👆 **Click** │ Char │

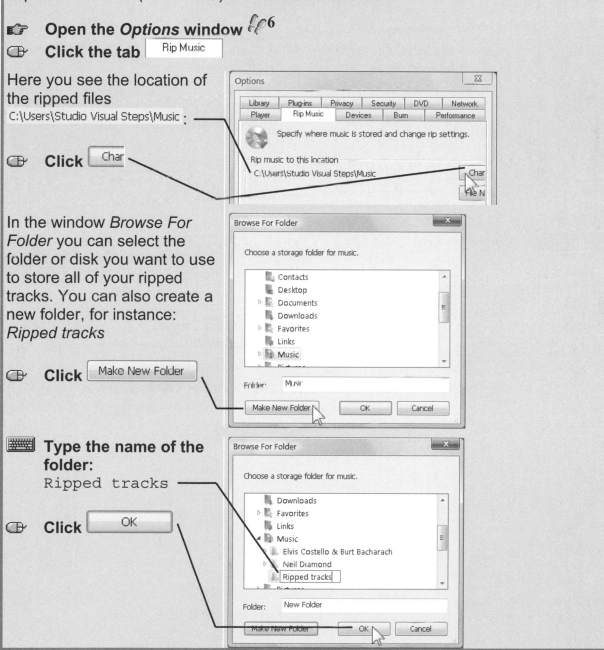

In the window *Browse For Folder* you can select the folder or disk you want to use to store all of your ripped tracks. You can also create a new folder, for instance:
Ripped tracks

👆 **Click** │ Make New Folder │

⌨ **Type the name of the folder:**
Ripped tracks

👆 **Click** │ OK │

💡 Tip

Adjusting the properties of the Music folder

When you create a new folder in the *Music* folder, this folder automatically gets the properties of a music folder. When you create a new folder for music files at another location, for example in *Documents* or on another disk, you can adjust the folder type to make the folder suitable for audio files:

🖰 **Right-click the new folder**

🖰 **Click** Properties

Browse For Folder		Send To ▶
		Cut
Choose a storage folde		Copy
■ Desktop		Delete
◢ 📒 Studio Visual		Rename
📒 Contacts		New ▶
📒 Desktop		Properties
◢ 📒 Documents		
📒 New music files		
▷ 📒 Practice files		

Folder: New Music Files

Make New Folder   OK   Cancel

🖰 **Click the tab** Customize

🖰 **Click** ▾

🖰 **Click** Music Details

🖰 **Click** OK

New music files Properties

General | Sharing | Security | Previous Versions | **Customize**

What kind of folder do you want?

Use this folder type as a template:

Documents ▾

All Items
Documents
Pictures and Videos
Music Details
Music Icons

Choose File...

Restore Default

Folder icons

You can change the folder icon. If you change the icon, it will no longer show a preview of the folder's contents.

Change Icon...

OK   Cancel   Apply

💡 **Tip**

Copy protection for WMA files
When you rip a CD in the WMA format, check beforehand if the copy protection is turned on. Copy protection makes it impossible to play the WMA files on an MP3 player for example, even when it is suitable for WMA files. When you create an audio CD using these files it can only be played on your computer. It is a lot more convenient to turn the copy protection off:

☞ **Open the *Options* window** *6

⬚ **Click the tab**
| Rip Music |

When the option
☑ Copy protect music **is check** marked:

⬚ **Click to remove the check mark at**
Copy protect music

Now the check mark is gone.

⬚ **Click** | OK |

Options   ✕

| Library | Plug-ins | Privacy | Security | DVD | Network |
| Player | Rip Music | Devices | Burn | Performance |

Specify where music is stored and change rip settings.

Rip music to this location

C:\Users\Studio Visual Steps\Music   Char

                                            File N

Rip settings

Format:

Windows Media Audio   ▼

☐ Copy protect music   Learn about copy protecti
☐ Rip CD when inserted
   ○ Only when in the Rip tab
   ○ Always
☐ Eject CD when ripping is complete
Audio quality:

Smallest   Be
Size   ▯   Qu

       Uses about 56 MB per CD (128 Kbps).

                        Compare formats online

     [OK]   [Cancel]   [Apply]   [Help]

Notes

Write down your notes here.

3. Working with the Library

In the *Library* of *Windows Media Player* you can easily manage your audio files. You can let the *Library* search for audio files and other media files that are already on the hard disk of your computer. You can use these files to create playlists with the tracks you like to listen to while you work on your PC.

You can rank your favorite tracks by giving them a one- to five-star rating. Using the auto playlists in the *Library* you can quickly create a list containing all five-star tracks for example. It is also possible to create an auto playlist containing the tracks of a certain genre or artist. You can select the criteria for your auto playlist yourself.

When you learn to use every possibility of the *Library*, your computer changes into a jukebox with endless possibilities!

In this chapter you learn how to:

- add files to the *Library*;
- view the tracks in the *Library*;
- add a track to the playlist by dragging;
- use different ways to add tracks to the playlist;
- add multiple tracks to the playlist;
- change the order of the playlist;
- remove a track from the playlist;
- save a playlist;
- rate tracks;
- use auto playlists;
- define an auto playlist;
- delete a playlist.

⇨ Please note:

In this chapter you will be using some of the practice files. The practice files can be found on the CD-ROM you received with this book. To be able to work through this chapter, you need to copy these files to the hard disk of your computer.
You can read how to do that in **Appendix A**.

3.1 Adding Files to the Library

In the *Library* you can easily manage, organize and view your audio files.

☞ **Open *Windows Media Player*** ⁀⁀⁵

You see the *Library* right away.

The tab ▭ Library ▭ is active:

If that is not the case on your computer:

☞ **Click** ▭ Library

⇨ **Please note:**

You may see different tracks in your *Windows Media Player* window, or the window itself may look different than the windows you see in the examples.

✕ **HELP! My Library looks very different.**

If you see only text instead of the images of the CD covers, you need to change the *view* setting of the *Library*:

☞ **Click** ▾ **beside** ▭

☞ **Click** ▭ **Expanded Tile**

3.2 Viewing the Tracks in the Library

The albums you rip are automatically added to the *Library*. The practice files you have copied from the CD-ROM you received with this book, have also been added to the *Library*. You can choose between different views for your library, for example the one based on *Genre*:

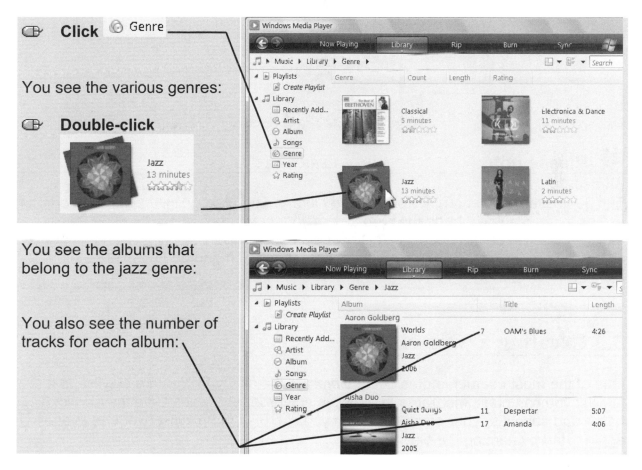

☞ **Click** ⊚ Genre

You see the various genres:

☞ **Double-click**

Jazz
13 minutes

You see the albums that belong to the jazz genre:

You also see the number of tracks for each album:

You can also display these tracks when you sort the *Library* in a different way, for example by *Songs*:

☞ **Click** ♪ Songs

You see the information
about the albums that have
been added to the *Library*:

➡️ **Please note:**

Shortcuts
The audio files are not really stored in the *Library*. The *Library* only contains shortcuts
to files located anywhere on the hard disk of your computer. Make sure you do not
move these files on the hard disk. Otherwise *Windows Media Player* will no longer be
able to find them. You will need to search for them again and add them once more to
the *Library*.

3.3 Creating a New Playlist

One of the most useful features of the *Library* is the ability to create a playlist. In a
playlist you can place the tracks in a row, in any order you want. Give the playlist a
name and save it to your computer. Then you can play the playlist over and over
again. Start by naming the playlist:

🖱️ **Click**

Now you can fill your playlist by using the tracks in the *Library*. To do so, you drag the selected tracks to the playlist:

An empty playlist opens on the right side of your window:

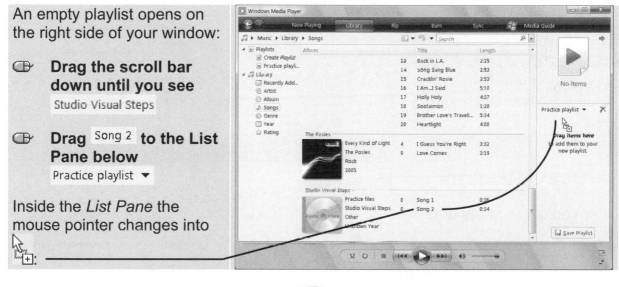

☞ **Drag the scroll bar down until you see** Studio Visual Steps

☞ **Drag** Song 2 **to the List Pane below** Practice playlist ▼

Inside the *List Pane* the mouse pointer changes into

The track Song 2 has been added to the playlist: ⎯⎯⎯

The track starts playing right away:

☞ **Stop playing the track** 👣2

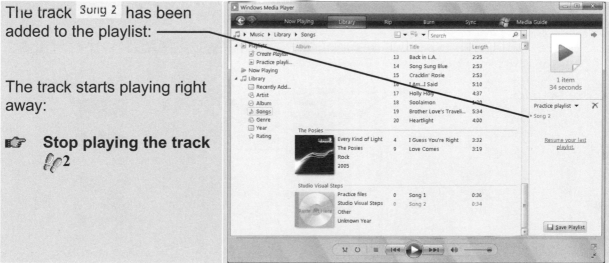

The list becomes very long when there are many albums in your *Library*. When you sort the *Library* by artist, you can add tracks from another artist more quickly. You can do that like this:

☞   **Click** ⚂ Artist _____

You see the names of the artists whose tracks are in the *Library*:

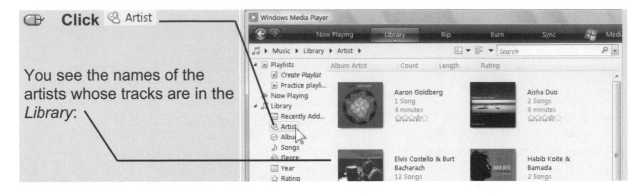

💡   **Tip**

Displaying only the names
When there are many artists the list becomes very long. You can also choose to display the names without the images:

☞   **Click** ▼ **beside** 🖼

☞   **Click** Details _____

Now you only see the details of the artists:

Now you can select the artist whose track you want to add to the playlist:

☞   **Double-click the name of an artist, for example**
Elvis Costello & Burt Bacharach

The tracks of this artist are displayed. You are going to select a random track and drag it to the playlist:

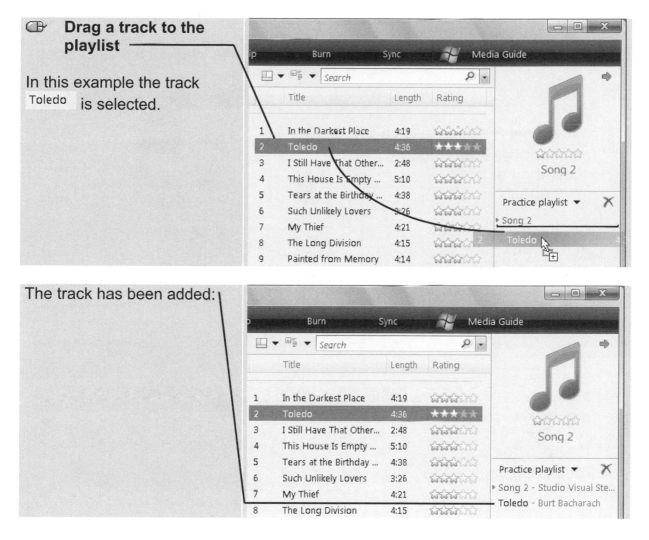

Drag a track to the playlist

In this example the track Toledo is selected.

The track has been added:

3.4 Different Ways to Add Tracks

In the previous section you have added tracks to the playlist by dragging them there. There are more ways to add tracks to a playlist. You are going to try that with a track from the second audio CD you ripped. First you display the tracks of the other artist:

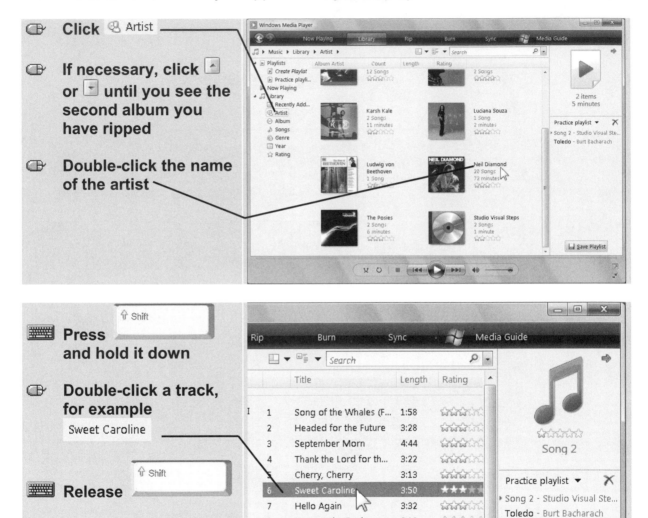

A third track has been added to the playlist:

3.5 Adding Multiple Tracks

You can also add tracks using the shortcut menu. That is very convenient when you want to add multiple files at once:

Click a track, for example Hello Again

Press and hold Ctrl

Click another track, for example America

Ctrl

Release

Now you can add both selected tracks to the playlist at the same time:

☞ **Right-click one of the selected tracks**

☞ **Click**

Add to 'Practice playlist'

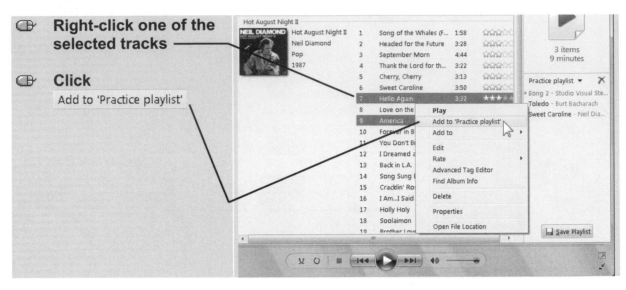

Both tracks have been added to the playlist:

💡 **Tip**

To select a number of consecutive tracks, you click the first track, and hold the Shift-key down while you click the last track.

💡 **Tip**

You can also right-click any single track and add it to the playlist using the shortcut menu.

You can also add all tracks of an artist or album to the playlist at the same time.
To add all tracks by Studio Visual Steps to the playlist:

☞ **Click** ⚲ Artist

☞ **If necessary, click** ▲
or ▼ **until you see**

Studio Visual S
2 Songs
1 minute

again

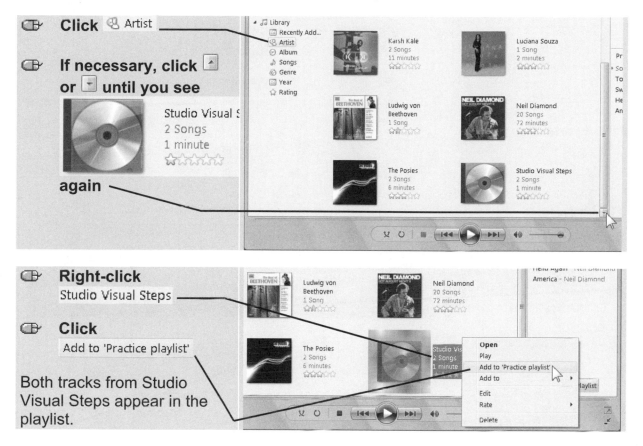

☞ **Right-click**
Studio Visual Steps

☞ **Click**
Add to 'Practice playlist'

Both tracks from Studio
Visual Steps appear in the
playlist.

3.6 Changing the Order of the Playlist

The order of the playlist has been decided by the order in which you added the
tracks. You can very easily change the order of the tracks. For instance, try moving
the last track to the top of the playlist:

☞ **Click** Song 1

☞ **Drag** Song 1 **to the top
of the playlist**

The mouse pointer changes
into :

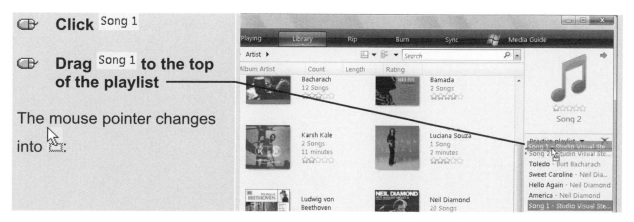

Now Song 1 is the first track on the playlist:

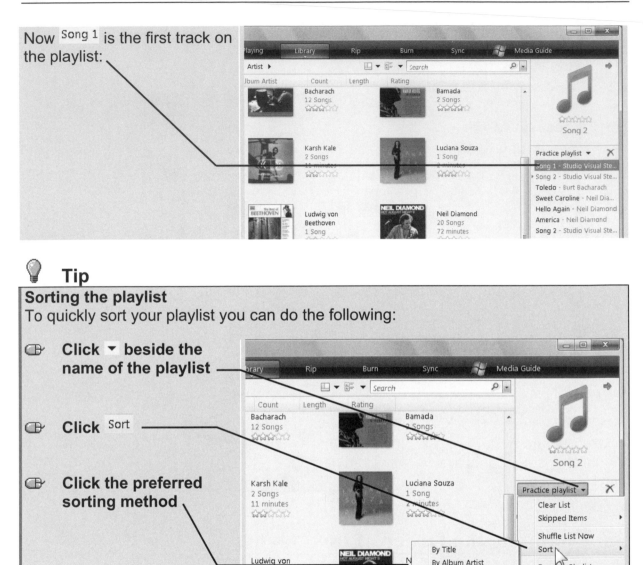

💡 Tip

Sorting the playlist
To quickly sort your playlist you can do the following:

☞ **Click** ▼ **beside the name of the playlist**

☞ **Click** Sort

☞ **Click the preferred sorting method**

3.7 Deleting a Track from the Playlist

When you decide you no longer want a track in the playlist, you can delete it. You are going to do that with Song 2, the track that was added to the playlist twice:

Click Song 2

Press Delete

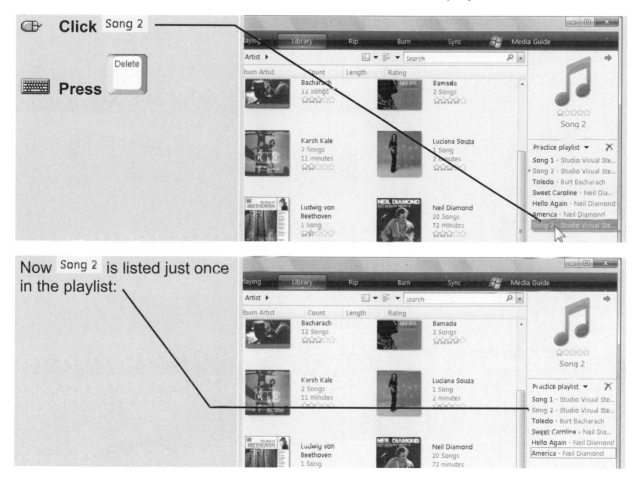

Now Song 2 is listed just once in the playlist:

3.8 Saving the Playlist

When you are satisfied with your playlist, you can save it. You do that like this:

Click 💾 Save Playlist

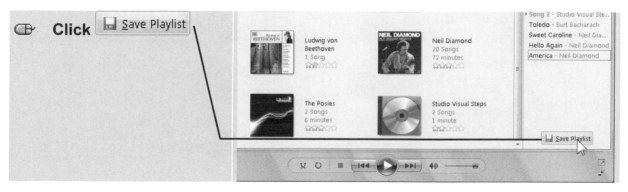

HELP! Nothing happens when I click [🖫 Save Playlist].

It may look like nothing happens when you click [🖫 Save Playlist], but *Windows Media Player* saves the playlist using the name you gave the playlist before: *Practice playlist*.

When you have saved the playlist, you can hide it:

🖱 Click ➡

💡 Tip

Changing the name of the playlist
If you do not like the name you gave to the playlist, you can change it:

🖱 Click ▼ beside the current name

🖱 Click [Rename Playlist]

⌨ Type the new name for your playlist

⌨ Press [Enter ↵]

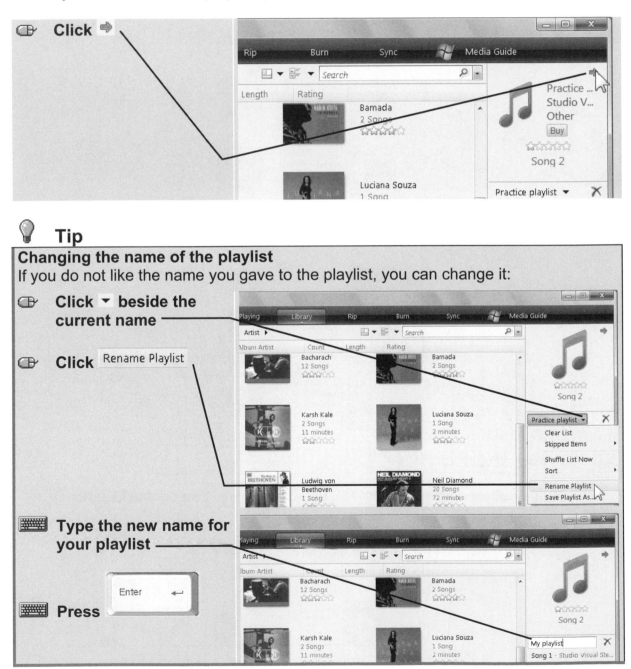

3.9 Opening the Playlist

When you want to look at the playlist *Practice playlist* again, you can open it in the left pane of *Windows Media Player*:

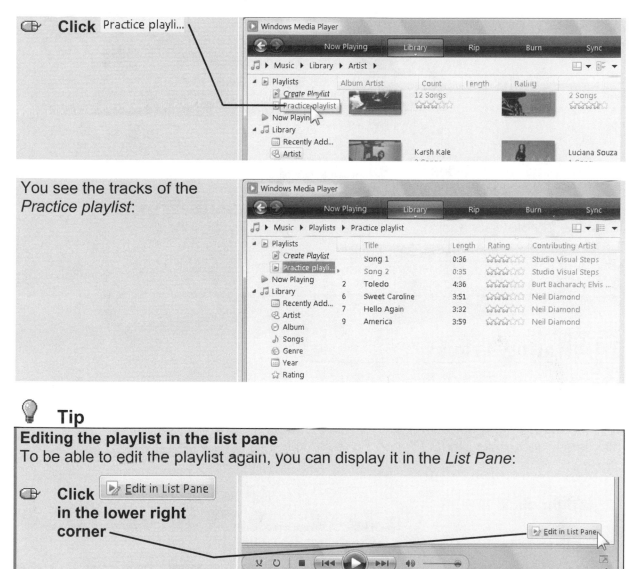

☞ **Click** Practice playli...

You see the tracks of the
Practice playlist:

💡 **Tip**

Editing the playlist in the list pane
To be able to edit the playlist again, you can display it in the *List Pane*:

☞ **Click** ▶️ Edit in List Pane
**in the lower right
corner**

💡 Tip

Show or hide playlists
When you have many playlists it can be useful to hide them temporarily. You can do that like this:

Click ◢ beside ▷ Playlists

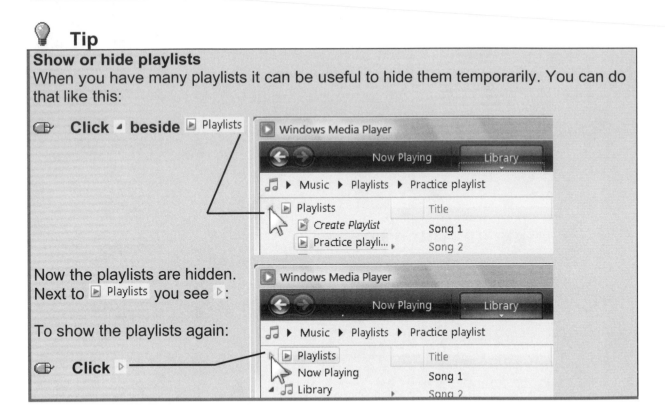

Now the playlists are hidden. Next to ▷ Playlists you see ▷:

To show the playlists again:

Click ▷

3.10 Rating Tracks

In *Windows Media Player* you can rate your tracks. You do that by giving stars to a track. The highest rating for a track is five stars; one star is the lowest rating. This classification will be especially useful when you learn how to work with the auto playlists in *Windows Media Player*. For example, this is how you give two stars to *Song 1*:

Right-click Song 1

Click Rate

Click 2 Stars

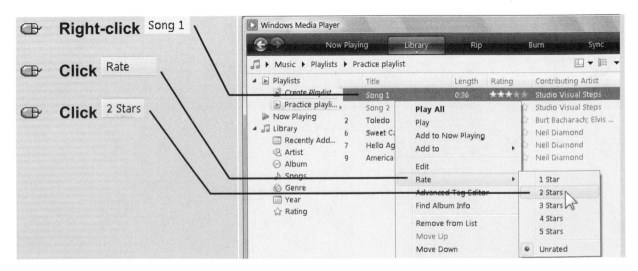

Song 1 now has two stars:

☞ **Give two stars to** Song 2 **as well** 🖐⁷

3.11 Creating an Auto Playlist

You can also create an automatic playlist. When you play this playlist, it is filled with tracks from the *Library* that match the criteria you have chosen. This is a simple way to play all tracks of a certain artist or genre for example. *Windows Media Player* collects the tracks that match the criteria. This is how you create an auto playlist:

☞ **Click** ▭▬ below 🖼 Library

☞ **Click** Create Auto Playlist

In the window *New Auto Playlist* you can enter the criteria the tracks have to meet to be added to the playlist. You start with the first criteria:

⌨ **Type:** Two stars

☞ **Click** [Click here to add criteria]

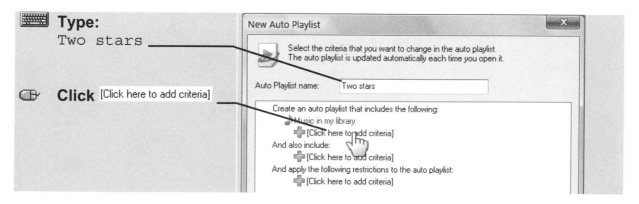

You only want to add tracks with a two-star rating to the playlist. You can set up this custom criteria as follows:

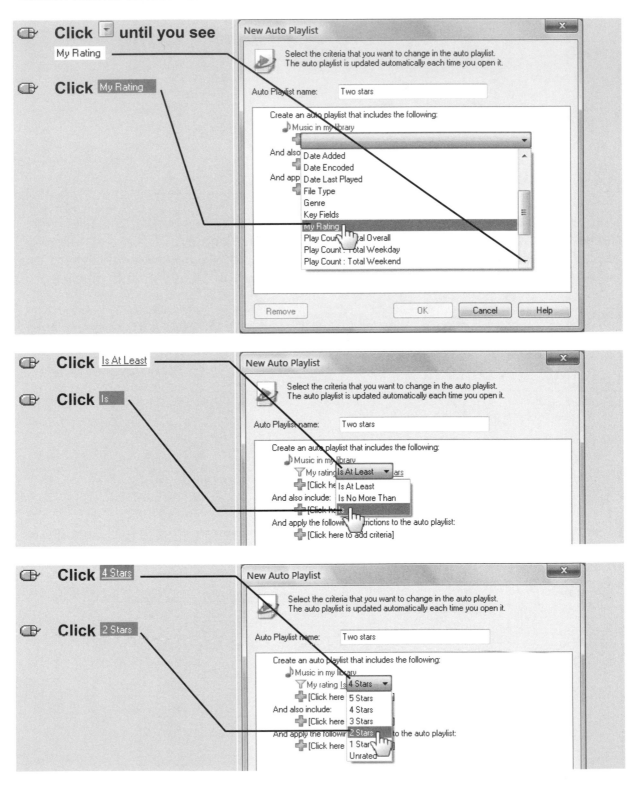

You see the criteria: ———

⬅ **Click** `OK`

New Auto Playlist

Select the criteria that you want to change in the auto playlist. The auto playlist is updated automatically each time you open it.

Auto Playlist name: `Two stars`

Create an auto playlist that includes the following:
 Music in my library
  My rating Is 2 Stars
  [Click here to add criteria]
And also include:
  [Click here to add criteria]
And apply the following restrictions to the auto playlist.
  [Click here to add criteria]

Remove   OK   Cancel   Help

Only the tracks that match the criteria are displayed:

The icon ⬚ indicates the playlist *Two stars* is an automatic playlist: ———

Windows Media Player

Now Playing Library Rip Burn Sync

Music ▸ Playlists ▸ Two stars

	Title	Length	Rating	Contributing Artist
▲ ▸ Playlists				
▸ Create Playlist	Song 1	0:36	☆☆☆☆☆	Studio Visual Steps
▸ Practice playli... ▸	Song 2	0:35	☆☆☆☆☆	Studio Visual Steps
⬚ Two stars				
▸ Now Playing				
▲ ♫ Library				
🖼 Recently Add...				
⚇ Artist				

➡ **Please note:**

You may see other tracks in this list as well, if they received two stars before.

💡 **Tip**

Playing an auto playlist
You can play this auto playlist by double-clicking ⬚ Two stars .

When you give another track a two-star rating, it will be added to this playlist:

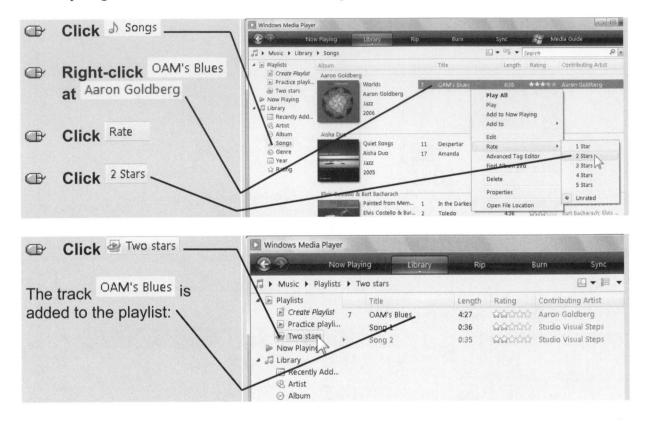

3.12 Changing an Auto Playlist

You can set different criteria and also combine criteria in an auto playlist. You can also exclude certain artists from your playlist. This is how you exclude the tracks of Aaron Goldberg, even if they have two stars:

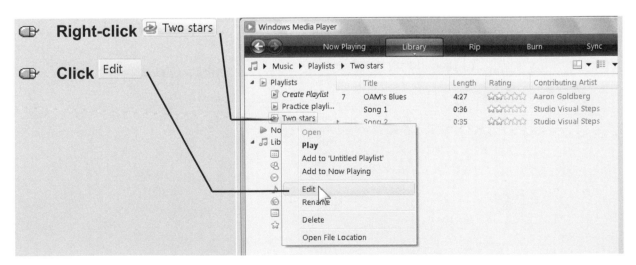

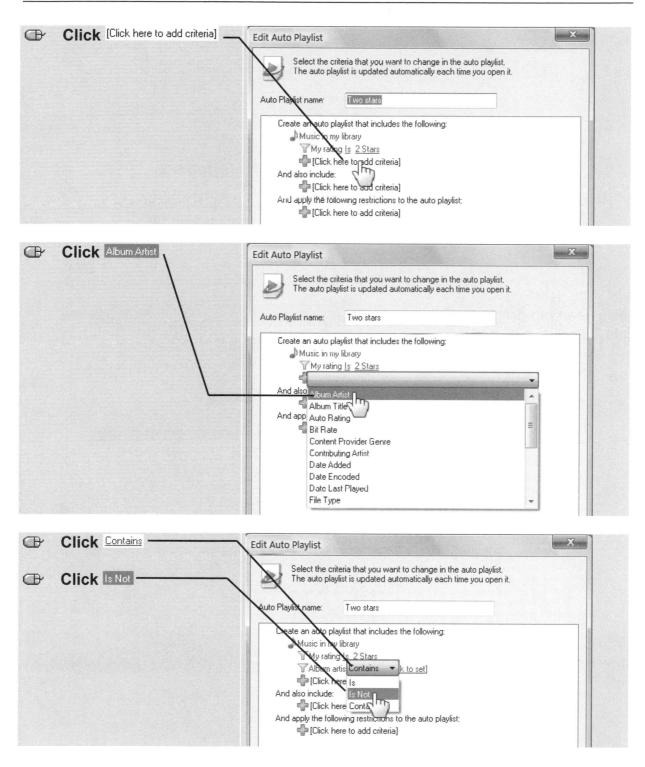

👆 **Click** [click to set]

👆 **Click** Aaron Goldberg

You see both criteria for this playlist:

👆 **Click** OK

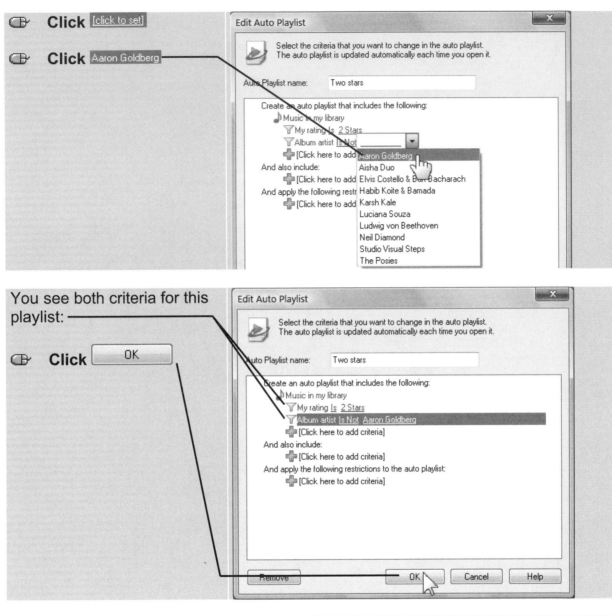

The track by Aaron Goldberg has been removed from this list.

3.13 Deleting a Playlist

The auto playlists and the playlists you create yourself can also be removed from the *Library*. This is how you delete the auto playlist you just created:

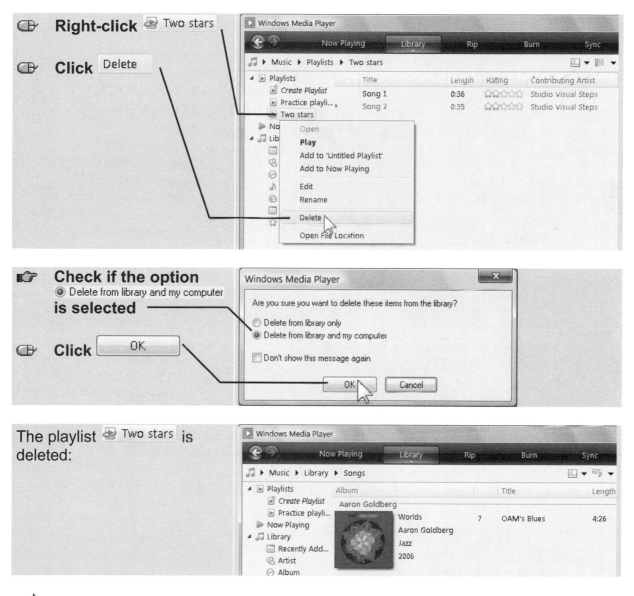

Right-click Two stars

Click Delete

Check if the option
● Delete from library and my computer
is selected

Click OK

The playlist Two stars is deleted:

➡ **Please note:**

When you choose the option ○ Delete from library only the playlist remains on your computer. When you search and add files to the *Library*, the playlist is added to the *Library* again.

☞ **Close *Windows Media Player*** ⁄ℓ³

3.14 Exercises

The following exercises help you to practice what you have learned in this chapter. Have you forgotten how to do something? Use the number beside the footsteps to look it up in the appendix *How Do I Do That Again?*

Exercise: Playlist

Creating playlists makes it very easy to group items from the *Library* according to specific criteria which you specify. You can make your own customized playlists for any occasion.

✔ Open *Windows Media Player*. $\ell\ell^5$

✔ Go to the *Library*. $\ell\ell^8$

✔ Display the tracks by *Songs*. $\ell\ell^9$

✔ Create a new playlist named *Exercise list*. $\ell\ell^{10}$

✔ Add a track to the *Exercise list*. $\ell\ell^{11}$

✔ Stop playing the track. $\ell\ell^2$

✔ Add an album to the *Exercise list*. $\ell\ell^{12}$

✔ Move the last track to the top of the *Exercise list*. $\ell\ell^{13}$

✔ Delete a track from the *Exercise list*. $\ell\ell^{14}$

✔ Delete the *Exercise list*. $\ell\ell^{15}$

✔ Close *Windows Media Player*. $\ell\ell^3$

3.15 Background Information

Glossary	
Auto playlist	An auto playlist is a type of playlist that changes automatically according to criteria you have specified.
Criteria	Conditions used to compile an auto playlist.
Library	A database in *Windows Media Player* that contains information about digital media files on a computer, a network drive, or the Internet.
List Pane	The part of the *Windows Media Player* window where you can edit a playlist.
Playlist	A list containing shortcuts to tracks or other digital media content. The playlist is displayed in the *Library* in *Windows Media Player*.
Rating	Appreciation given to tracks by yourself or by *Windows Media Player*, ranging from one star (low) to five stars (high). Ratings are used by *Windows Media Player* to help you quickly find and organize your favorite tracks, videos and photos.

Source: Windows Help and Support

Difference between regular and auto playlist
When you add, change or remove items from your *Library*, the content of the auto playlist is updated automatically, depending on the criteria you have defined for the list. For example, you can create an auto playlist containing all songs by your favorite artist rated with four or more stars. When you add or remove a song by this artist, or change a rating, the content of the auto playlist will automatically reflect the changes.

The contents of a regular playlist do not change, unless you manually add items to or remove items from the playlist.

3.16 Tips

💡 Tip

Adding files to the Library again?

You can add files to the *Library* as often as you want. Use the [F3] key on your keyboard to open the window for selecting media files on your computer:

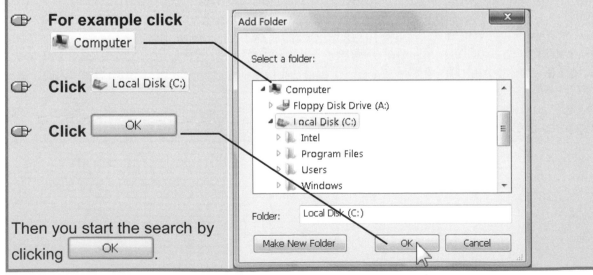

You see the folders that have already been added to the *Library*:

☞ **Click** My folders and those of others that I can access

☞ **Click** Add...

In the next window you select the folders or disks you want to have searched. If you store audio files in other folders or on other disk drives, you can choose to have the entire C-drive searched:

☞ **For example click** 🖳 Computer

☞ **Click** 💾 Local Disk (C:)

☞ **Click** OK

Then you start the search by clicking OK.

💡 Tip

Deleting player history

By default, *Windows Media Player* keeps track of which tracks you play and how often you play them. This information is used to compile auto playlists. You can delete the *History* that is saved by *Media Player*. Here is how to do that:

👉 **Click** below **Library**

👉 **Click** More Options...

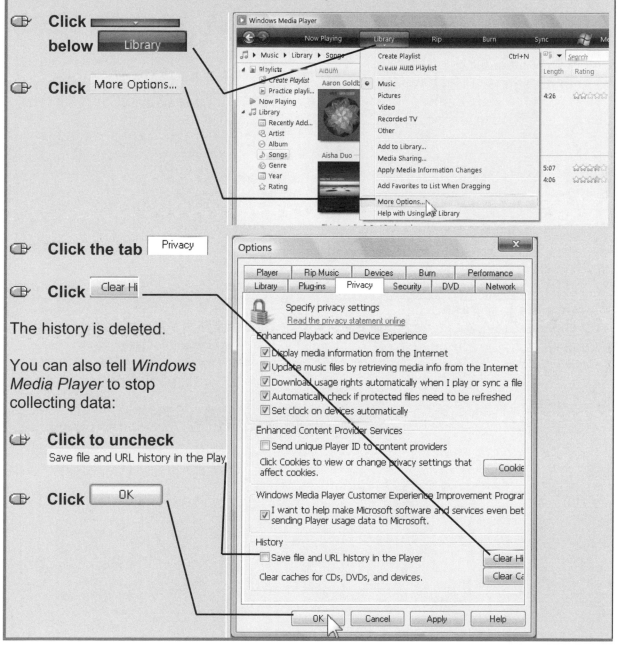

👉 **Click the tab** Privacy

👉 **Click** Clear Hi

The history is deleted.

You can also tell *Windows Media Player* to stop collecting data:

👉 **Click to uncheck**
Save file and URL history in the Play

👉 **Click** OK

💡 Tip

Displaying media files
You can also organize other types of media files in the *Library*, the same way you did with the audio files in this chapter. Select another file type like this:

☞ **Click** ▭ ▭
below ▭ Library

Select the media files you
want to display: ↙

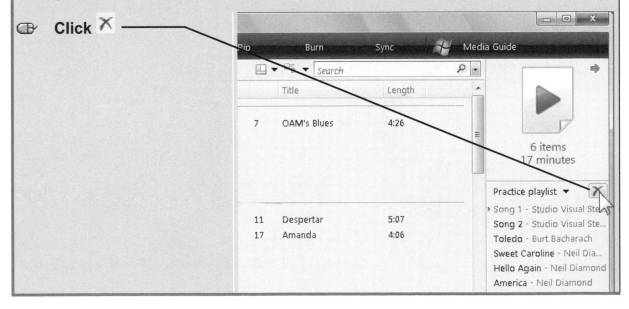

💡 Tip

Clearing the List Pane
You can clear the *List Pane* of the *Library*, for example when you want to create a new playlist. If you already saved the playlist in the *List Pane* it will remain in the *Library*, but the *List Pane* is cleared. You can clear the *List Pane* like this:

☞ **Click** ✕

4. Burning an Audio CD

In addition to playing and ripping CDs, you can also use *Windows Media Player* to *burn* audio CDs. You can use the tracks in your *Library* for that. *Burning a disc* means copying files to a writeable disc.

For example, you can burn an audio CD containing a compilation of tracks or the playlist you created containing your favorite tracks. It is also possible to burn a previously ripped CD, to an audio CD. In this way you can make a copy of your own CD.

Audio CDs can also be played in most audio equipment, like the CD player in your stereo set or your car.

In this chapter you learn the following:

- select a playlist to burn to an audio CD;
- use volume leveling;
- burn a playlist to an audio CD;
- check the audio CD;
- create a *Burn list*;
- clear the *Burn list*;
- add all tracks of a ripped CD to the *Burn list*;
- burn a copy of a ripped CD;
- update the album information.

⇨ Please note:

To be able to work through this chapter you need to have a CD or DVD burner installed in your computer. You will also need two blank discs available of the type CD-Recordable (CD-R). This type can be used in most devices.

It is better not to use a CD-Rewritable (CD-RW). This type of disc may cause problems in older CD playing devices.

You can buy blank CD-R discs in computer stores, discount department stores and other retail outlets.

4.1 Selecting a Playlist

In the previous chapter you created the playlist *Practice playlist*. You are going to burn this playlist to an audio CD.

⇨ **Please note:**

The process of transferring data to a CD or DVD disc is commonly referred to as *burning*. In computing, *optical disc authoring* is the process of recording source material – video, audio or other data – onto an optical disc: compact disc (CD) or DVD. The device used for burning data to a disc is called a *writer* or *burner*.

☞ **Open *Windows Media Player*** 📖⁵

In the *Windows Media Player* window you see a separate tab for burning CDs:

☞ **Click** Burn

In the *List Pane* the *Burn list* appears:

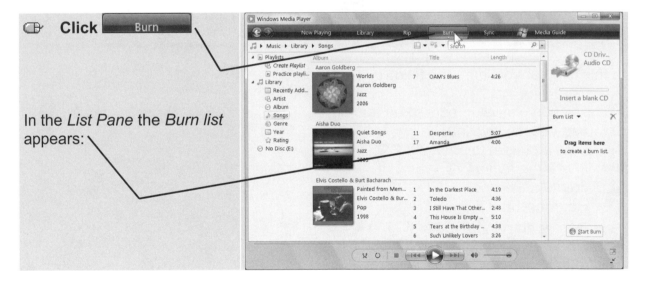

You add the *Practice playlist* to the *Burn list*:

☞ **Right-click**
▷ Practice playli...

☞ **Click** Add to 'Burn List'

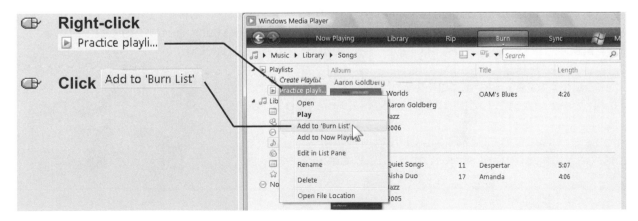

You see the tracks of the
Practice playlist:

💡 **Tip**

Adjusting the playlist
When you are not happy with the playlist you created before, you can still make changes following the steps learned in the previous chapter.

4.2 Adjusting the Burn Settings

Before you start burning the files to CD, you first choose the type of CD you want to create. You choose an audio CD:

Click below Burn

Click Audio CD

Check before you burn the files to CD if the *volume leveling* is turned on. Volume leveling is a very useful feature when the audio files on your computer originate from different sources. There may be differences in volume between the audio files you downloaded or ripped. This can be annoying when you take the time to burn the files to an audio CD and then later when you test it, you hear these volume differences.

When you apply volume leveling across tracks on audio CDs, possible differences in volume are reduced. This only works for MP3 and WMA files that contain a value for volume leveling. When you rip tracks using *Windows Media Player* this value is added automatically. This feature may not work with audio files obtained illegally.

You can check the volume leveling setting like this:

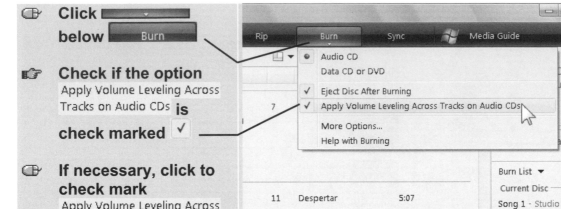

☞	**Click** below **Burn**
☞	**Check if the option** Apply Volume Leveling Across Tracks on Audio CDs **is** **check marked** ✓
☞	**If necessary, click to check mark** Apply Volume Leveling Across Tracks on Audio CDs

4.3 Burning the Playlist to an Audio CD

Now you can burn the playlist to an audio CD.

☞   **Insert a blank CD-Recordable in the CD/DVD burner of your computer**

⇨   **Please note:**

Do you see this window?
This window may appear when you insert a blank CD-R disc:

☞   **Then click** ▉ X ▉

If necessary, check the Tip at the end of this chapter for information on how to prevent this window from appearing when you insert a blank CD-R disc.

Before you start burning the CD you can name the *Burn list*. This name will be given to the audio CD, making it easier to identify it when you play it.

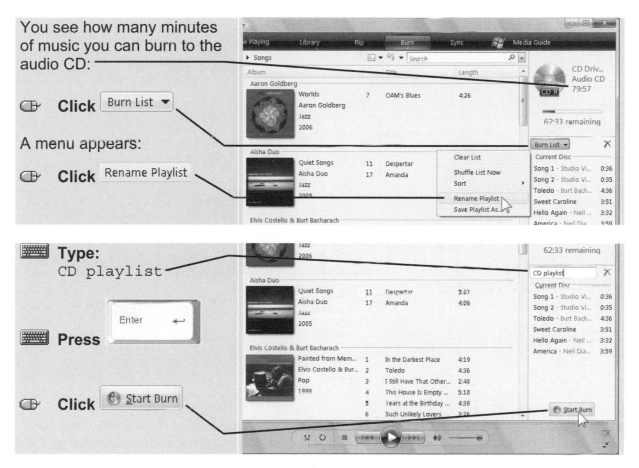

You see how many minutes of music you can burn to the audio CD:

⊞▶ **Click** Burn List ▼

A menu appears:

⊞▶ **Click** Rename Playlist

⌨ **Type:** CD playlist

⌨ **Press** Enter ⏎

⊞▶ **Click** 🔵 Start Burn

Windows Media Player starts the burning process. One after another, the tracks are analyzed and converted to CDA files. CDA files are files that can be played in your home or car CD player. After this conversion, the tracks are burned to the CD.

⇨ **Please note:**

Do not open the drawer of the CD burner during the burning process. Opening the drawer will cause the burning process to fail.

⇨ **Please note:**

Do not click 🚫 Stop Burn during the burning process. If you do, the burning process is interrupted. You cannot use the CD-R disc again. Data can be burned to this type of disc only one time!

You see the progress of the burning for each track:

Here you see the progress of the burning for the full CD:

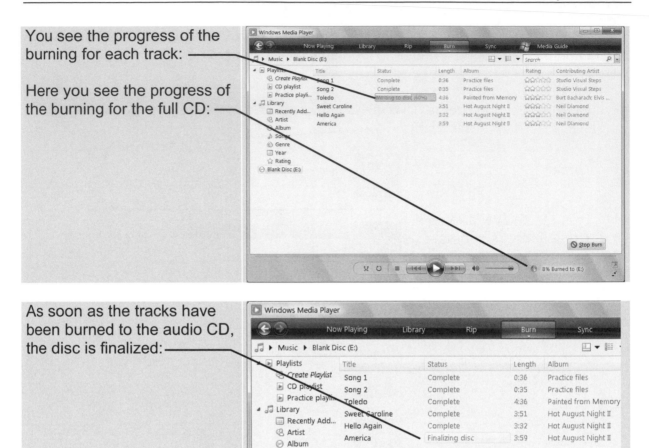

As soon as the tracks have been burned to the audio CD, the disc is finalized:

After the burning process the CD is finalized automatically. This means you can no longer add tracks, even when there is still some space left on the disc. Discs that have not been finalized cannot be played in some devices, like certain types of portable CD and DVD players, regular CD players and car CD and DVD players.

When the burning process has completed you see this window:

4.4 Checking the Audio CD

When the burning process has finished, the drawer of the CD burner opens. Now you can check if the files have been transferred to the audio CD correctly.

☞ **Close *Windows Media Player* ℓℓ³**

☞ **Leave the new audio CD in the CD/DVD burner and close the drawer**

Windows Media Player opens and you see the track details. The name of the CD is also displayed: —————

The first track is played.

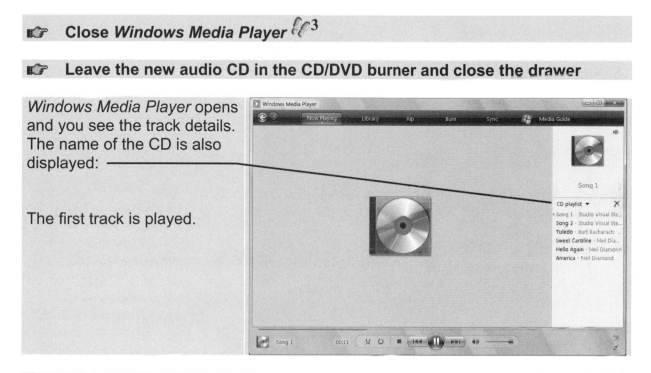

☞ **Stop playing the CD ℓℓ²**

☞ **Remove the CD from the CD/DVD burner**

⇨ **Please note:**

> If your stereo system is equipped with an older model CD player, you may not be able to play this audio CD. Older CD players may not be compatible with CD-R (CD-Recordable) or CD-RW (CD-Rewritable) discs. Please check the manual of your CD player to determine if it is possible to play an audio CD that you have burned.

You have created an audio CD containing the playlist you saved earlier. In the next section you are going to compile an audio CD directly using the *Burn list*.

4.5 Creating a Burn List Yourself

When you are going to burn tracks to an audio CD, it is not necessary to create a playlist first. You can also add the tracks to the *Burn list* straight away:

☞ **Go to the *Library* $\ell\ell^8$**

☞ **Click** Burn

Now you can select the tracks to be added to the *Burn list*. You select the tracks the same way you selected tracks for a playlist:

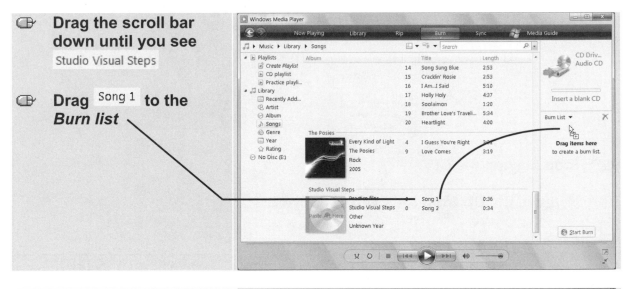

☞ **Drag the scroll bar down until you see** Studio Visual Steps

☞ **Drag** Song 1 **to the Burn list**

The first track has been added to the *Burn list*:

Now you can add more tracks to the *Burn list*. You do that the same way you created a regular playlist.

💡 **Tip**

Maximum playing time

Pay close attention to the maximum playing time of the CD-R disc you want to use when you create a *Burn list.* Most CD-R discs allow you to burn up to eighty minutes of music. It does not matter what bit rate was used to create the tracks. On a 700 MB CD-R disc you can fit eighty minutes of music, regardless of the bit rate and file size.

When the *Burn list* extends beyond eighty minutes, *Windows Media Player* will ask you to insert another CD-R disc to complete the burning process.

💡 **Tip**

Naming the Burn list

Are you making an audio CD with specific music or for a special occasion? Then it is a good idea to name the *Burn list* before you start burning the CD 🖋16.
After the burning process is finished, you can no longer change the name.

4.6 Creating a Copy of a CD

Previously you have ripped two CDs from your own collection and added the tracks to the *Library.* You can use these audio files to create a copy of one of these CDs. Say for example you want to take a favorite CD along with you on a trip, but you are afraid of damaging the original CD. Then you can listen to a copy of the CD in your car CD player, while the original stays safely at home.

It is best to start with an empty *Burn list* to make sure only the tracks of your favorite CD end up in the list:

📖 **Click** ✗

The *Burn list* is cleared.

		Title	Length	
	14	Song Sung Blue	2:53	
	15	Cracklin' Rosie	2:53	
	16	I Am...I Said	5:10	
	17	Holly Holy	4:37	
	18	Soolaimon	1:20	
	19	Brother Love's Traveli...	5:34	
	20	Heartlight	4:00	
it	4	I Guess You're Right	3:32	

Rip — Burn — Sync — Media Guide

CD Driv... Audio CD

Insert a blank CD

Burn List ▼

Current Disc

Song 1 - Studio Vi... 0:36

You can add all tracks of a ripped CD to the *Burn list* using a shortcut menu:

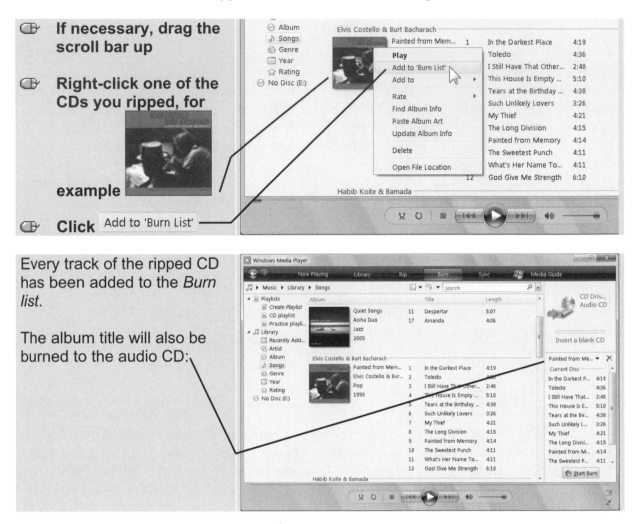

☞ **If necessary, drag the scroll bar up**

☞ **Right-click one of the CDs you ripped, for example**

☞ **Click** Add to 'Burn List'

Every track of the ripped CD has been added to the *Burn list*.

The album title will also be burned to the audio CD:

💡 **Tip**

Changing the Burn list
You can still change the *Burn list* before you actually burn the audio CD. Perhaps you want to change the order of the tracks, remove a track, or add another track when space allows. In this case, the resulting audio CD will not be the same as the original.

☞ **Insert a blank CD-R disc in the CD/DVD burner**

☞ **If necessary, close the *AutoPlay* window** 💾³

Now you are going to burn the copy of the CD straight from the *Library. Windows Media Player* uses the burner and the type of CD you selected earlier:

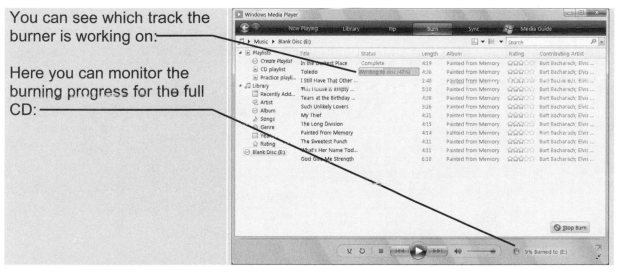

The tracks are analyzed and converted to CDA files. Then the burning process begins.

You can see which track the burner is working on:

Here you can monitor the burning progress for the full CD:

As soon as the burning process has finished, the message Complete appears after each track title:

The drawer of the CD burner opens.

Now you can check the audio CD by playing it:

☞ **Close the drawer of the CD burner**

Windows Media Player automatically starts playing the audio CD.

Is that not the case?

☞ **Start playing the audio CD** 👣¹

☞ **Stop playing the CD** 👣²

4.7 Updating Album Information

If you want to see the CD cover and media information for this copied CD as well, you can retrieve it from the Internet when the information does not appear automatically.

⇨ **Please note:**

To be able to download the information from the Internet, you need a functioning Internet connection. If you do not have that, you can just read through this section.

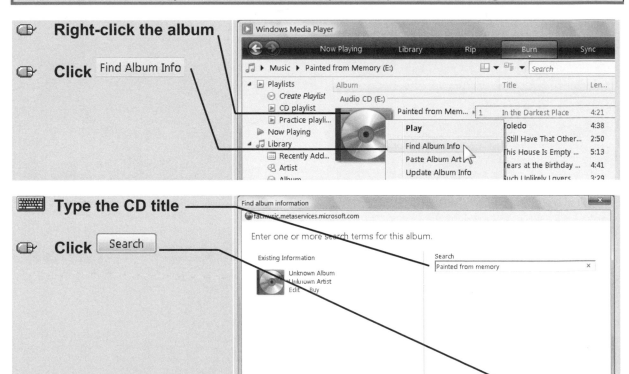

Did you find the correct album in the list of search results?

☞ **Click the album**

☞ **Click** | Next |

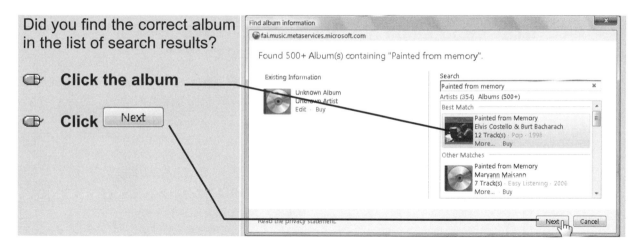

If the correct album was not found:

👉 **Check your search term and search again**

You see the album information:

☞ **Click** | Finish |

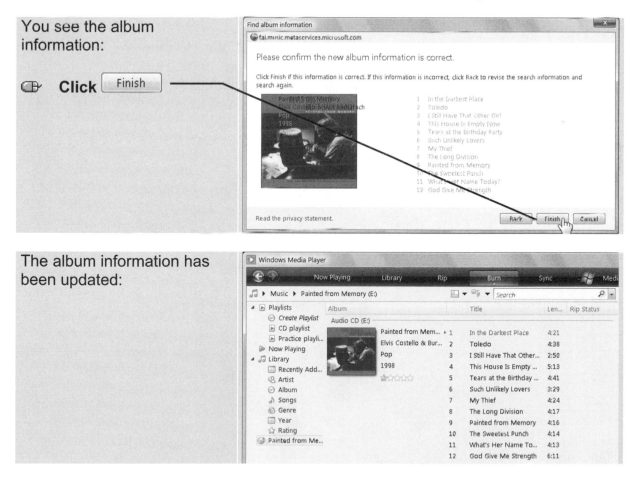

The album information has been updated:

HELP! The information has not been updated.

When the information is not updated right away, you can do the following:

☞ **Right-click the album**

☞ **Click** Update Album Info

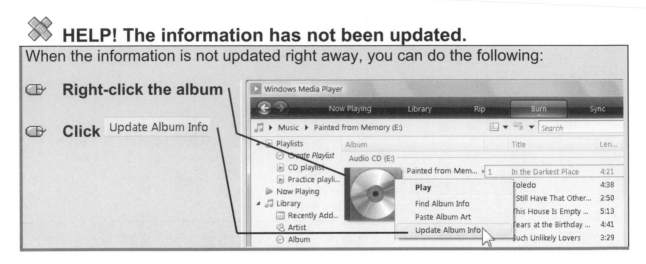

☞ **Remove the CD from the CD burner**

☞ **Close** *Media Player* 🦶³

In this chapter you have used the audio files from the *Library* to burn two audio CDs. These CDs can also be played in your regular CD player. In the next chapter you can read how to use *Windows Media Player* to copy audio files to an MP3 player.

4.8 Exercises

The following exercises help you to practice what you have learned in this chapter. Have you forgotten how to do something? Use the number beside the footsteps to look it up in the appendix *How Do I Do That Again?*

Exercise: Burning an Audio CD

In the *Library* you can compile and burn audio CDs that you can play in your home or car CD player.

✓ Open *Windows Media Player*. [5]

✓ Go to the *Library*. [8]

✓ Open the *Burn list*. [17]

✓ Add an album you ripped to the *Burn list*. [18]

✓ Add another track to the *Burn list*. [19]

✓ Change the name of the *Burn list* to *Practice CD*. [16]

✓ Select *audio CD* as the type of CD you want to burn. [20]

✓ Insert a CD-R disc in your CD or DVD burner.

✓ Burn the *Burn list* to the CD-R disc. [21]

✓ Close the drawer of the burner with the audio CD in it.

✓ Stop playing the CD. [2]

✓ Remove the audio CD from the CD or DVD burner.

✓ Close *Windows Media Player*. [3]

4.9 Background Information

Glossary	
Audio CD	Music CD in the standard *Red Book* audio format. Audio CDs can be played in most computers and in home and car CD players that play CD-R and CD-RW discs. You can burn an audio CD from either WMA (*Windows Media Audio*), MP3, or WAV file formats.
Burning	The process of burning data to a writable CD. The words *copying, writing* or *transferring* may refer to the same process.
CD-Recordable CD-R	A type of writable CD on which files can be copied, but not erased or replaced.
CD-Rewritable CD-RW	A type of writable CD on which files can be copied, erased, and replaced.
CDA files	This abbreviation stands for *CD Audio*. These are the audio files you find on a regular audio CD. In this format the files can be played in regular CD players like home or car CD players. CDA files have excellent quality.
Volume leveling	When you burn files that were originally recorded at different volume levels, you can use volume leveling to reduce the differences in volume between the tracks on the audio CD. Then you do not have to adjust the volume when you play the CD.
Writing	Copying files to a writable CD, also called *burning*.

Source: Windows Help and Support

Copy protection

To prevent new CDs from being copied and spread in bulk, some artists choose to add copy protection to their CDs. This protection should make sure that the CD cannot be ripped.

Usually copy protection is a playback restriction that aims to make the CD unusable in computers with CD-ROM drives, leaving only dedicated audio CD players for playback. Copy protection also prevents creating a copy for your own use.

Copy protection is not always watertight. Some people consider it a challenge to crack and disable the copy protection.

Is a copied CD illegal?

It is not allowed to copy a CD and give, rent or sell that copy to someone else. However, it is allowed to make a copy for your own use. A 1992 law allows music listeners to make some personal digital copies of their music. You do not need to ask the permission of the copyright holder to make these copies.

A copy is not a personal digital copy when:
- you make more than a few copies;
- you have a commercial objective, such as selling or renting;
- you copy for another reason than strictly personal use.

An artist or composer's income is dramatically impacted because their work is copied and distributed in bulk. That is why recording companies collect royalties on the blank media used for this purpose. For every digital audio tape (DAT), blank audio CD, or minidisc sold, a few cents will go to the recording companies.

Kazaa, LimeWire and viruses

Downloading music using MP3 websites and programs like *Kazaa* and *LimeWire* is **illegal**! No royalties are paid for the files that are distributed on *Kazaa* and *LimeWire*. This means artists sell less CDs because many illegal copies are spread, and their revenues are depleted.

There are plenty of ways to download music in a **legal** way, so you do not need the MP3 websites, *Kazaa* and *LimeWire*.

You are also at risk when you download files using programs like *Kazaa* and *LimeWire*, or from other MP3 websites. Stories appear frequently in newspapers and elsewhere about the spread of viruses and other unwanted and harmful software by these kinds of websites and programs.

4.10 Tips

 Tip

MP3 CDs

Many new portable CD players can play both audio CDs and MP3 CDs. An MP3 CD is a data CD containing MP3 files that have not been converted to the CDA file format.

Since MP3 files are a lot smaller, you can store many more MP3 tracks on an MP3 CD. You are not limited to a maximum capacity of eighty minutes that applies to an audio CD.

Some portable CD players not only play CDs containing MP3 files, but WMA files as well:

When there is no indication on the outside of your player, you can check your user manual to determine what types of media files are supported.

You need to choose the data CD format to burn an MP3 CD:

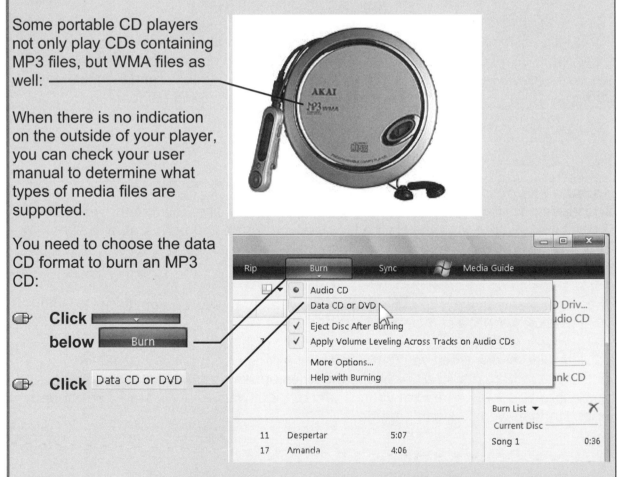

☞ **Click** [▾] **below** [Burn]

☞ **Click** [Data CD or DVD]

The tracks you burn to a data CD are not converted to CDA files and therefore cannot be played on all devices.

MP3 CDs are becoming increasingly popular. There are many home and car CD players on the market that are capable of playing MP3 CDs.

💡 Tip

Setting the speed of the CD burner
If your computer frequently freezes during the burning process, and you are wasting too many CD-R discs, then it is a good idea to lower the burning speed of your burner. This may also be the solution when burning errors occur during the burning process. You can lower the burning speed like this:

Click [▼] below [Burn]

Click [More Options...]

Click [Fastest ▼] next to [Burn speed:]

Click a lower speed, for example [Medium]

Click [OK]

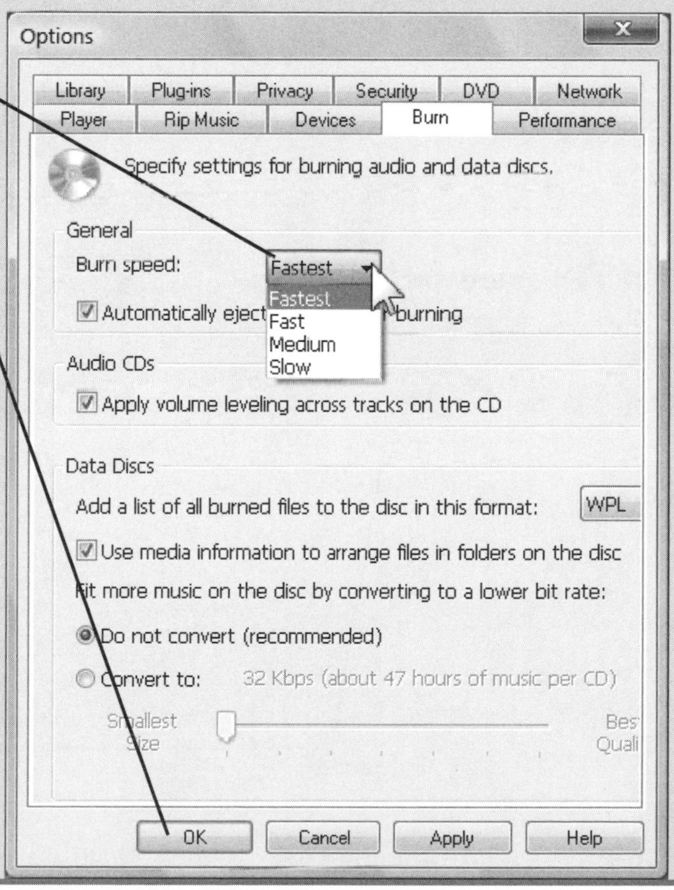

💡 Tip

Changing the AutoPlay default setting for inserting blank CDs
When you insert a blank CD-R disc, the *AutoPlay* window of *Windows Vista* may appear automatically. This window gives you a list of various things you can do with the blank disc. You can change the default *AutoPlay* setting to instruct *Windows Vista* to take **no** action when you insert a blank disc:

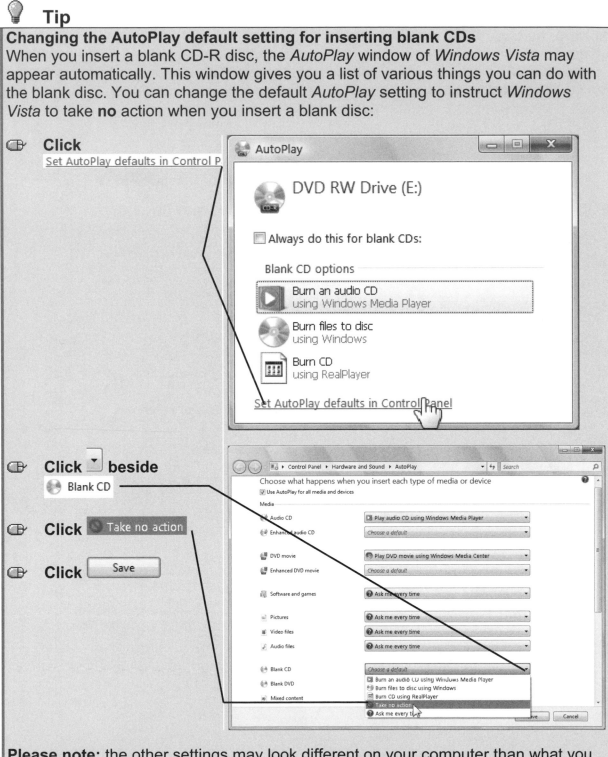

👆 **Click**
Set AutoPlay defaults in Control P

👆 **Click** ▾ **beside**
💿 Blank CD

👆 **Click** 🚫 Take no action

👆 **Click** Save

Please note: the other settings may look different on your computer than what you see in this example. Leave the other settings unchanged.

5. The MP3 Player

First it was a walkman, then the portable CD player. Now the MP3 player is the latest development in portable audio. Whether you are traveling, working out or gardening, these small players make it easier than ever to have your favorite music on hand.

There are inexpensive MP3 players on the market. They may be as small as a cigarette lighter but can store up to 32 hours worth of music! Larger players have even more capacity. There are players with a 20 to 40 Gigabyte hard disk, big enough to store your entire CD collection. Although the name indicates otherwise, most MP3 players play both MP3 and WMA files.

Windows Media Player makes it easy to maintain the audio files on your MP3 player. You can copy an existing playlist to the MP3 player. It is also possible to create a *Sync list* especially for the MP3 player. You can synchronize the MP3 player with this list automatically or manually.

In this chapter you learn how to:

- adjust the settings for the MP3 player;
- synchronize the MP3 player with a playlist manually;
- create a new *Sync list*;
- delete tracks from the MP3 player;
- adjust the settings for automatic synchronization;
- synchronize the MP3 player automatically.

⇨ **Please note:**

To be able to work through this chapter, you need an MP3 player. This device should be supported by *Windows Vista* and *Windows Media Player*. Keep in mind that many older MP3 players are not compatible with *Windows Vista*. Please refer to the manual you received with your MP3 player for information on how to connect the player to your computer.
In the examples provided, a simple USB MP3 player by *Samsung* is used:

If you do not have an MP3 player you can just read through this chapter.

5.1 Setting Up the MP3 Player

Before you transfer music to your MP3 player, you need to adjust some settings first.

☞ **Start** *Media Player* 𝒾𝒾5

You can use the *Sync* tab to manage the contents of your MP3 player:

☞ **Click** **Sync**

Windows Media Player starts
to search for an MP3 player,
but is unable to find it:

☞ **Connect your MP3 player to the computer**

In this example *Windows
Media Player* recognizes the
MP3 player:

HELP! I see a different window.

When you connect your MP3 player for the first time, *Windows Media Player* needs to install your MP3 player. Then you see this window:

Follow the instructions in the windows to install your MP3 player. Sometimes the necessary drivers are available in *Windows Vista*, but for newer models you may have to install the driver from the CD-ROM you received with your MP3 player.

HELP! My MP3 player is not recognized.

When *Windows Media Player* does not recognize your MP3 player, it is possible that your player is not compatible with *Windows Vista* or *Windows Media Player*. Please note that many older MP3 players will not be able to work with *Windows Vista*. You can try to make the connection manually:

 Click **Sync** **below**

 Click Refresh Devices

If your MP3 player is still not recognized, check the website of the manufacturer of your MP3 player. Perhaps you can download a new driver there, to enable communication between your computer and your MP3 player. After installing this new software, your MP3 player will often be able to communicate with *Windows Vista* and *Windows Media Player*.

Before you sync your MP3 player with *Windows Media Player*, you check a couple of settings:

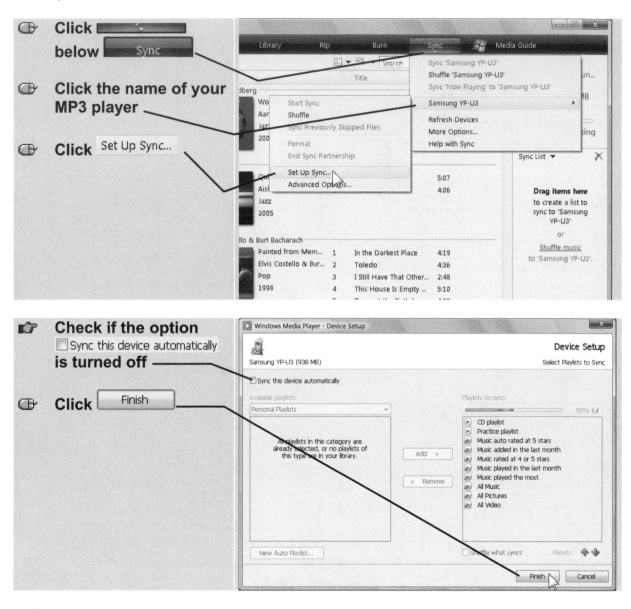

☞ **Click ▬▬▬ ▾**
    below [Sync]

☞ **Click the name of your**
    MP3 player

☞ **Click** [Set Up Sync...]

👉 **Check if the option**
    ☐ Sync this device automatically
    is turned off

☞ **Click** [Finish]

⇨ **Please note:**

When you choose to sync your MP3 player automatically, you may lose tracks on your MP3 player. You can read more about this subject in section
5.5 Automatic Synchronization.

You can store a large number of tracks on an MP3 player. You can use separate folders for the tracks, just like on your computer. When you store each album in a separate folder, it will be easier to find specific tracks, or play all tracks on one album. To do so, check the following setting for the MP3 player:

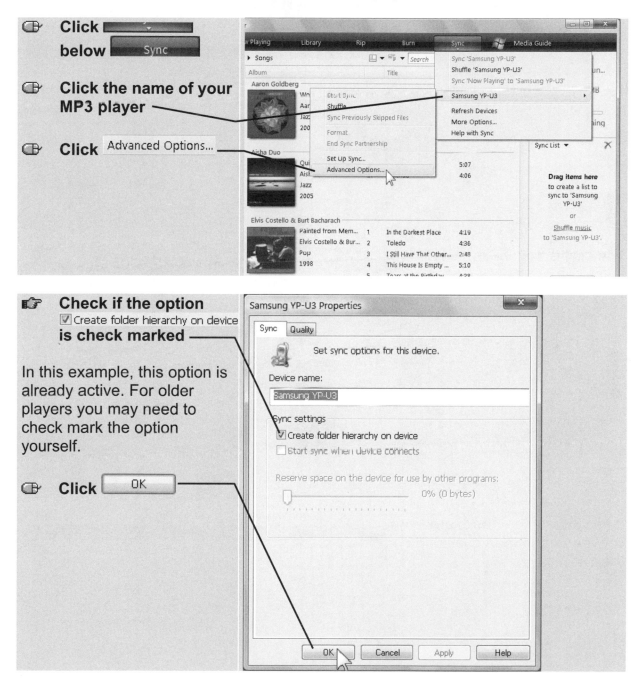

Click below `Sync`

Click the name of your MP3 player

Click `Advanced Options...`

Check if the option ☑ Create folder hierarchy on device **is check marked**

In this example, this option is already active. For older players you may need to check mark the option yourself.

Click `OK`

The tracks you copy to your MP3 player will now be sorted by album.

5.2 Copying a Playlist to the MP3 player

Now that *Windows Media Player* has recognized your MP3 player, you can copy a playlist to the MP3 player. First you add the playlist to the *Sync list*:

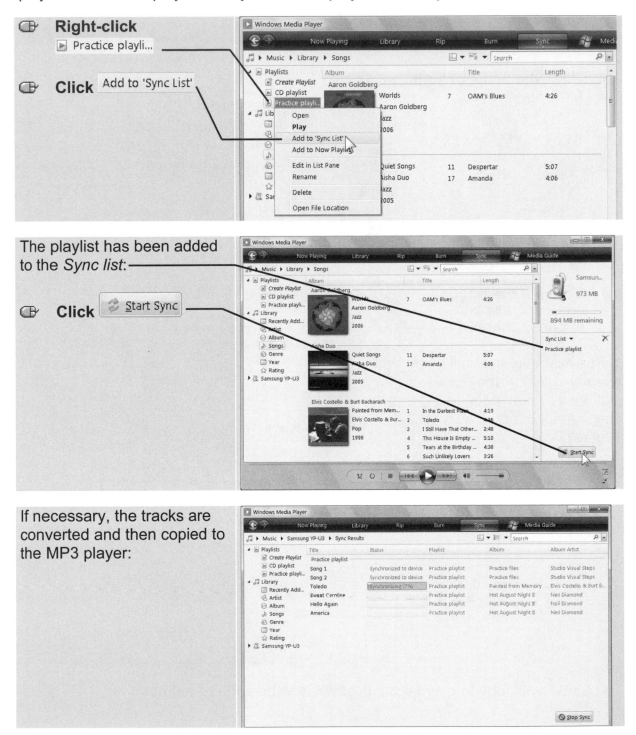

☞ **Right-click**
  ▶ Practice playli...

☞ **Click** Add to 'Sync List'

The playlist has been added to the *Sync list*:

☞ **Click** ⟳ Start Sync

If necessary, the tracks are converted and then copied to the MP3 player:

➡️ **Please note:**

Files will only be converted if the files need to have a certain quality level or format optimized for playback on the specific device. Conversion does not affect the original file.

After synchronization you see the message

> You can now disconnect 'Samsung YP-U3'.

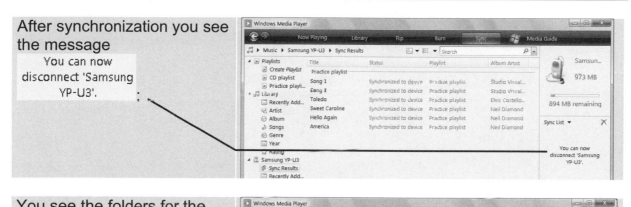

You see the folders for the MP3 player 🖳 Samsung YP-U3 :

👆 **Click** ♪ Songs **below your MP3 player** ——

You see the albums and tracks on your MP3 player:

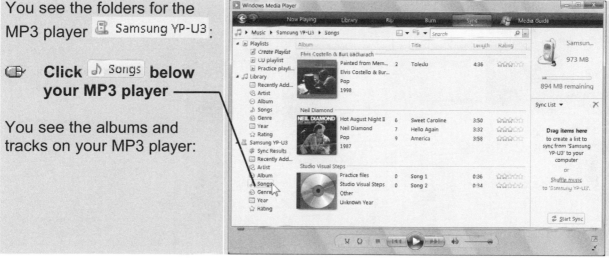

❌ **HELP! I do not see any folders.**

It is possible that your MP3 player does not support the folder structure. In that case, you can choose to sync without folder hierarchy in the window *Properties*.

👆 **Click to remove the check mark for**
☐ Create folder hierarchy on device

Please note: this is not possible with every MP3 player.

5.3 Creating a New Sync List

Previously you have learned how to create a playlist and a *Burn list*. You can create a *Sync list* the same way:

Click ⊙ Album **in the** 🎵 Library

Right-click an album, for example

Click Add to 'Sync List'

All tracks are added to the *Sync list*:

Click 🔄 Start Sync

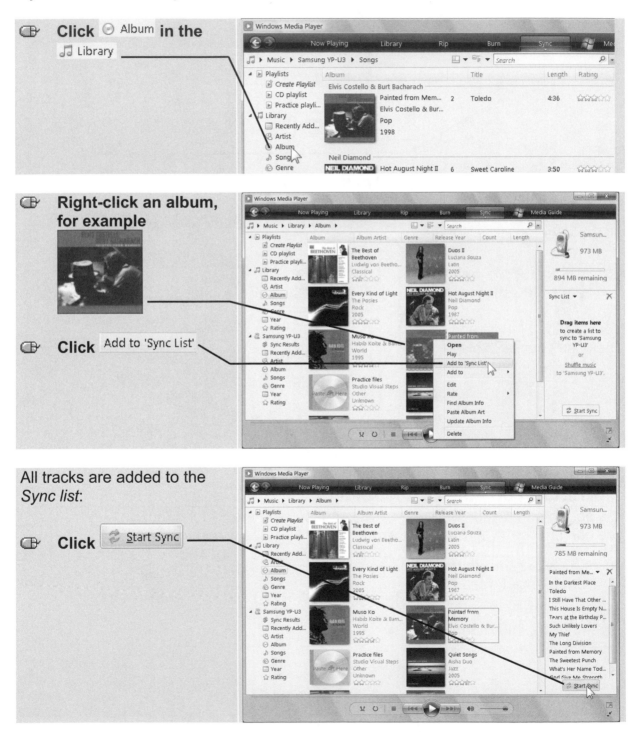

The tracks from the *Sync list* have been copied to the MP3 player:

The *Sync list* is cleared again.

Here you see which tracks have been added. Track 2 was skipped because it was already on the MP3 player:

💡 Tip

Double tracks
When you sync your MP3 player with a playlist, it may contain tracks that are already on your MP3 player. That is no problem. As you see, *Windows Media Player* skips these tracks and avoids double tracks on your MP3 player.

5.4 Deleting Tracks from the MP3 Player

When you manually sync an MP3 player with a playlist, tracks are only added. The tracks that are on your MP3 player, but not in the playlist, will not be deleted. The tracks you no longer want on your MP3 player can be deleted manually. Try that with one of the tracks you just added:

Click ♪ Songs **below your MP3 player**

Click a track

Press Delete

Click OK

The track has been removed:

You can also remove several tracks at the same time like this:

Click the first track of an album

Press and hold ⇧ Shift

Click the fourth track

Release ⇧ Shift

Now four tracks are selected:

Press Delete

The four tracks are deleted from the MP3 player at the same time.

👆 **Click** [OK]

Windows Media Player [x]

Are you sure you want to delete the 4 selected items from 'Samsung YP-U3'?

☐ Don't show this message again

[OK] [Cancel]

💡 **Tip**

Selecting several tracks separately

When you hold the [⇧ Shift] key down, you can select a clock of consecutive tracks. When the tracks you want to delete are not in a row, you hold the [Ctrl] key down to add separate tracks to the selection.

You have manually synchronized your MP3 player with your favorite tracks. It is also possible to synchronize your MP3 player automatically. You can read more about that in the next section.

5.5 Automatic Synchronization

When you synchronize your MP3 player automatically, it is automatically filled with every track in the *Library*. In case these tracks do not fit on your MP3 player, they are copied to the MP3 player according to a priority list. Priority is based on the available playlists.

➡️ **Please note:**

When you use automatic synchronization, not only audio files are synchronized, but also photos and video. This is of course only useful when your MP3 player is capable of showing photos or videos.

👆 **Click** [▾]
below [Sync]

👆 **Click the name of your MP3 player**

👆 **Click** [Set Up Sync...]

In the window *Device Setup* you can see in which order the tracks of the playlists in the *Library* will be copied to your MP3:

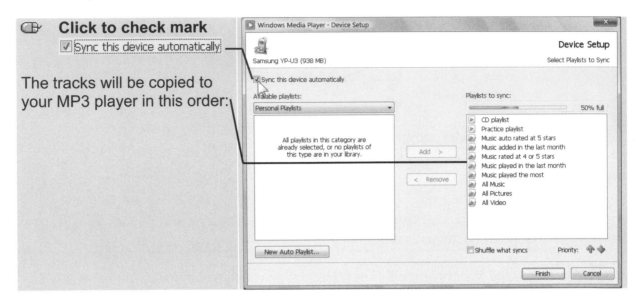

Click to check mark
☑ Sync this device automatically

The tracks will be copied to your MP3 player in this order:

In this example the tracks from your own playlists are synchronized first, then *Music auto rated at 5 stars*, then *Music added in the last month*, etcetera. Synchronization will continue until your MP3 player is full or every track has been copied. This may take some time if you have many files in your *Library*.

You can also exclude playlists from synchronization by removing them from the list:

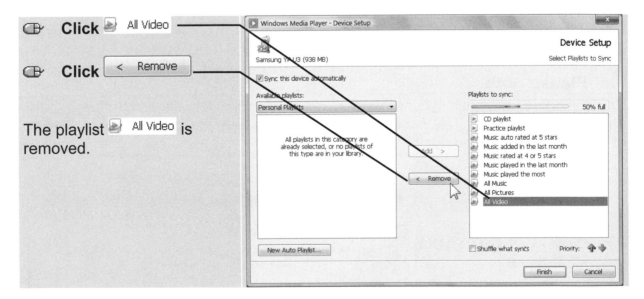

Click 🔲 All Video

Click < Remove

The playlist 🔲 All Video is removed.

HELP! I removed the wrong list.

Did you remove the wrong playlist? Then you can easily restore it like this:

Click ▼ beside `Personal Playlists`

Click `Sync Playlists`

Click the playlist you want to restore

Click `  Add  >  `

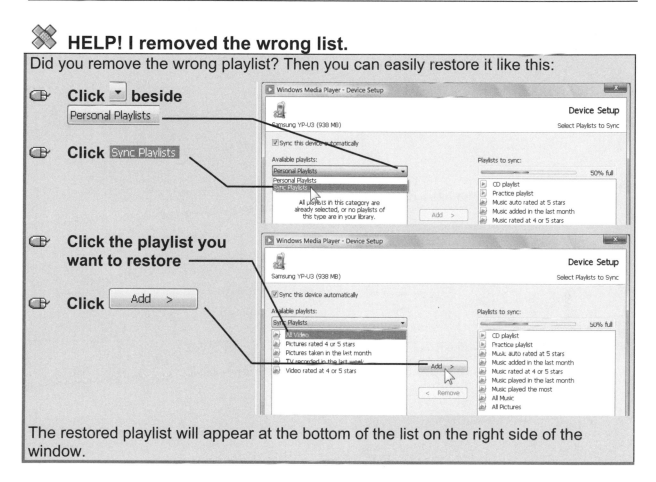

The restored playlist will appear at the bottom of the list on the right side of the window.

You can change the priority of the playlists by moving them up or down. You can move the playlist with music you played most to the top like this:

Click `⊞ Music played the most`

Click ⬆ until `⊞ Music played the most` **is at the top**

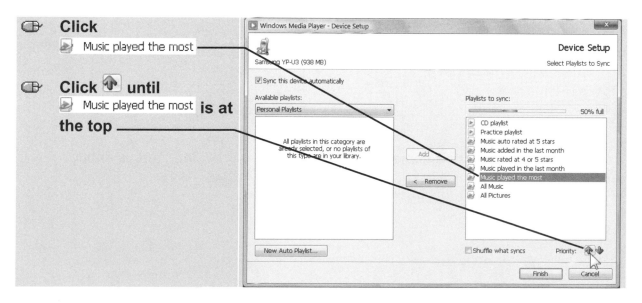

`Music played the most` is at the top of the list: ———

☞ **Click** [Finish]

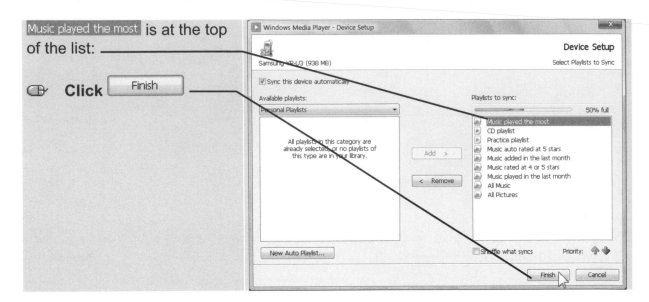

💡 **Tip**

Sync in random order
Would you like to play random tracks from the different playlists? Then you can choose to shuffle the tracks that sync:

☞ **Click** ☑ Shuffle what syncs

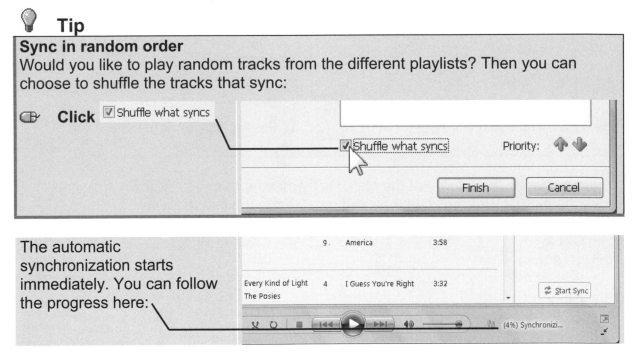

The automatic synchronization starts immediately. You can follow the progress here: ↘

Each track in the *Library* is copied to your MP3 player, provided there is enough space.

The current setting is *automatic* synchronization. This will start as soon as you open *Windows Media Player* and connect your MP3 player. If you want to prevent synchronization from starting automatically, change the setting like this:

☞ **Click** below **Sync**

☞ **Click the name of your MP3 player**

☞ **Click** Advanced Options...

☞ **Click to uncheck** ☐ Start sync when device connects

☞ **Click** OK

Now you can synchronize your MP3 player like this:

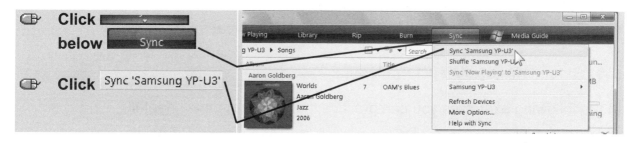

☞ **Click** below **Sync**

☞ **Click** Sync 'Samsung YP-U3'

Synchronization will take place according to the playlists set.

When the synchronization process has completed you see the message 🔄 Sync Complete :

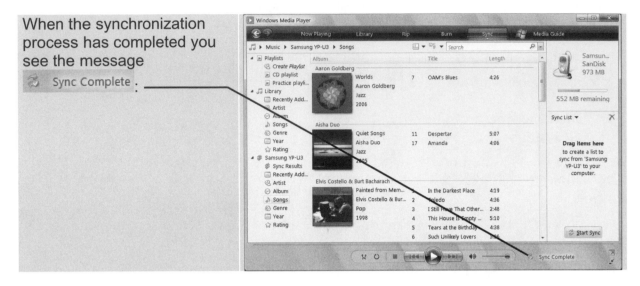

➡ **Please note:**

During the automatic synchronization process, lower priority tracks will be removed from your MP3 player to make space for higher priority tracks. Tracks you removed from your computer are also removed from your MP3 player. It is possible to lose tracks when you sync automatically!

➡ **Please note:**

Each *Windows Media Player Library* can be synchronized with up to sixteen devices. This means every family member can set up his own synchronization or you can use multiple devices yourself. When you try to synchronize another device and the limit of sixteen has been reached, an error message will be displayed.

Synchronization is a practical way to exchange files with your MP3 player. Most of the time manual synchronization will be preferred, but when you make good use of your playlists, you can have them synchronized automatically as well. Then you can automatically add the newest tracks or the tracks you play most to your MP3 player. That way you always have new tracks or your current favorites on your player.

☞ **Disconnect the MP3 player from the computer**

☞ **Check the audio files that are on your MP3 player**

☞ **Close *Windows Media Player* 👣³**

In the following exercises you can practice the tasks from this chapter.

5.6 Exercises

The following exercises help you to practice what you have learned in this chapter. Have you forgotten how to do something? Use the number beside the footsteps to look it up in the appendix *How Do I Do That Again?*

Exercise: Synchronization

Synchronization is a simple and convenient way to maintain your MP3 player.

- ✔ Open *Windows Media Player*. [5]
- ✔ Go to the *Library*. [8]
- ✔ Create a new playlist named *Travel music*. [10]
- ✔ Add a track to the playlist. [11]
- ✔ Add one of the albums you ripped to the playlist *Travel music*. [12]
- ✔ Save the playlist. [38]
- ✔ Go to the *Sync* tab. [39]
- ✔ Connect your MP3 player.
- ✔ Add *Travel music* to the *Sync list*. [40]
- ✔ Sync the player with *Travel music*. [41]
- ✔ Remove a track from the player. [42]
- ✔ Disconnect the MP3 player from the computer.
- ✔ Close *Windows Media Player*. [3]

5.7 Background Information

Glossary	
Conversion	Transforming files to a different file format or quality level that is optimized for playback on the device. Conversion does not affect the original file.
Driver	Software that enables hardware or devices (such as a printer, mouse, MP3 player or keyboard) to work with *Windows*. Every device needs a driver in order for it to work.
Sync / Synchronize	In *Windows Media Player*, the process of maintaining digital media files on a portable device based on the rules or actions specified by the user. This may require copying digital media files from a computer to a device, updating information on the device, or deleting files from the device.

Source: Windows Help and Support

Automatic synchronization

When you connect a device to the computer for the first time, *Windows Media Player* selects the sync method (automatic or manual) that is most suitable for this type of device. This depends on the storage capacity of your MP3 player and the size of your *Library*. If the storage capacity exceeds 4 Gigabytes (GB) and your total *Library* can fit on it, the entire *Library* is synchronized automatically.

If the storage capacity of the device is less than 4 GB or if the total *Library* does not fit on the device, manual synchronization is selected by *Windows Media Player*.

You can adjust these settings yourself like you have learned in this chapter.

What kind of MP3 players are there?

MP3 players are very popular. More and more types are released. Below you see a few examples:

MP3 Flash Players

These players are very small and lightweight, with a built-in flash memory card

Here you see the *Creative Nano Plus 1GB*, with built-in FM tuner.

MP3 Jukeboxes

These MP3 players have a hard disk ranging in size from 4 to 40 Gigabyte.

Here you see *Creative Zen* with 20 GB hard disk on the left.

On the right you see the *iRiver H340 SE* with 40 GB, hard disk and a color display to view photos.

Please note: the players above are possibly not (yet) compatible with *Windows Media Player 11*. When you buy an MP3 player, look for the specifications 'compatible with *Windows Vista* and *Windows Media Player 11*' and ask the salesperson about it.

MP3 CD player

An MP3 CD player is a portable CD player *(discman)* that plays regular CDs as well as MP3 files. You burn the MP3 files on a data CD for that. This way you can fit up to 700 MB of MP3 files on one CD-R.

Which MP3 player is suitable for you?
If you want to buy a (new) MP3 player, you have to consider a few things. Do you only want to play MP3 and WMA files? Then you need to consider how many tracks you want to be able to store on the MP3 player. The storage capacity of an MP3 player is measured in an amount of MB (Megabyte) or GB (Gigabyte). For a good quality track you need about 4 MB. This means that you can fit about 120 tracks on a 512 MB MP3 player, roughly eight hours of music.

Many MP3 players can do a lot more than just play audio files. You can ask yourself if you want to use any of these functions. The additional functions can be:

- a built-in FM tuner;
- a voice recorder you can use to record a speech for example;
- the possibility to store photos and view these on a small screen;
- record directly in MP3 format from any analog or digital source;
- an equalizer to adjust the sound of your favorite music.

Aside from these additional functions you can also consider the following:
- is it possible to extend the memory of the MP3 player?
- can the *firmware* (internal software) of the MP3 player be updated when new functions are added or new file formats are developed?
- is it a *Plug 'n Play* device, or do you need to install software on your computer to be able to transfer files to the player?

Always make sure that the MP3 player is compatible with *Windows Vista* and *Windows Media Player 11*.

In general: the larger the memory, the more expensive the MP3 player. The same thing goes for the extra functions: the more you can do with the player, the more expensive it will be.

Nonprofit organization *Consumer Reports* as well as diverse computer magazines and websites such as Cnet.com publish comparative tests of MP3 players on a regular basis. These articles provide up-to-date information about these devices.

5.8 Tips

💡 **Tip**

You can find more practical information about synchronization in the *Windows Media Player* help windows. In *Media Player* you can open a help window like this:

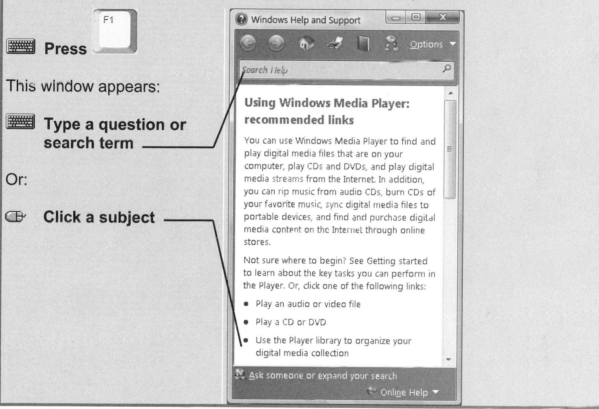

Press `F1`

This window appears:

Type a question or search term

Or:

Click a subject

💡 **Tip**

Reverse Sync

You can also use the new reverse sync feature of *Windows Media Player* to transfer files from your MP3 player or another device to the *Library*.

For example audio recordings you made with your MP3 player, or perhaps part of a radio show you recorded from the radio in your MP3 player. Or files you copied from another computer. In addition, many mobile phones can be used as MP3 player and camera, so you can use the reverse sync to copy your photos to the *Library*.

First you add these files to the *Sync list*, and then you copy them to the *Library* using the button ⟳ Copy from Device.

Notes

Write down your notes here.

6. The Appearance of Windows Media Player

It is very easy to have *Windows Media Player* run unobtrusively in the background while you are busy with other programs. You can listen to your favorite music as you work in *Word* for example. It is not necessary to have the *Windows Media Player* window in full view all of the time. When you have a smaller computer screen every bit of screen space may be needed by a program you are running. Fortunately, you can adjust the display mode of *Windows Media Player* to smaller sizes and still have all the conveniences of the player right at hand.

Perhaps you are a little tired of the same old *Windows Media Player* window. Did you know that you can customize its appearance to suit your own taste? Not only can you adjust size and colors but other aspects of the program can be 'decorated' as well. You can have your player look like an old fashioned radio or a cartoon character.

In this chapter you learn the following:

- switch to compact mode;
- switch to skin mode;
- display *Windows Media Player* full screen;
- display the visualization full screen;
- activate the mini player on the taskbar;
- change the colors;
- what a *skin* is;
- how to choose a different skin.

6.1 The Compact Mode

Windows Media Player has five different display modes:
- full (the default view)
- skin
- compact
- full screen
- mini player

You can easily switch back and forth between modes to suit your preferences.

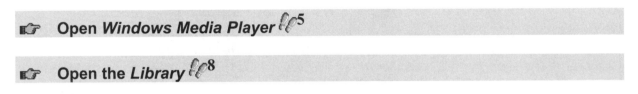

So far you have worked in the *full mode*. You can switch to the *compact mode* with one mouse click:

This view displays only the most important buttons and no visualization. With just one mouse click you can return to the full mode:

6.2 The Skin Mode

When you do not need the full mode, but you want to see more than you did in the compact mode, you can choose the skin mode:

☞ **Play a track** ✍¹

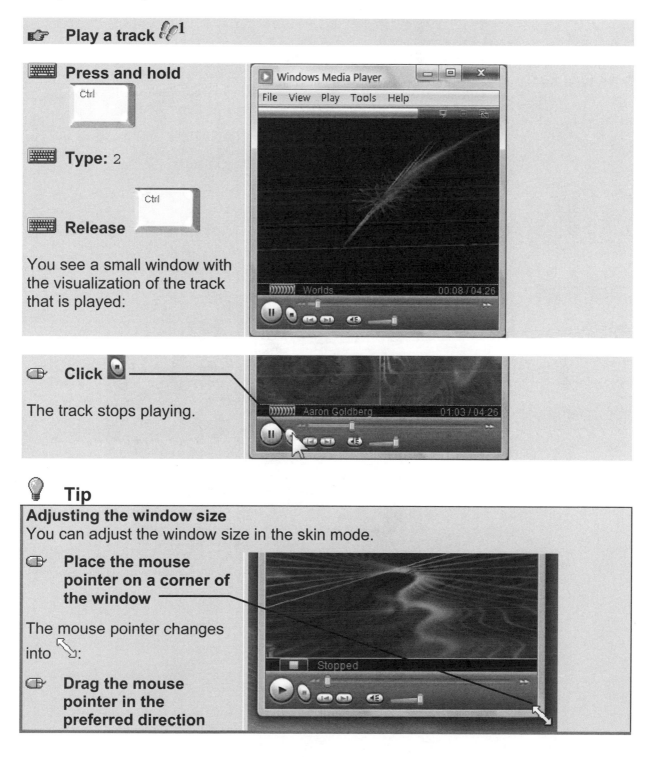

Press and hold

Ctrl

Type: 2

Ctrl

Release

You see a small window with the visualization of the track that is played:

Click ⊙

The track stops playing.

💡 **Tip**

Adjusting the window size
You can adjust the window size in the skin mode.

☞ **Place the mouse pointer on a corner of the window**

The mouse pointer changes into ↘:

☞ **Drag the mouse pointer in the preferred direction**

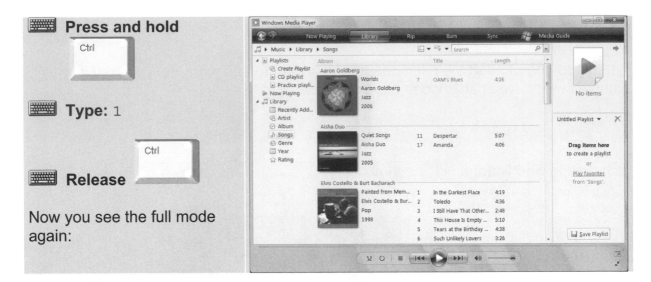

Press and hold Ctrl

Type: 1

Release Ctrl

Now you see the full mode again:

6.3 Full Screen

You can also display *Windows Media Player* full screen. This is only possible when you display a visualization:

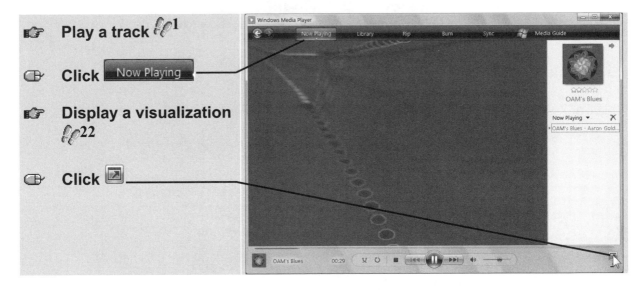

☞ **Play a track** 𝄞1

🖱 **Click** Now Playing

☞ **Display a visualization** 𝄞22

🖱 **Click** ▣

The window fills the entire screen:

☞ **Do not move the mouse pointer**

After a few moments the bar at the bottom of the screen also disappears and the *Visualization* window is displayed full screen.

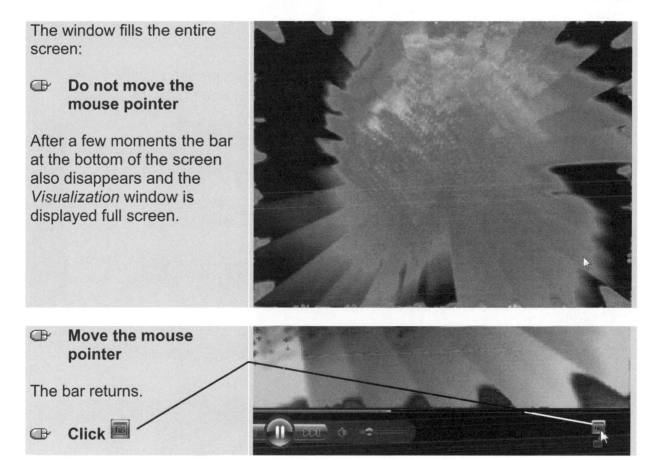

☞ **Move the mouse pointer**

The bar returns.

☞ **Click** 🖾

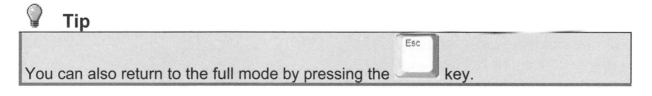

You see the full mode again.

💡 **Tip**

You can also return to the full mode by pressing the [Esc] key.

6.4 Mini Player Mode

To make the most amount of screen space available while working, place *Windows Media Player* in its smallest mode right on your taskbar. Here is how to do that:

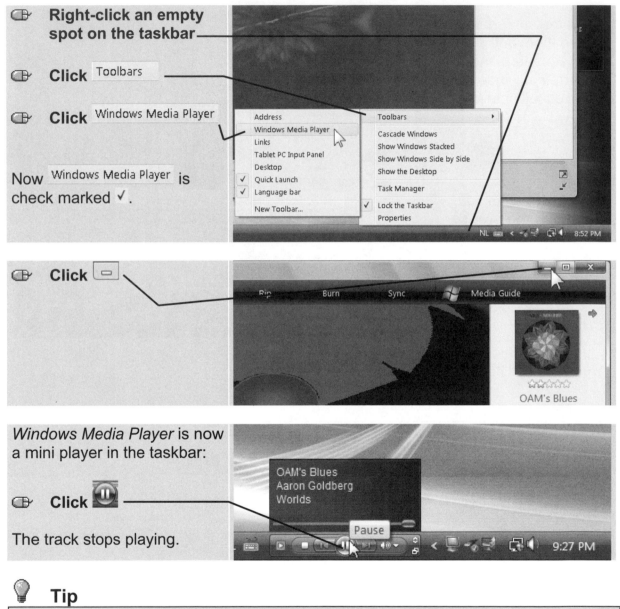

☞ **Right-click an empty spot on the taskbar**

☞ **Click** Toolbars

☞ **Click** Windows Media Player

Now Windows Media Player is check marked ✓.

☞ **Click** ⬜

Windows Media Player is now a mini player in the taskbar:

☞ **Click** ⏸

The track stops playing.

💡 **Tip**

| **Display track information** |
| When you point to the mini player, a small window appears above it. This window displays track information for the track that is currently being played. |

Now the screen is free for other programs, while every button you need to play tracks is in the taskbar. To return to the full mode:

⇨ **Please note:**

Every time you minimize the *Windows Media Player* window by clicking ⬜, it will be displayed as a mini player in the taskbar. You can turn off the mini player by removing it from the taskbar:

Right-click an empty part of the taskbar

Click Toolbars

Click Windows Media Player

Windows Media Player is no longer check marked.

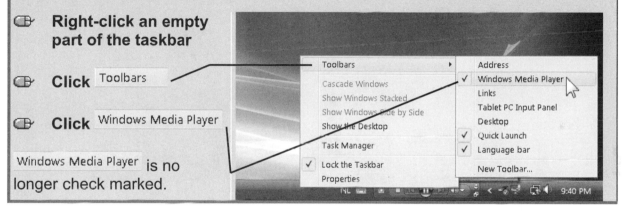

6.5 Changing the Colors

By default, *Media Player* has a black menu bar with blue buttons. You can adjust the color of the buttons yourself:

Click below Now Playing

Click Enhancements

Click Color Chooser

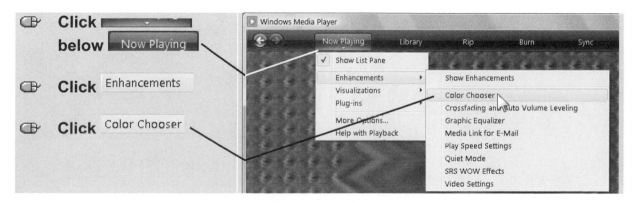

👆 **Click** Next preset

The button has changed color.

👆 **Click** Next preset **a couple of times**

You see that the color of the buttons keeps changing:

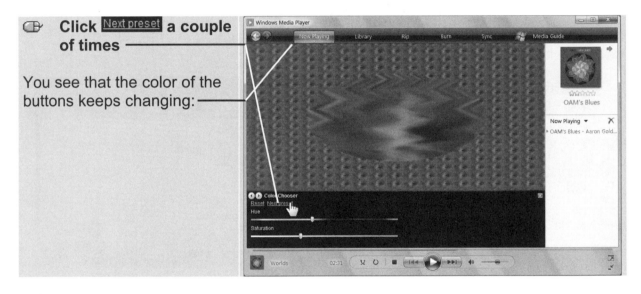

➡️ **Please note:**

Sometimes just one button changes color and sometimes all buttons do.

To go back to the color you are used to:

👆 **Click** Reset

You see the familiar blue buttons again.

💡 **Tip**

Do-It-Yourself
With the sliders for 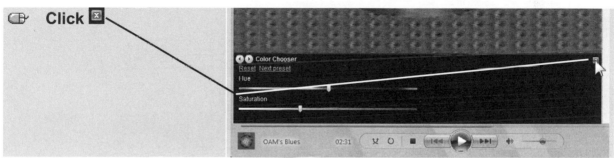 Hue and Saturation you can create a color scheme yourself.

Moving the Hue slider a little bit to the left or the right changes the color of one or all buttons.

🖰 **Click** ⊠

6.6 Choosing a Different Skin

If you are tired of the appearance of the default skin for *Windows Media Player,* you can easily select a different one:

🖰 **Right-click an empty part of the bar at the bottom of the window**

🖰 **Click** View

🖰 **Click** Skin Chooser

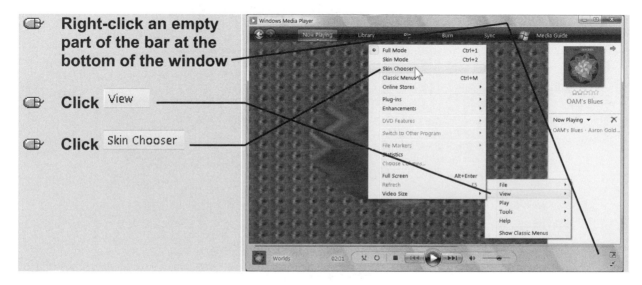

Click Revert

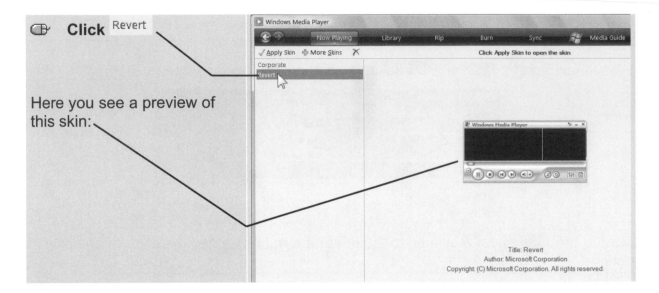

Here you see a preview of this skin:

➡️ **Please note:**

You probably see more skins in the list. Try Revert first to practice applying skins.

Click ✓ Apply Skin

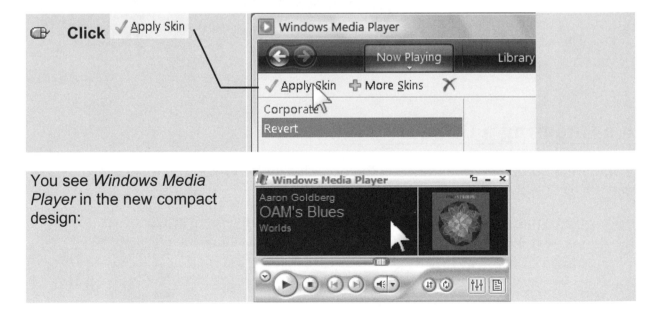

You see *Windows Media Player* in the new compact design:

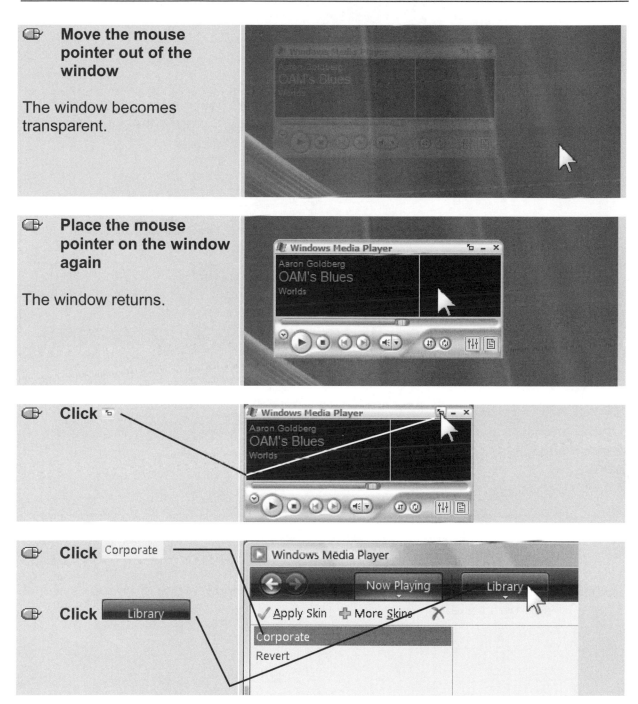

Move the mouse pointer out of the window

The window becomes transparent.

Place the mouse pointer on the window again

The window returns.

Click 🗗

Click Corporate

Click Library

You see the familiar *Windows Media Player* window again.

💡 **Tip**

Downloading more skins
If this was the first time you visited the *Skin chooser*, there are only a few skins to choose from. On the *Microsoft* website *Skins for Media Player* you can download and install skins quickly and easily. This is a free service. To go to that website:

☞ **If necessary, connect to the Internet**

👉 **Click** ➕ More Skins

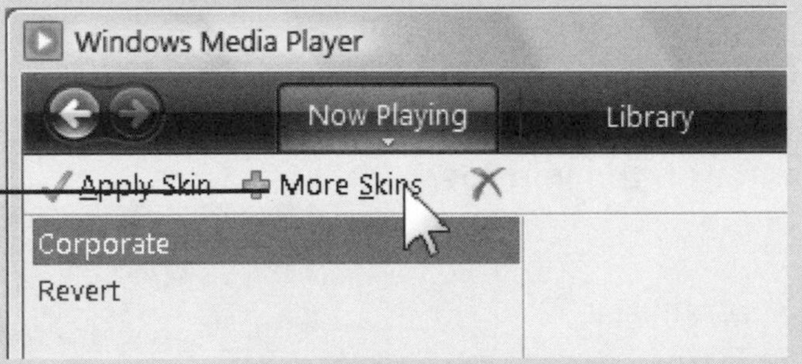

👉 **If necessary, click** Extras

👉 **Click** Skins

On this website you can choose and download a new skin.

☞ **Close Windows Media Player** 👣³

In this chapter you have seen how you can adjust the appearance of *Windows Media Player* to your own taste.

6.7 Exercises

The following exercises help you to practice what you have learned in this chapter. Have you forgotten how to do something? Use the number beside the footsteps to look it up in the appendix *How Do I Do That Again?*

Exercise: Choosing a Display Mode

By choosing another display mode, you give *Windows Media Player* a new look.

✔ Open *Windows Media Player*. $\ell\ell^5$

✔ Go to the *Library*. $\ell\ell^8$

✔ Play a track. $\ell\ell^1$

✔ Switch to the skin mode. $\ell\ell^{23}$

✔ Go back to the full mode. $\ell\ell^{24}$

✔ Open the tab *Now Playing*. $\ell\ell^{25}$

✔ Display *Windows Media Player* in full screen. $\ell\ell^{26}$

✔ Go back to the full mode. $\ell\ell^{27}$

✔ Open the color chooser. $\ell\ell^{28}$

✔ Change the color of the buttons by changing the hue. $\ell\ell^{29}$

✔ Go back to the default colors. $\ell\ell^{30}$

✔ Close the color chooser. $\ell\ell^{31}$

✔ Stop playing the track. $\ell\ell^2$

✔ Close *Windows Media Player*. $\ell\ell^3$

6.8 Background Information

Glossary	
Color chooser	Part of the window where you can change the color of *Windows Media Player* as it appears in full mode.
Full mode	The default operational state of *Windows Media Player* from which all of its features are available. *Media Player* can also appear in skin mode, mini player mode, or full screen mode.
Skin	A user interface that provides an alternative appearance and customized functionality for software such as *Windows Media Player*.
Source: Windows Help and Support	

Codec

A codec is software that is used to compress or decompress a digital media file such as a song or a video. *Windows Media Player* and other programs use codecs to create and play digital media files.

For example, when you rip a song from an audio CD to your computer, *Windows Media Player* uses the *Windows Media Audio codec* to compress the song into a compact WMA file. When you play that WMA file, *Media Player* uses the *Windows Media Audio codec* to decompress the file so the music can be played through your speakers.

If you get a message that says that your computer is missing a codec, you are probably trying to play, burn, or sync a file that was compressed by using a codec that *Windows* or *Windows Media Player* does not include by default. In many cases, you can download and install the missing codec by clicking the *Web Help* button in the error message dialog box.

Source: Windows Help and Support

6.9 Tips

💡 Tip

Windows Media Player always on top

When you are working with another program, you can keep *Windows Media Player* on top of your other windows. The compact mode is very suitable for this.
You can adjust the setting like this:

☞ **Click** [▮▮▮▮▮▮] **below** [Library]

☞ **Click** [More Options...]

☞ **Click the tab** [Player]

☞ **Click to check mark**
Keep the Player on top of other wir

☞ **Click** [OK]

💡 Tip

Full screen visualization
When you display *Windows Media Player* in full mode, you can let the visualization fill the entire window.
You can do that by closing the *List Pane*:

Click ⇨

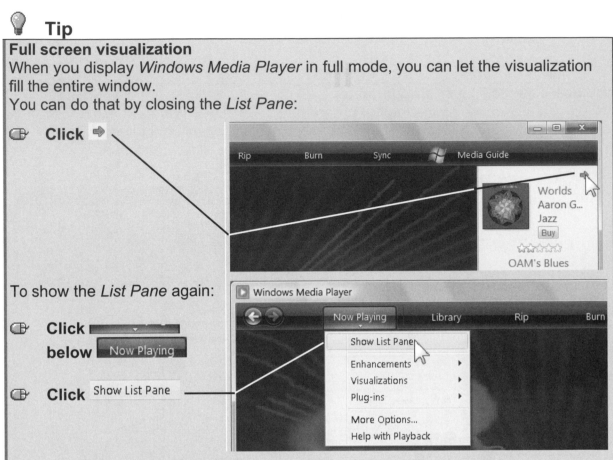

To show the *List Pane* again:

Click ▬▬▬▬ ▾
below [Now Playing]

Click [Show List Pane]

Please note the difference between *full mode* and *full screen mode*:

- *full mode* is the default operational state of *Windows Media Player* from which all of its features are available. The full mode does not have to be displayed full screen.
- *full screen mode* means the entire screen is filled, for example by a visualization or video.

💡 Tip

Problems with Windows Media Player?
Windows Media Player contains an extensive Help feature where you can find more information about the program features. Refer to the Help section when you need specific information about the functionality of parts of the program. You can quickly access the Help section using the F1 key.

When you do experience a problem with the program, you can find self-help options, technical support and a section containing Frequently Asked Questions on this web page:
http://www.microsoft.com/windows/windowsmedia/player/windowsvista/troubleshooting.aspx

7. Video, DVD and Radio in Windows Media Player

Windows Media Player can be used for more than just listening to music. The program is also well suited for watching videos. In *Windows Media Player* you can play video files from the hard disk of your computer as well as movies on DVD.

This feature is especially interesting for *Windows Vista Home Basic* users. Users of other *Windows Vista* editions have the more extensive *Windows Media Center* at their disposal.

You can use *Windows Media Player* to listen to radio stations from around the world on the Internet. Some radio stations broadcast exclusively on the Internet, others broadcast both their normal broadcast and one (or more) for the Internet.

In this chapter you learn how to:

- watch a video file;
- adjust the display settings;
- view the video full screen;
- watch a DVD on your computer;
- listen to a radio station;
- add a radio station to *My stations*;
- find a radio station with a certain theme.

7.1 Opening a Video File

In the previous chapter you have used the *Library* in *Windows Media Player* for audio files. Now you are going to use the *Library* for video files:

☞ **Open *Windows Media Player*** ⅇℓ⁵

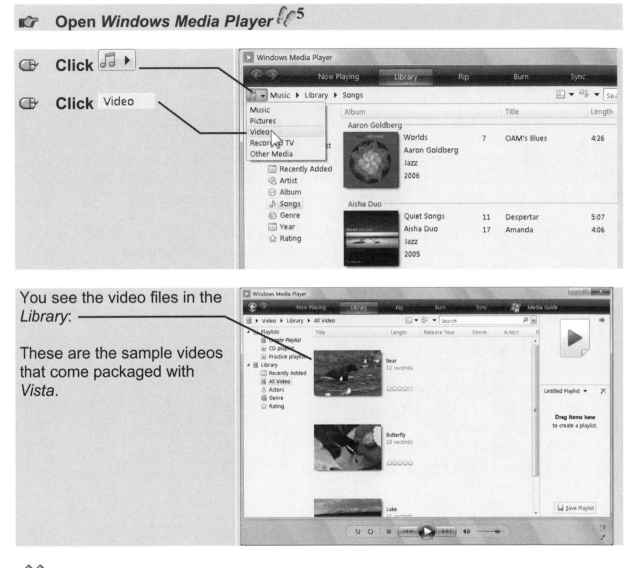

☞ **Click** 🎵 ▶

☞ **Click** Video

You see the video files in the *Library*:

These are the sample videos that come packaged with *Vista*.

HELP! I do not see these video files.

It is possible that you do not see these files on your computer, but other files instead. The video files you see in the example can also be found on the CD-ROM you received with this book. Please refer to **Appendix A** for instructions on how to copy these video files to the correct location. Remember you have to search and add the files to the *Library* after you copy them to the hard disk of your computer.

※ HELP! I see each file twice.

If you already copied the practice files from the CD-ROM to the hard disk of your computer, these files are possibly stored in two locations: the location where *Vista* stored the original sample video files and the location where you copied the practice files. This will not pose a problem.

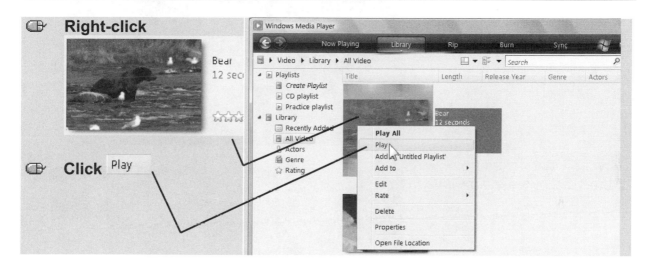

☞ **Right-click**

☞ **Click** Play

➡ Please note:

When you click Play All all video files from the *Library* are played in a row.

The short video is played. Play the video again:

☞ **Click** ▶

※ HELP! The video keeps repeating.

If the video does not stop automatically, but is played repeatedly, then the *Repeat* feature is turned on. You can turn it off like this:

☞ **Click** ⟳

HELP! I can hardly see the video.

Is the video displayed very small in *Windows Media Player*? You can correct that by changing a setting:

☞ **Right-click in the video**

☞ **Point to** Video Size

☞ **Click** Fit Video to Player on Resize

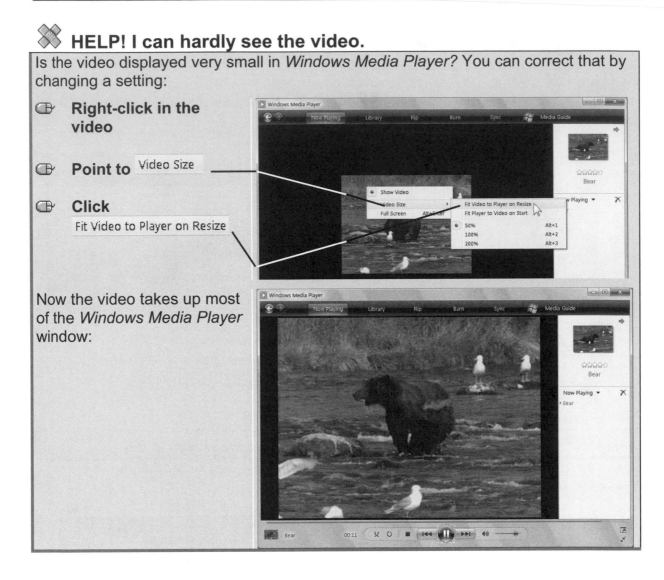

Now the video takes up most of the *Windows Media Player* window:

7.2 Displaying a Video File Full Screen

The *Windows Media Player* contains a couple of bars and panes that limit the size of the video. This can be very annoying when you watch a video. It is very easy to enlarge the window. For example, close the *List Pane*:

☞ **Click** ➡

The video now fills the complete *Windows Media Player* window. You can even enlarge the video to full screen:

☞ **Play the video again**
𝄞¹

👆 **Click** 🔲 ———————

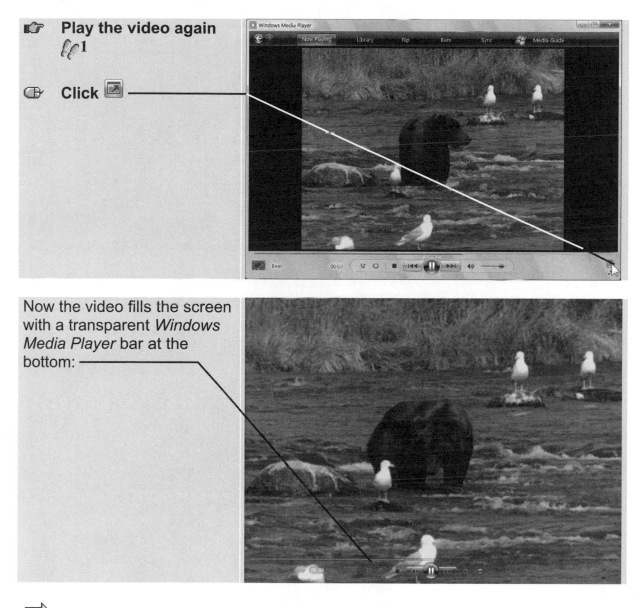

Now the video fills the screen with a transparent *Windows Media Player* bar at the bottom: ——————

⇨ **Please note:**

The sharpness of the video image when it is stretched to full screen depends on the quality of the video.

☞ **Do not move the mouse**

The bar disappears as well.

When you move the mouse, the bar will appear again at the bottom of the screen. Now you can reduce the size of the *Windows Media Player* window again:

☞ **Click** ▣

You see *Windows Media Player* in full mode again.

You have tried out several possibilities for watching video. In the next section you can read how to play a DVD in *Windows Media Player*.

☞ **Close *Windows Media Player*** ℓℓ³

7.3 Playing a DVD

You are not limited to playing videos stored on the hard disk of your computer with *Windows Media Player*. You can also use it to play regular DVDs.

⇨ **Please note:**

To be able to work through this section you need to have a DVD drive installed in your computer.

You can recognize it by this sign:

You also need a DVD with a movie, for example:

If you do not have either one, you can just read through the following sections.

☞ **Insert a DVD in the DVD drive of your computer**

Windows Vista recognizes the disc you just inserted in the DVD drive as a DVD. You are going to play the DVD in *Windows Media Player* just once:

☞ **Make sure the option**
☐ Always do this for DVD movies
is not check marked

🖰 **Click**
▶ Play DVD movie
using Windows Media Player

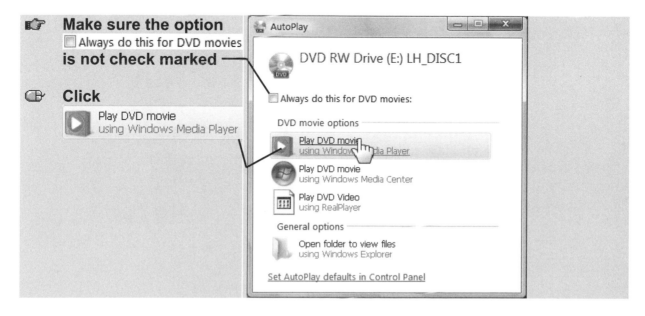

Windows Media Player opens and you see the opening sequence of the DVD in full screen mode.

Most DVDs have a main menu where you can choose which part of the DVD you want to play. The main menu appears after the copyright warnings.

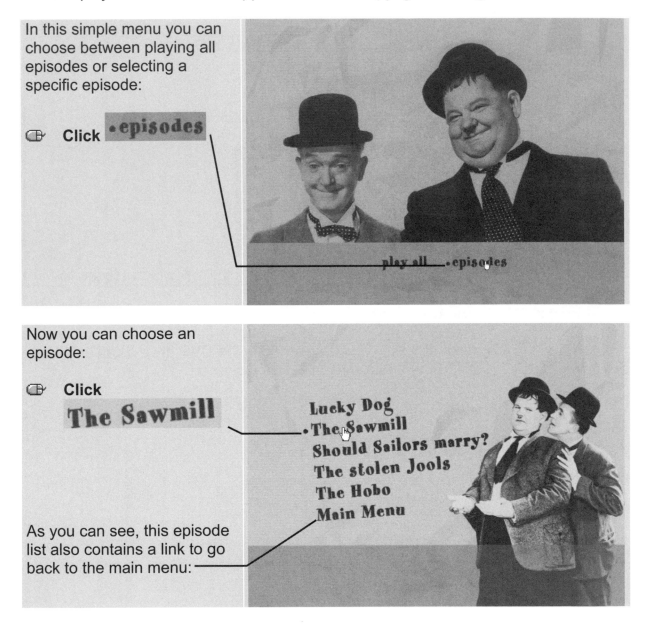

In this simple menu you can choose between playing all episodes or selecting a specific episode:

☞ **Click** •episodes

Now you can choose an episode:

☞ **Click** The Sawmill

As you can see, this episode list also contains a link to go back to the main menu:

The episode starts playing:

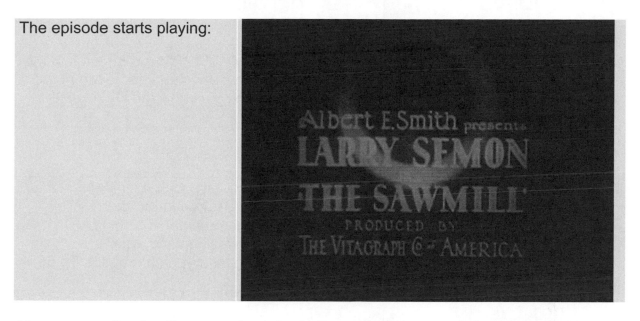

You can use the familiar controls at the bottom of the screen to pause the DVD, or to go to the next scene. The transparent bar appears when you move the mouse:

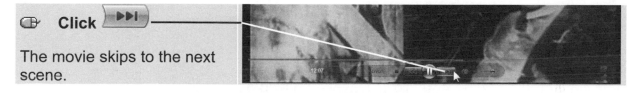

☞ **Click** ▶▶❙

The movie skips to the next scene.

You can also go back to the main menu using this bar:

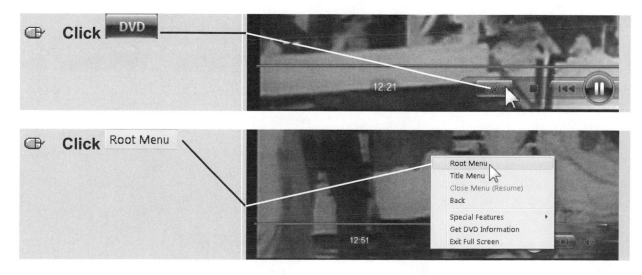

☞ **Click** DVD

☞ **Click** Root Menu

The main menu appears again.

⇒ **Please note:**

On some DVDs you need to choose `Title Menu` instead of `Root Menu` to go back to the main menu. Usually one gives access to the main menu, and the other to the menu where you can choose an episode. This varies depending on how the DVD you are playing was set up.

※ **HELP! The DVD will not play!**

If the DVD refuses to play and you encounter an error message that indicates the DVD video cannot be played or that you are missing a DVD decoder, then there is probably no compatible DVD decoder installed on your computer. To play DVDs, you must have a DVD decoder compatible with *Windows Vista* and *Windows Media Player* installed on your computer. At the end of this chapter you can read a Tip on how to download and install a decoder on your computer.

☞ **Go back to full mode** ℓℓ²⁷

☞ **Close *Windows Media Player*** ℓℓ³

🔅 **Tip**

Downloading DVD information
Just like you did earlier for audio CDs, you can also download information about the DVDs you play from the Internet.

☞ **If necessary, connect to the Internet**

⊕ **Click** ⬛ Library

⊕ **Click** ⊙ Unknown DVD (E:)

⊕ **Right-click** 💿

⊕ **Click** Find DVD Info

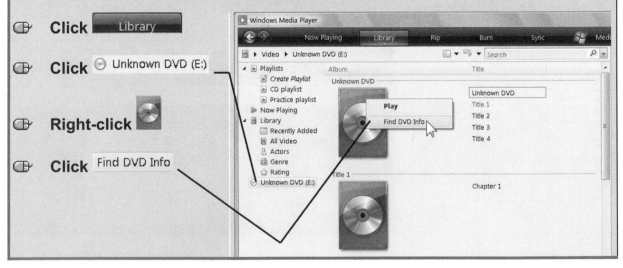

7.4 Radio

You can use the Internet to listen to radio stations from all over the world.

⇨ **Please note:**

To be able to follow the examples in this chapter, you need a high-speed Internet connection, for example DSL or cable Internet.

☞ **Open *Windows Media Player***

☞ **If necessary, connect to the Internet**

☞ **Click** `Media Guide`

Does this button have a different name on your computer?

☞ **Then click** ▬▬▬▼▬▬▬ **below the button**

☞ **Click** Media Guide

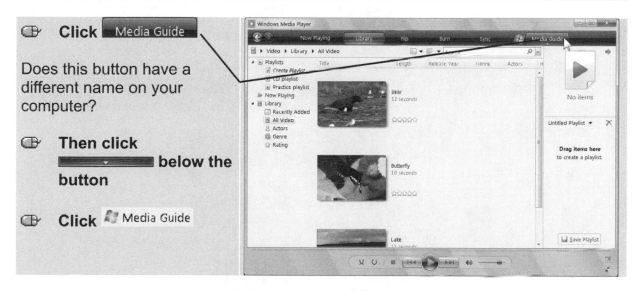

☞ **Click** ▸ Internet Radio

The welcome screen of *Internet radio* contains a number of hyperlinks to popular radio stations. You can try listening to one of these now:

☞ **Click ⩔ beside**
  ▷ NPR National Public Radio

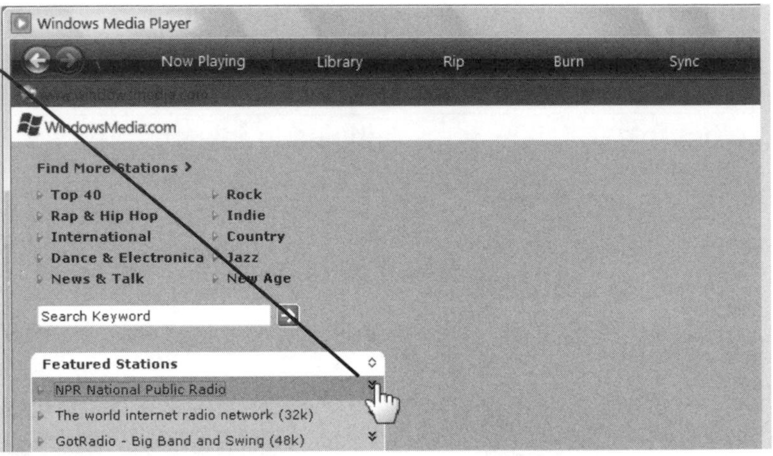

You see more information about this radio station:

☞ **Click ▷ Play**

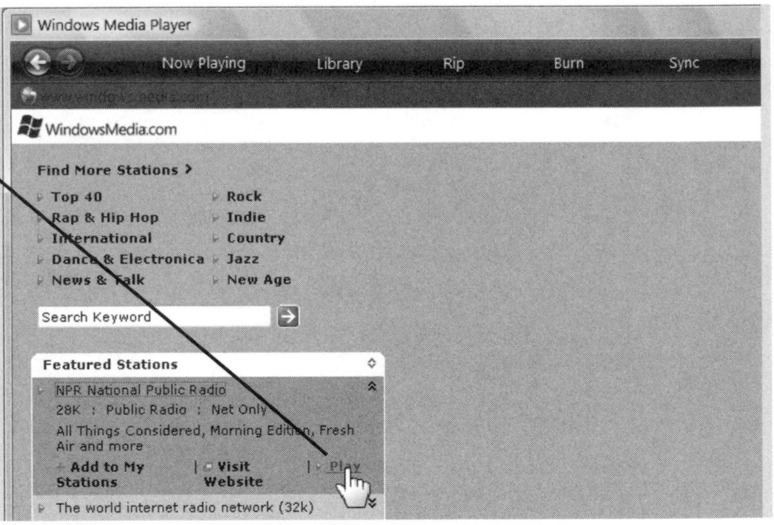

You hear the broadcast of *NPR National Public Radio*. You can stop listening to this broadcast like this:

☞ **Click** ■

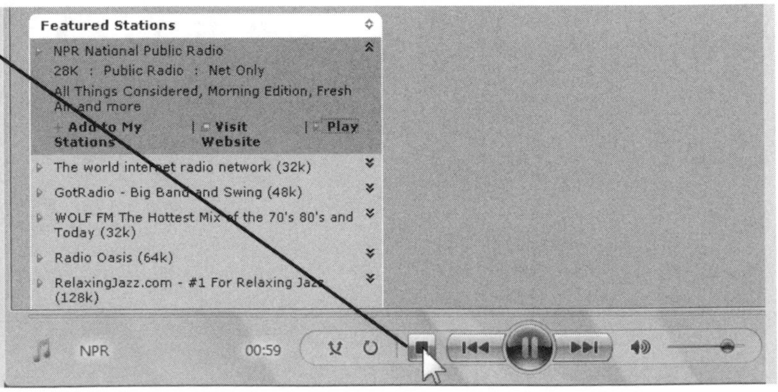

7.5 Adding a Radio Station to My Stations

You can add your favorite radio stations to the page *My Stations*. Then you can find them more easily next time you want to listen to a broadcast.

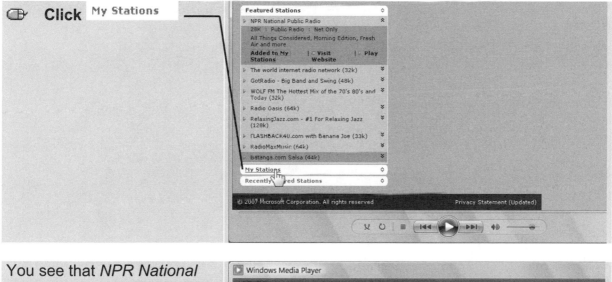

The radio station has been added to your favorite stations. You can verify this:

7.6 Finding a Radio Station

There are several ways to find a radio station in *Windows Media Player*. You can search by genre, keyword or ZIP code. For example, search for the stations that play jazz music:

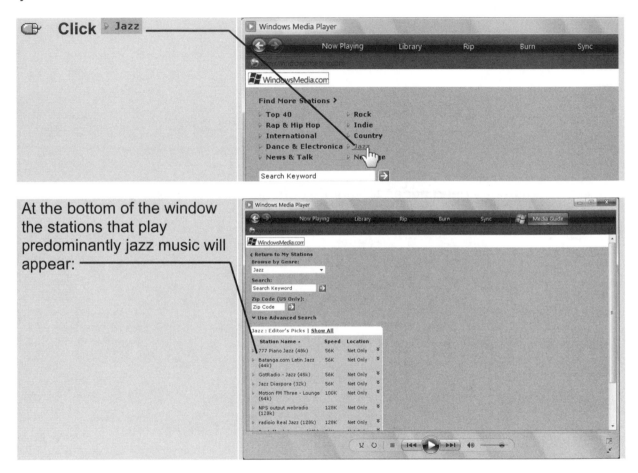

Click ▷ Jazz

At the bottom of the window the stations that play predominantly jazz music will appear:

When there is no section for the station you are looking for, you can try searching by keyword. For example, look for the stations that play country music:

Click
Search Keyword
below Search:

Type:
country

Click ➡

A long list of stations featuring country music appears:

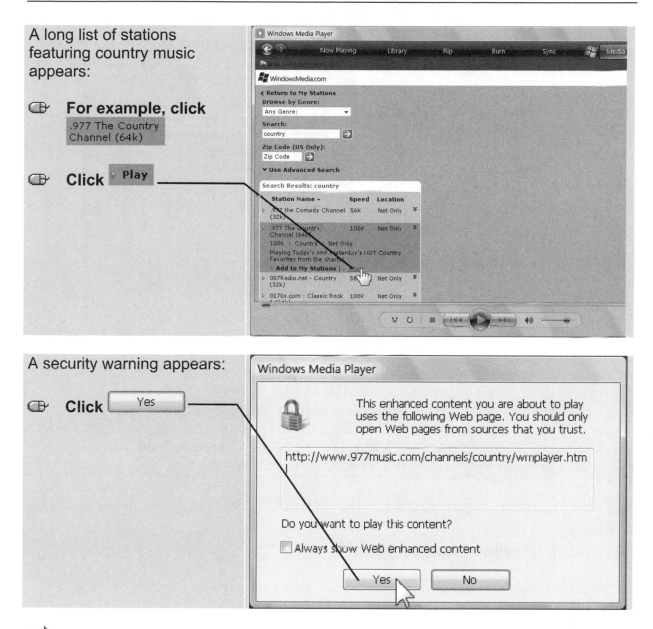

For example, click **.977 The Country Channel (64k)**

Click **Play**

A security warning appears:

Click **Yes**

⇨ **Please note:**

Most Internet radio stations will often have diverse marketing strategies in action. You may see popup windows with offers for free toolbars, virus checks, lotteries etcetera. Do not click on these types of hyperlinks, ignore them and close the extra windows.

The tab *Now playing* displays the website of this radio station:

You can stop listening to the radio broadcast now:

 Click ■ ——————

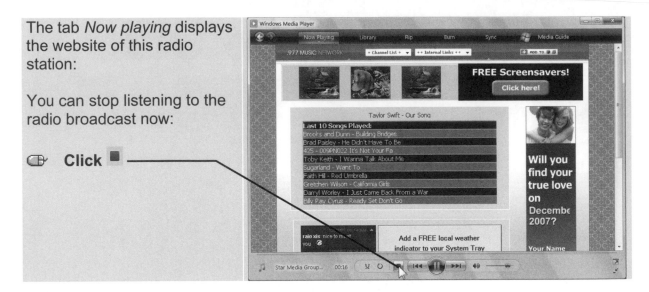

Tip

More radio stations
In *Windows Media Player*, most of the stations listed are Internet radio stations. To be able to listen to your favorite local FM radio station when you go on vacation for example, you can go to the website of that station. The web address is usually the same as the name of the station, for example www.knx1070.com (Los Angeles' KNX 1070) or www.wnyc.org (New York's WNYC 93.9 FM). On the website you will find hyperlinks to listen to the live radio broadcasts (*streaming audio*).

☞ **If necessary, disconnect from the Internet**

☞ **Close *Windows Media Player*** ✍️³

In this section you have learned how to find and listen to radio stations in *Windows Media Player*.

7.7 Exercises

The following exercises help you to practice what you have learned in this chapter. Have you forgotten how to do something? Use the number beside the footsteps to look it up in the appendix *How Do I Do That Again?*

Exercise: Playing a Video

✓ Open *Windows Media Player*. $\ell\ell^5$

✓ Go to the *Library*. $\ell\ell^8$

✓ Display the videos in the *Library*. $\ell\ell^{32}$

✓ Play a video. $\ell\ell^{33}$

✓ Enlarge the window to full screen. $\ell\ell^{26}$

✓ Stop playing the video. $\ell\ell^2$

Exercise: Listening to Internet Radio

✓ Go to the *Media Guide*. $\ell\ell^{34}$

✓ Go to the *Internet Radio* page. $\ell\ell^{35}$

✓ Search by keyword for stations that broadcast *sports* reports. $\ell\ell^{36}$

✓ Listen to a station. $\ell\ell^{37}$

✓ Stop listening to the broadcast. $\ell\ell^2$

✓ Close *Windows Media Player*. $\ell\ell^3$

7.8 Background Information

DVD decoder	A DVD decoder is another name for an MPEG-2 decoder. The content on DVD-Video discs is encoded in the MPEG-2 format, as is the content in DVR-MS files (*Microsoft Recorded TV Shows*) and some AVI files. To play these items in *Windows Media Player*, you need a compatible DVD decoder installed on your computer.
Streaming audio/video	A method of delivering digital media across a network in a continuous flow. The digital media is played on the computer as it is received, for example in *Windows Media Player*. Typically, streaming makes it unnecessary for users to download a file before playing it.

Source: Windows Help and Support

Video and sound card

Every computer contains a video (graphics) card and a sound card. These cards control your monitor and speakers. Sometimes they are separate cards, but often they are combined in one card. They can also be built in on the motherboard (*on-board*).

These cards determine the performance of your computer when you play or create audio or video files. No matter how fast your computer is, when the video card is too slow you may experience 'traffic jams' with the rendering of sound and images. It may also happen that sound and video are not played in sync.

If you plan to work frequently with video, it is advisable to choose a computer with a separate video card that is not built into the motherboard. Separate cards are faster and have more memory. Furthermore, it is easier to upgrade the drivers, which may be necessary when installing new hardware or software. In *laptops* and *notebooks* these cards are usually built into the motherboard, due to the limited space available.

7.9 Tips

💡 Tip

DVD decoder

If the DVD refuses to play and you encounter an error message indicating that the DVD video cannot be played or that a DVD decoder is missing, then there is probably no compatible DVD decoder installed on your computer. To play DVDs, you must have a DVD decoder compatible with *Windows Vista* and *Windows Media Player* installed on your computer.

In *Windows Vista Home Premium* and *Windows Vista Ultimate* this decoder is available by default. When you work with *Windows Vista Home Basic*, *Windows Vista Business*, or *Windows Vista Enterprise* you can purchase and download a DVD decoder for about $15 (price subject to change) on this *Microsoft* webpage:

www.microsoft.com/windows/windowsmedia/player/plugins.aspx#DVDDecoder

On this page you can find hyperlinks to websites of several companies that offer DVD decoders.

The supplier for example has a website with clear instructions on how to order, purchase and download:

When you are not in the U.S. you can click ▼ and select your country from the list:

You will be led through a series of steps as you complete the download procedure.

Because websites change quickly, the pages may look different than what you see in these examples.

💡 Tip

Increasing and decreasing the window size by dragging

The size of the *Windows Media Player* window can be increased or decreased in skin mode as well as in full mode. You can drag both the corners and the edges of the window.

☞ **Place the mouse pointer on** ◣

The mouse pointer changes into 🢔:

☞ **Drag the window in the preferred direction**

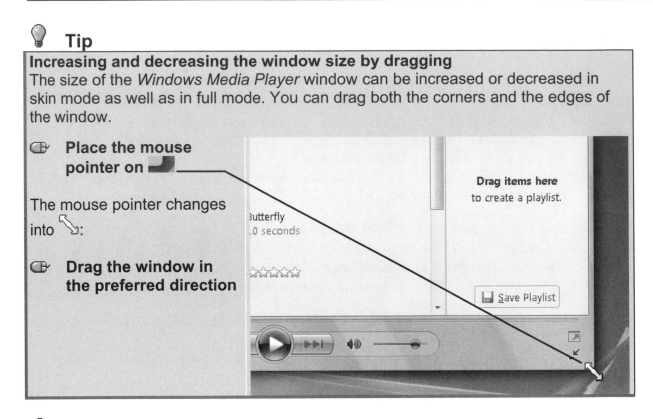

💡 Tip

FAQ

On the website **http://www.microsoft.com/ windows/windowsmedia/ player/faq/default.mspx** you can find a large number of Frequently Asked Questions about different features, known problems and solutions for *Windows Media Player*.

For more self-help options and specific technical support in troubleshooting *Windows Media Player* you can refer to this website:
http://www.microsoft.com/windows/windowsmedia/player/windowsvista/troubleshooting.aspx

8. Windows Movie Maker and DVD Maker

Digital video editing has become increasingly popular in recent years. For this purpose *Windows Vista* is equipped with the program *Windows Movie Maker*.

You can use this program to edit the videos on your hard disk as well as the footage you have on your digital video camera. You can use this program to rearrange your rough clips in the order you prefer and trim the clips to the right size. You can also add titles, transitions, effects, narrations and music to the movie.

When you have finished editing the movie, you can save the result to the hard disk of your computer. This is called *publishing* the movie.
You can also send the movie directly by e-mail without saving it.

You can use *Windows DVD Maker* to burn your movie to DVD, so you can play it in your regular DVD player and watch it on television. *Windows DVD Maker* is not available in *Windows Vista Home Basic*.

In this chapter you learn the following:

- open *Windows Movie Maker*;
- import video files, photos and music;
- edit a movie;
- split and trim video clips;
- add transitions, effects and titles;
- add music and a narration;
- play a movie;
- publish a movie;
- send a movie by e-mail;
- burn a movie to DVD with *Windows DVD Maker*.

⇨ **Please note:**

In this chapter the sample videos that come packaged with *Windows Vista* are used. If you do not have these files on the hard disk of your computer, you can copy the files from the CD-ROM you received with this book. In **Appendix A** at the end of this book you can read how to do that.

8.1 Opening Windows Movie Maker

You can open the program *Windows Movie Maker* like this:

☞ **Click**

☞ **Point to** ▶ All Programs

☞ **Click** 🎬 Windows Movie Maker

🔷 HELP! Movie Maker does not start.

Does *Movie Maker* not start?

Then you can download an alternative version of *Movie Maker* from the *Microsoft* website:

> **Windows Movie Maker**
>
> ⚠ Windows Movie Maker kan niet worden uitgevoerd omdat er onvoldoende videogeheugen beschikbaar is. Sluit ongebruikte, geopende programma's af of start de computer opnieuw op.
>
> Meer informatie over de vereisten voor de videokaart.
>
> OK

☞ **Open *Internet Explorer* and surf to www.microsoft.com/downloads**

⌨ **Type in the *Search Box*:** Windows Movie Maker 2.6

Search All Downloads ▼ Windows Movie Maker 2.6 [Go]

☞ **Click** [Go]

On the webpage that appears, click the link **Windows Movie Maker 2.6**. On the page that follows, click **Download**. Then follow the instructions to download and install this special version of *Movie Maker*.

Please note: version *Movie Maker 2.6* is only meant for *Windows Vista* users that have a computer which does not run the *Vista* version of *Movie Maker*. When *Movie Maker* opens normally on your computer, you must **not** download this version 2.6.

The images you see in this chapter do not match the screen prints of *Movie Maker 2.6*. You can download a supplement to this chapter by going to the news page of the website of this book: **www.visualsteps.com/photovista**.

You see the *Windows Movie Maker* window:

Tasks Pane:

Contents Pane (for video clips and effects):

Preview monitor:

Storyboard:

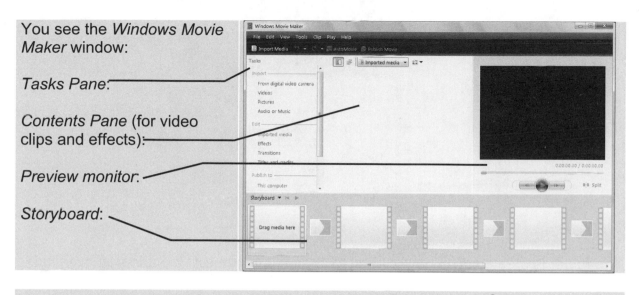

☞ **If necessary, enlarge the *Windows Movie Maker* window** 🦶**56**

8.2 Importing Video Files

Before you import video files, create a new folder where you can store all of the project's files. You can do that like this:

🖐 **Click** [View]

A menu appears:

🖐 **Click** [🔧 Collections]

The *Tasks Pane* has changed into the *Collections pane*:

☞ **Right-click**
  Imported media

A menu appears:

☞ **Click**
  New Collection Folder

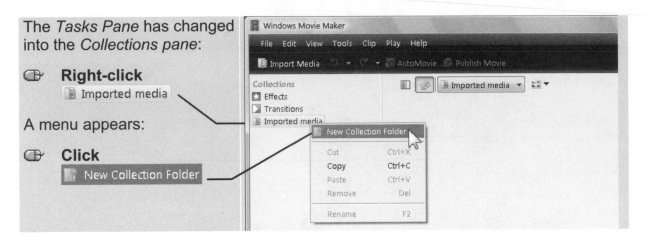

The folder is created. You do not need to change the name of the folder at this time.

☞ **Click** View

A menu appears:

☞ **Click** Tasks

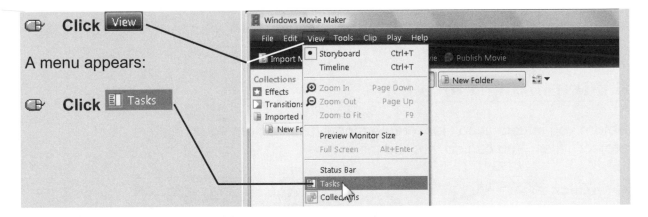

You see the *Tasks Pane* again. The new folder is opened. You can use this folder for all of the files that belong to this project.

To be able to edit a video file, you need to import it into *Windows Movie Maker* first. You can use the video files on the hard disk of your computer for that. You can also import a video file directly from your digital video camera. In **section 8.18 Importing Video from Your Digital Video Camera** you can read how to connect your camera to the computer.

In this chapter you will get to know the basic features of *Windows Movie Maker* using the *Windows Vista* sample video files. You can find these on the hard disk of your computer.

Click Videos

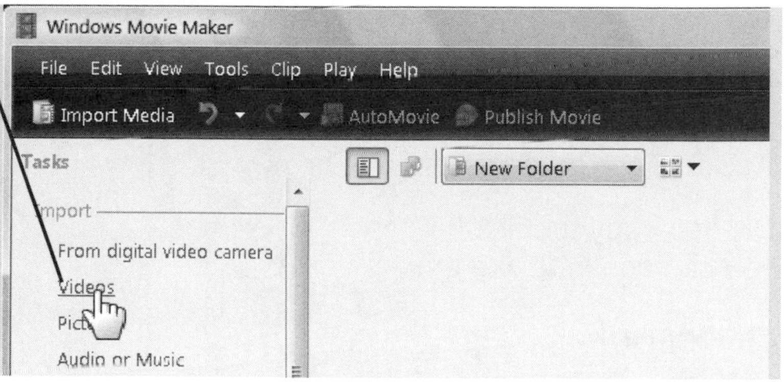

You see a window displaying the contents of the *Videos* folder. In the folder *Videos* you find a shortcut to the sample videos.

Double-click

Sample Videos

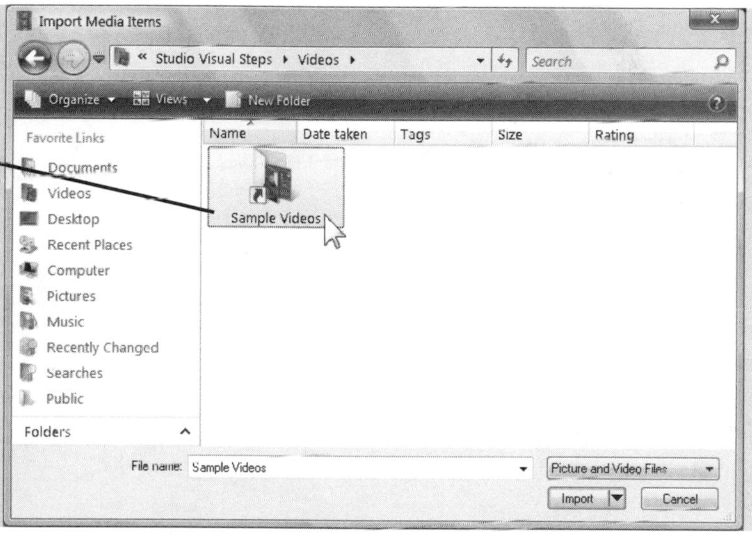

Now you see the sample videos:

Click Bear

Click Import ▼

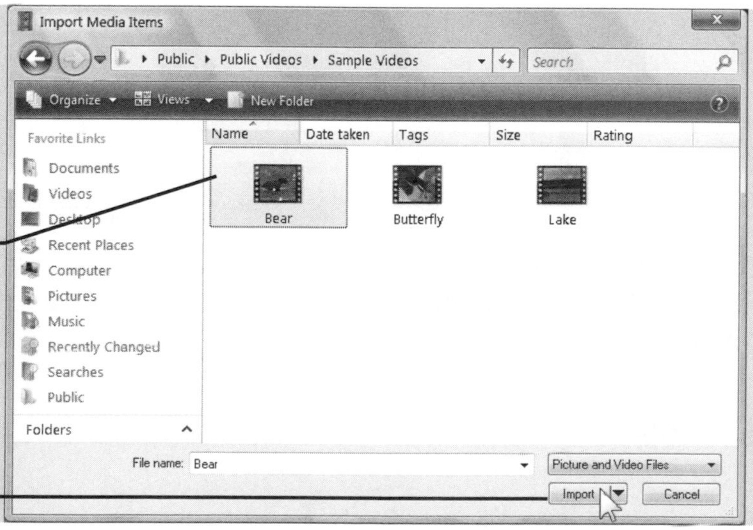

✖ HELP! I do not have these files.

If the practice files are not on the hard disk of your computer, you can copy them from the CD-ROM you received with this book. You can read how to do that in **Appendix A** at the end of this book.

Did you copy the files? Then you can continue like this:

☞ **Click** 📄 Documents

☞ **Double-click**
   📁 Practice files

You find the practice files in the folder 📁 Video :

☞ **Double-click** 📁 Video

Now you can import the video clip *Bear*.

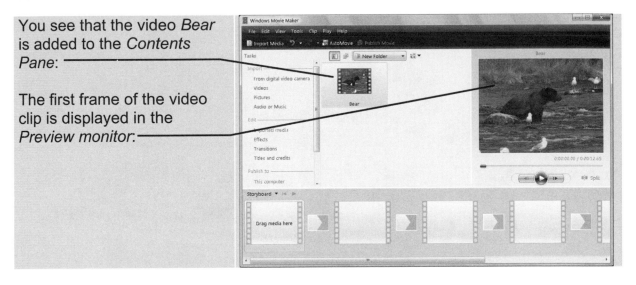

You see that the video *Bear* is added to the *Contents Pane*:

The first frame of the video clip is displayed in the *Preview monitor*:

One of the handy things possible with *Windows Movie Maker* is that you can combine several video clips in one movie. In the next step, you will import a few more video clips.

☞ **Import the file *Lake*** 👣57

☞ **Import the file *Butterfly*** 👣57

The three clips are now displayed in *Windows Movie Maker*:

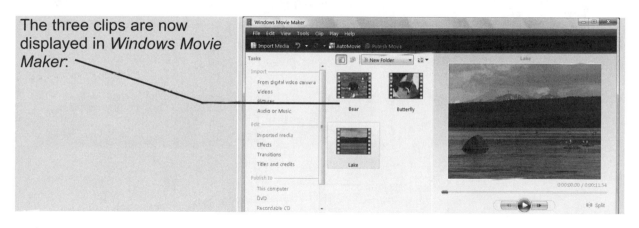

⇨ **Please note:**

Windows Movie Maker does not store an actual copy of the source files. Instead, a shortcut to the original source file is created. This shortcut appears in *Windows Movie Maker* as a clip.

Any edits that you make in *Windows Movie Maker* do not affect the original source file. You can edit audio clips, video clips, or pictures in *Windows Movie Maker* and be confident that the original audio, video, or picture source files remain unchanged.

While you are working on a movie it is very important that you do not move or delete the original files. If you do, the shortcuts are no longer correct. *Movie Maker* can no longer find the original files and you will end up with an empty project.

8.3 Importing Photos

Not only video files, but photos as well can be used in your movie. For example, you can interrupt a movie of a family gathering with a couple of pictures taken the same day. You can import photos the same way you import video clips:

Click Pictures

The folder *Pictures* is opened. Here you see a shortcut to the *Windows Vista* sample files. If you do not have these sample pictures, you can also use one of your own photos.

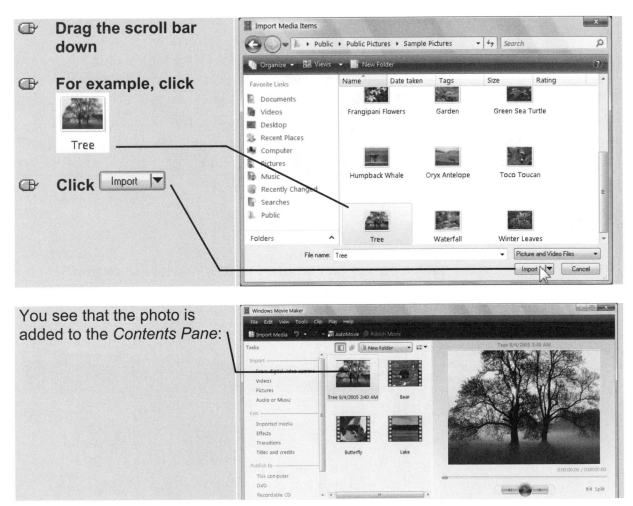

☞ **Double-click**

Sample Pictures

Select one of the sample pictures.

☞ **Drag the scroll bar down**

☞ **For example, click**

Tree

☞ **Click** Import ▼

You see that the photo is added to the *Contents Pane*:

8.4 Editing a Movie

The *Storyboard* is your work area in *Windows Movie Maker*. You can drag the clips from the *Contents Pane* to the *Storyboard* and arrange them in any order you want. You can do that like this:

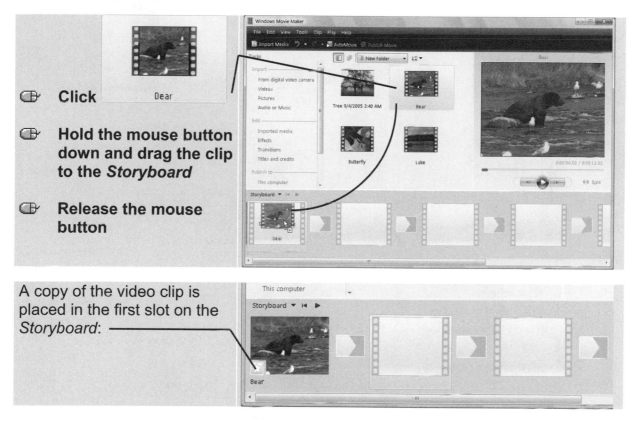

☞ **Click**   Bear

☞ **Hold the mouse button down and drag the clip to the *Storyboard***

☞ **Release the mouse button**

A copy of the video clip is placed in the first slot on the *Storyboard*:

Now you can add another clip:

☞ **Click**   Tree 4-9-2005 3:40

☞ **Drag the clip to the second slot**

☞ **Release the mouse button**

You can copy more clips to the *Storyboard*. Using the Shift key you can quickly select a row of consecutive clips:

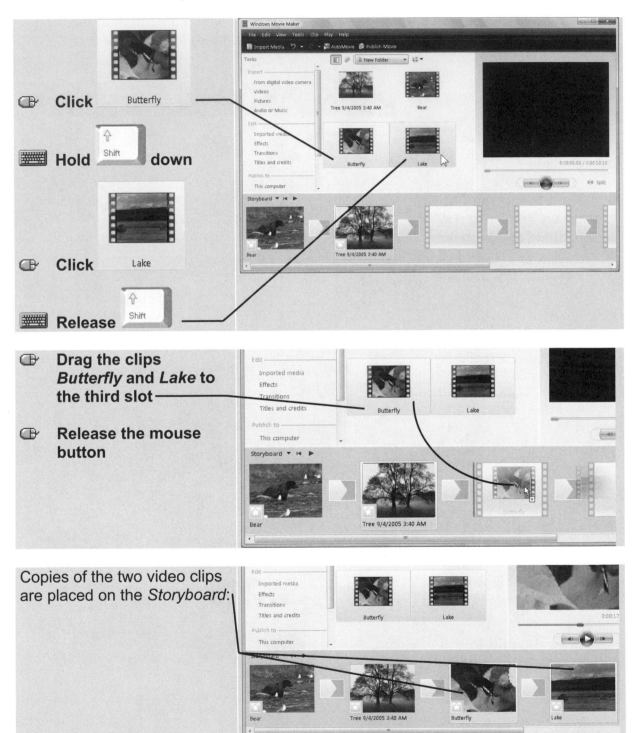

Click   Butterfly

Hold Shift down

Click Lake

Release Shift

Drag the clips *Butterfly* and *Lake* to the third slot

Release the mouse button

Copies of the two video clips are placed on the *Storyboard*:

Tip

Deleting clips

You can remove a clip from the *Storyboard* like this:

Click the clip ⎯⎯⎯

Press Delete

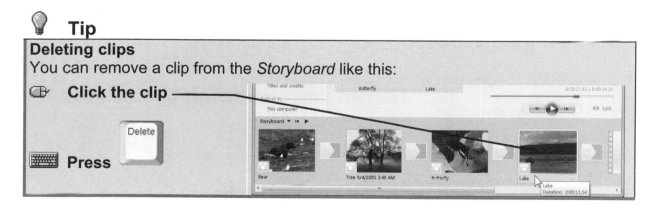

8.5 Playing a Movie

You have assembled a 'rough' movie by copying a couple of video clips to the *Storyboard*. You can play this movie in the *Preview monitor*, on the right side of the window. Take a closer look at the *Preview monitor* below:

Monitor: ⎯⎯⎯

Frame counter: ⎯⎯⎯

Search bar: ⎯⎯⎯

Controls: ⎯⎯⎯

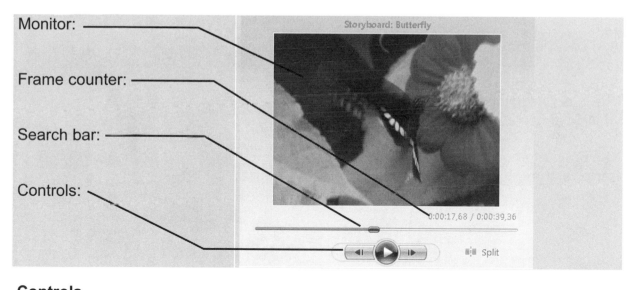

Controls

▶	Play
❚❚	Pause
◀❙	Previous frame
❙▶	Next frame
Split	Split a clip into two parts at exactly the point displayed in the *Preview monitor*

Before you start editing the movie, it is a good idea to watch the entire movie first. That will give you an idea of what needs to be done to improve the movie:

First you select the first clip:

⊕ **Click** Bear

Now you can play the entire movie:

⊕ **Click** ▶

The movie is played:

You see the movie in the *Preview monitor*:

The *Storyboard* shows you which clip is currently playing:

The counter shows which frame is currently displayed:

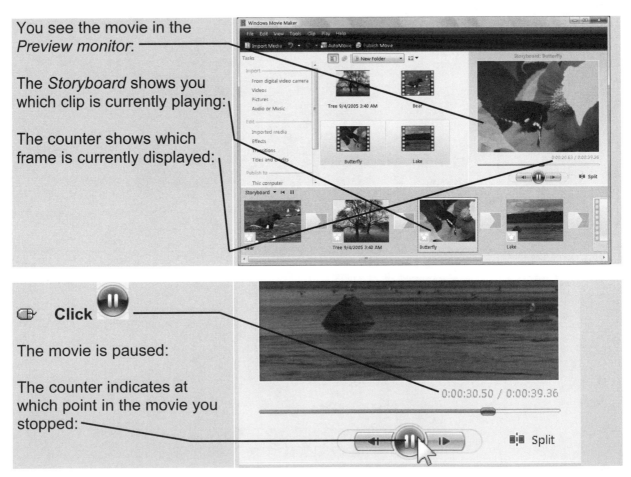

⊕ **Click** ⏸

The movie is paused:

The counter indicates at which point in the movie you stopped:

Now you can go through the movie frame by frame:

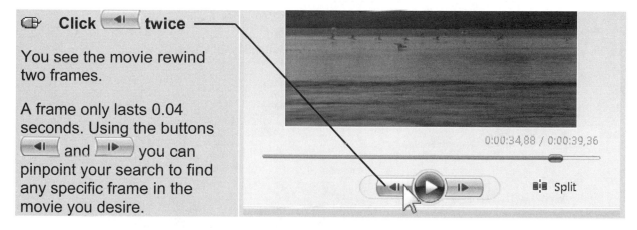

☞ **Click** ◀∥ **twice**

You see the movie rewind two frames.

A frame only lasts 0.04 seconds. Using the buttons ◀∥ and ∥▶ you can pinpoint your search to find any specific frame in the movie you desire.

You can also use the slider to find a certain point in the movie:

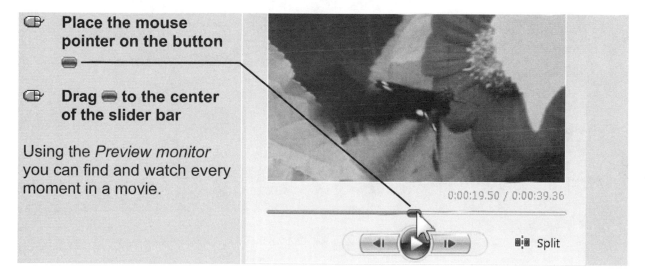

☞ **Place the mouse pointer on the button**
━

☞ **Drag** ━ **to the center of the slider bar**

Using the *Preview monitor* you can find and watch every moment in a movie.

💡 **Tip**

Play separate clips
You can also play the separate clips in the *Contents Pane*:

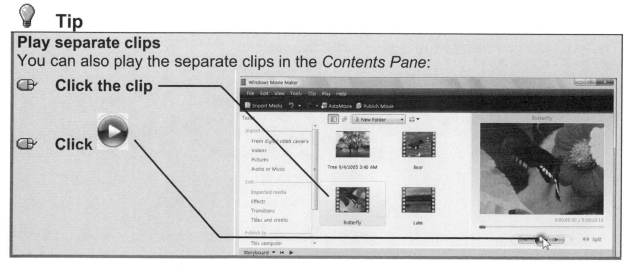

☞ **Click the clip**

☞ **Click** ▶

8.6 Splitting a Clip

When a clip is too long, you can split it. You are going to try that with the clip *Lake*. First you search for the exact frame where you want to split the clip.

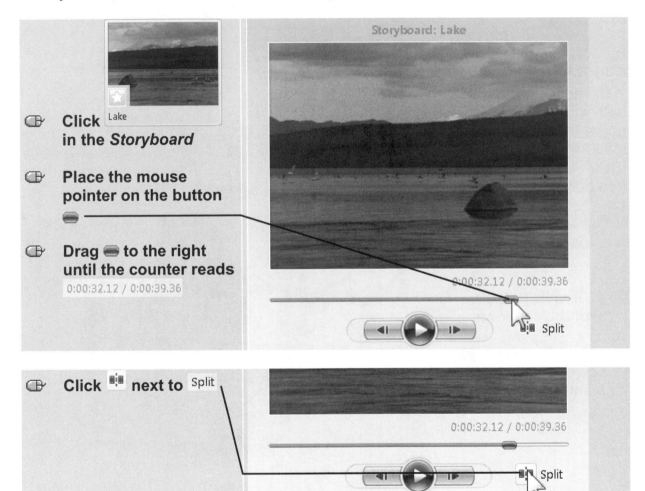

☞ **Click** Lake **in the *Storyboard***

☞ **Place the mouse pointer on the button**

☞ **Drag** 🔘 **to the right until the counter reads** 0:00:32.12 / 0:00:39.36

☞ **Click** 🔳 **next to** Split

The clip is split. You can see that in the *Storyboard*:

Now there are two clips named *Lake* in the *Storyboard*:

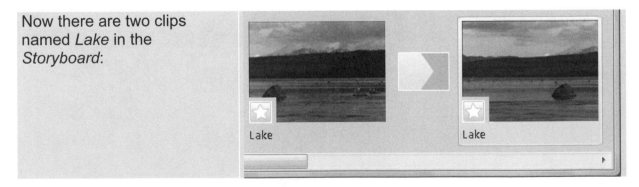

8.7 Moving a Clip

In the *Storyboard* you can change the order of the clips. For example, you can move the first part of the clip *Lake* to the beginning of the movie.

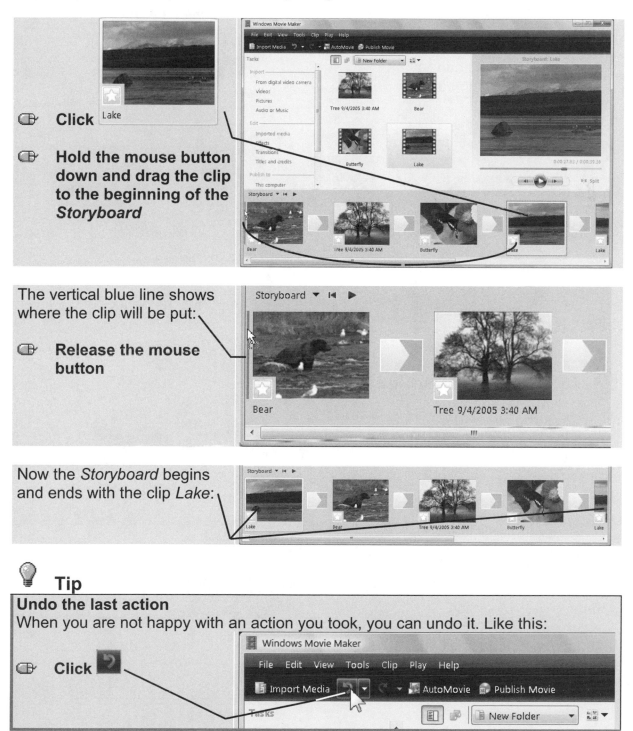

☞ **Click** Lake

☞ **Hold the mouse button down and drag the clip to the beginning of the Storyboard**

The vertical blue line shows where the clip will be put:

☞ **Release the mouse button**

Now the *Storyboard* begins and ends with the clip *Lake*:

💡 **Tip**

Undo the last action
When you are not happy with an action you took, you can undo it. Like this:

☞ **Click** 🔁

8.8 Trimming Clips

Often movie clips will not have exactly the right length. There may be a part at the beginning or at the end that needs to be cut off. You can do this by trimming the clip. You will need to switch to the *timeline view* first. Right now *Movie Maker* is still in the *Storyboard view*:

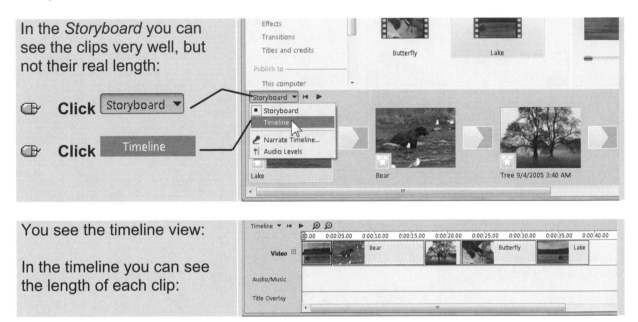

In the *Storyboard* you can see the clips very well, but not their real length:

☞ **Click** `Storyboard ▼`

☞ **Click** `Timeline`

You see the timeline view:

In the timeline you can see the length of each clip:

To illustrate how to trim, you can use the second clip.

☞ **Click the second clip**

The second clip is selected:

Two *trim handles* ▶ ◀ appear:

Using these trim handles you can trim the clip at the left and right edge.

☞ **Place the mouse pointer at the right trim handle** ————

The mouse pointer changes into ⬚⬌⬚ :

☞ **Drag the mouse pointer to the left until the counter reads** `0:00:15,60` ————

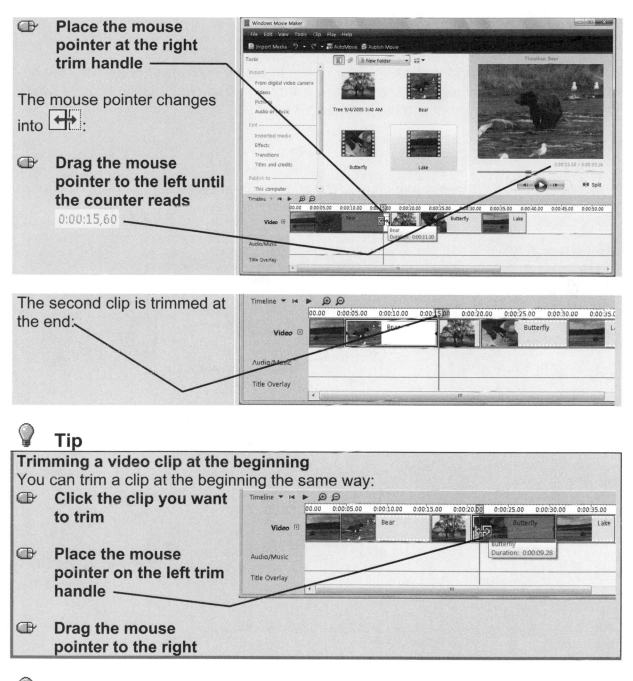

The second clip is trimmed at the end:

💡 **Tip**

Trimming a video clip at the beginning
You can trim a clip at the beginning the same way:

☞ **Click the clip you want to trim**

☞ **Place the mouse pointer on the left trim handle** ————

☞ **Drag the mouse pointer to the right**

💡 **Tip**

Trimming the display time of photos
When you combine video clips and photos in a movie, you should take into account that a photo can only be trimmed at the end. There is no left trim handle.

8.9 Adding a Transition

It is also possible to add a *transition* to a movie in *Movie Maker*. A transition is the effect that is shown when your movie plays from one video clip or picture to the next. To add a transition, go back to the *Storyboard view*.

☞ **Click** `Timeline ▼`, `Storyboard`

You can choose between many different transitions. You can add a transition between the second and third clip like this:

☞ **Click** `Transitions`

☞ **Click a transition, for**

example `Bars, Vertical`

☞ **Drag the transition between the second and third clip**

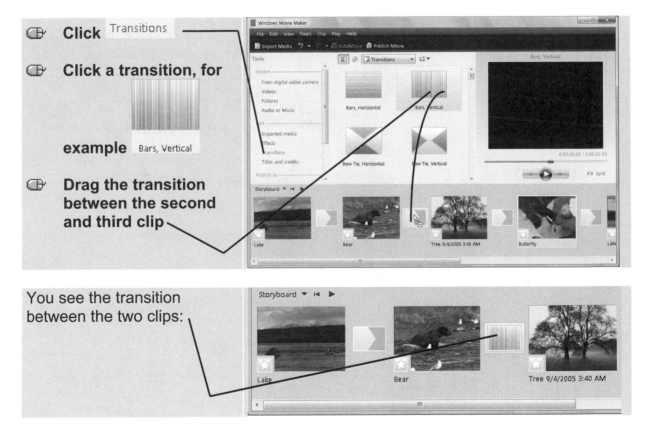

You see the transition between the two clips:

Later in this chapter you can see what this transition looks like when you play the video clips.

8.10 Adding an Effect

You can also add *effects* to the clips you use. You can make a video clip look like an old-time movie, for example.

Here you can also choose one of the many different effects. This is how you add an effect to the fourth clip:

Click `Effects`

Drag the vertical scroll bar down

Click `Film Age, Old`

Drag the effect to the fourth clip

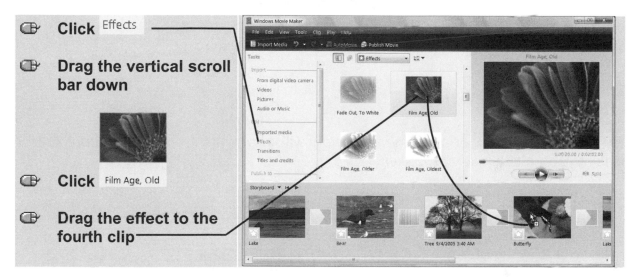

You can add multiple effects to the same clip. To make the clip look extra old:

Drag the vertical scroll bar down

Click `Sepia Tone`

Drag the effect to the fourth clip

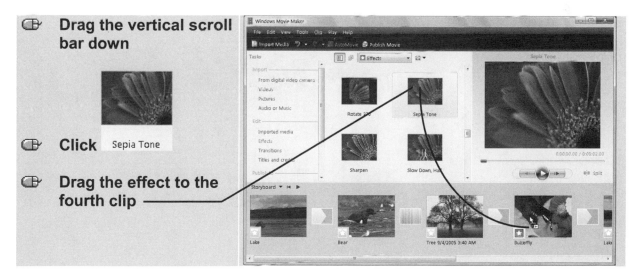

Both effects have been added to the video clip. You can see the result like this:

8.11 Adding a Title

By adding a title to your movie, your viewers will know what the movie is about. It is easy to add a title in *Movie Maker*.

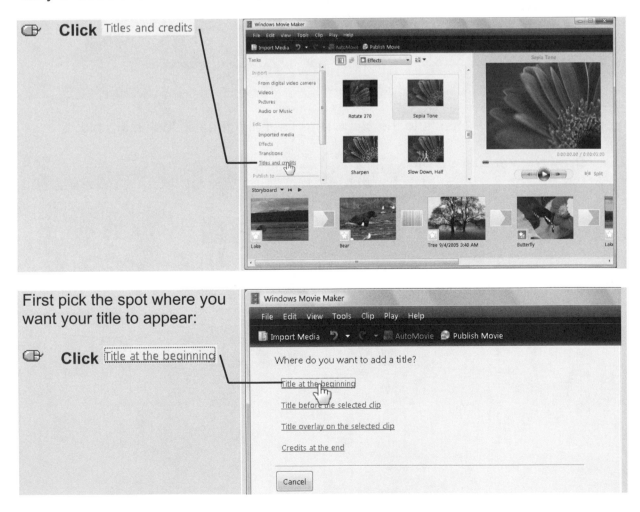

Now you can type the text for the title:

Type:
The Beauty of
Nature

Click
Change the title animation

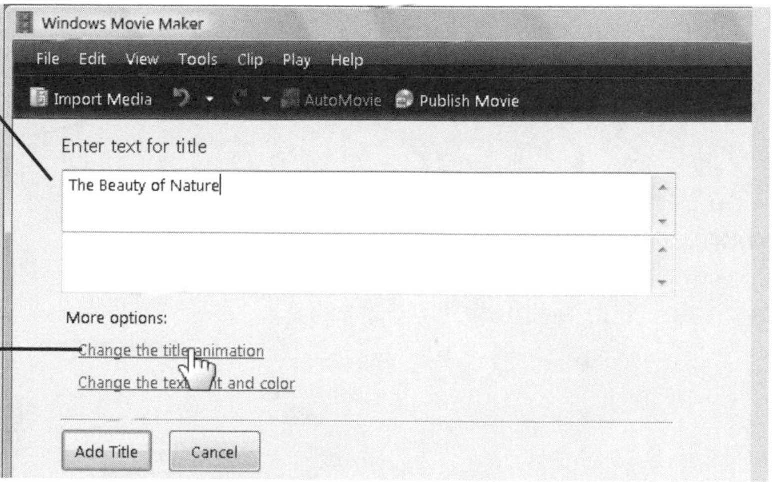

The *title animation* controls how the title text will appear. Just like with the transitions you can choose between many animations. The title animation Fade, In and Out is selected by default. To select a different animation:

If necessary, drag the vertical scroll bar down

For example, click
Moving Titles, Layered

In the *Preview monitor* you see the effect of the selected animation right away:

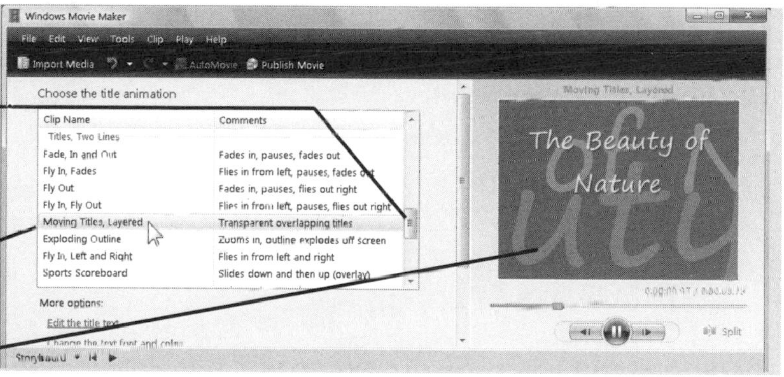

You can also change the font and color of the title:

Click
Change the text font and color

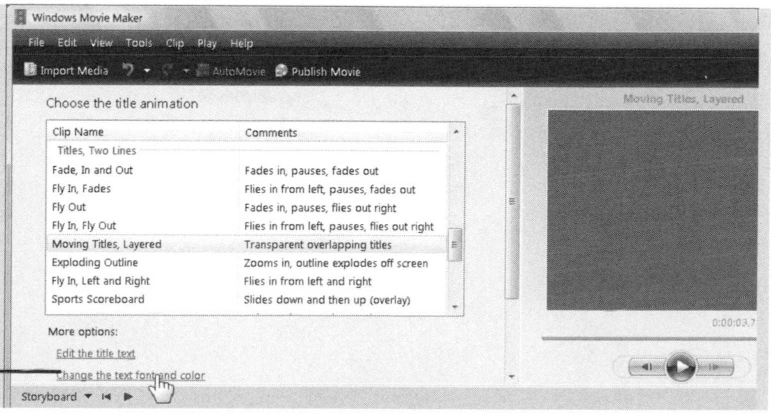

Select the font *Tahoma*:

☞   **Click** ▼

☞   **Click** `Tahoma`

You can see in the *Preview monitor* what the font looks like combined with the selected title animation.

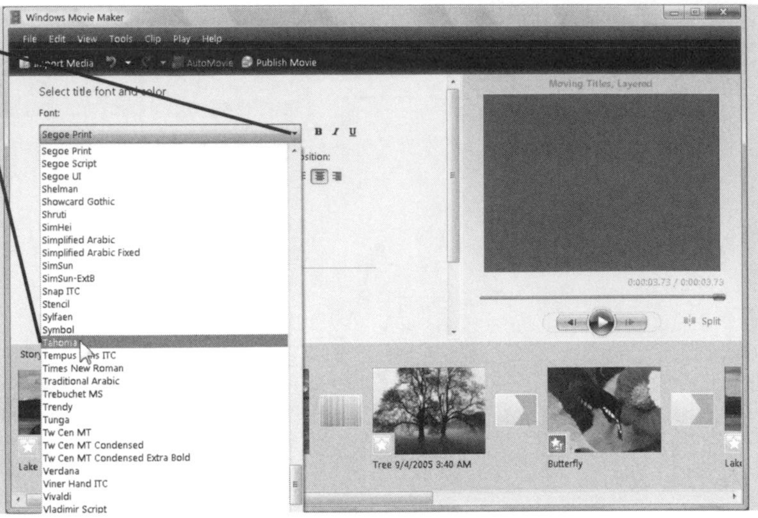

You can also increase the text size:

☞   **Click** A⁺ **below** `Size:`

The text size has increased one step. You can see the effect in the *Preview monitor*.

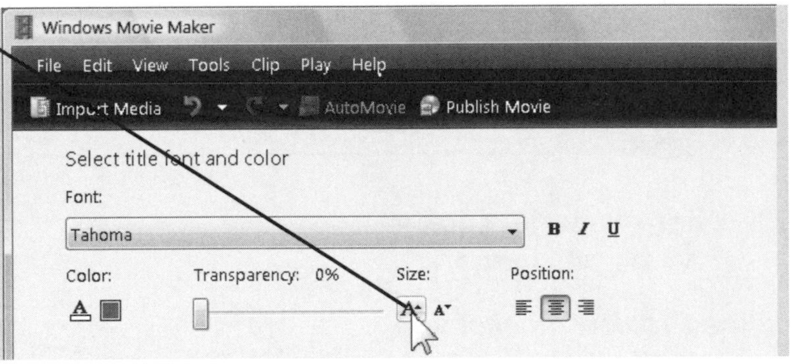

By default the title is displayed as white text on a blue background. You can change that for example to green text on a white background.

☞   **Click** ■ **below** `Color:`

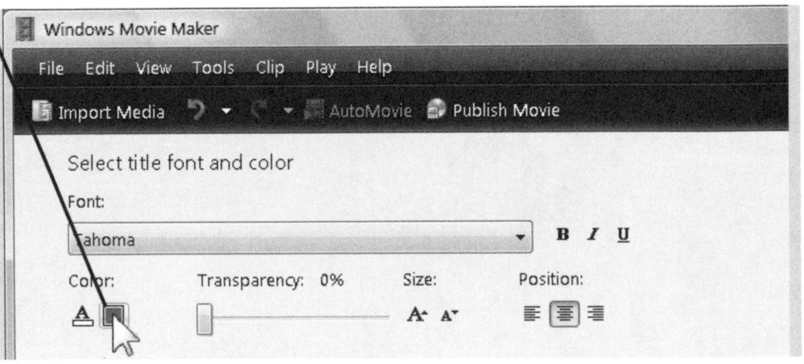

You select white:

☞ **Click** ☐ ────

☞ **Click** [OK]

The background is now white. You can change the color of the text the same way:

☞ **Click** ⚊A below Color:

You see the window *Color* again. There you select dark green text:

☞ **Click dark green** ■, **then** [OK]

The last step is adjusting the transparency of the text:

☞ **Drag the slider** ⬜
below Transparency: **to**
the right to 40%

The title is ready to be added to the movie:

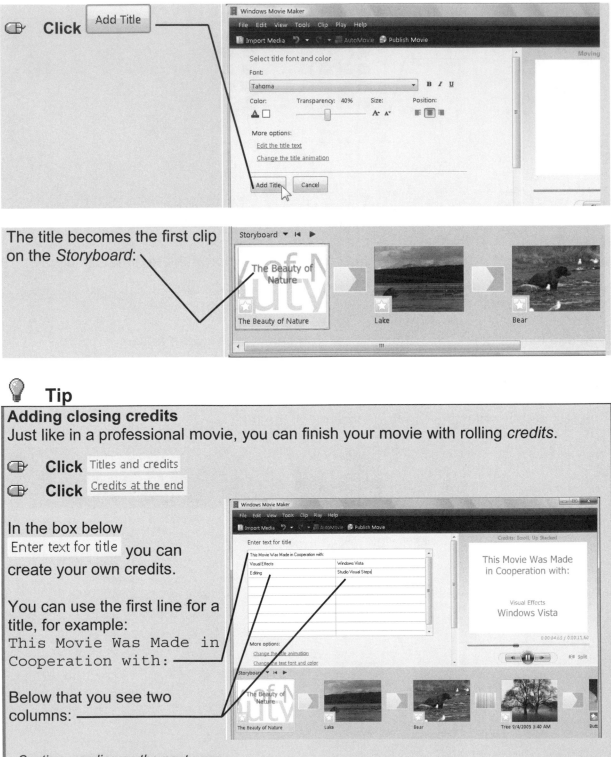

Click Add Title

The title becomes the first clip on the *Storyboard*:

💡 **Tip**

Adding closing credits
Just like in a professional movie, you can finish your movie with rolling *credits*.

Click Titles and credits

Click Credits at the end

In the box below Enter text for title you can create your own credits.

You can use the first line for a title, for example:
`This Movie Was Made in Cooperation with:`

Below that you see two columns:

- Continue reading on the next page -

You use the first column for a description, for example `Visual Effects`.
In the second column you enter a name, for example `Windows Vista`.

In the *Preview monitor* you can view while you type what the rolling credits will look like. Just like with the title you added to your movie before, the animation, font and text color can be adjusted to suit your preferences.

When the closing credits are finished:

⬛ **Click** `Add Title`

The closing credits have been added as a clip at the end of the *Storyboard*:

8.12 Collections

You can use *Collections* to organize the items you use in your movie. A collection behaves just like a regular folder. But a collection does not contain real video or audio files. It contains the shortcuts to files that are located somewhere else on the hard disk of your computer. Every user account on your computer has its own *Collection* file. You can quickly display your collections like this:

⬛ **Click**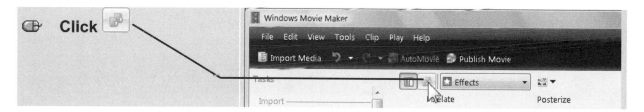

Your collections in *Windows Movie Maker* consist of three separate parts:
- the imported media – your video clips, audio clips and photos
- the transitions
- the effects

Your collections now look like this:

The video clips and the photo you imported previously are placed in the folder
New Folder.

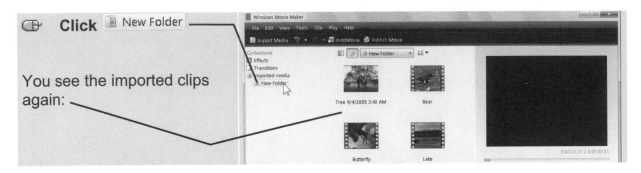

☞ **Click** New Folder

You see the imported clips
again:

Now is a good time to give the folder New Folder a more meaningful name:

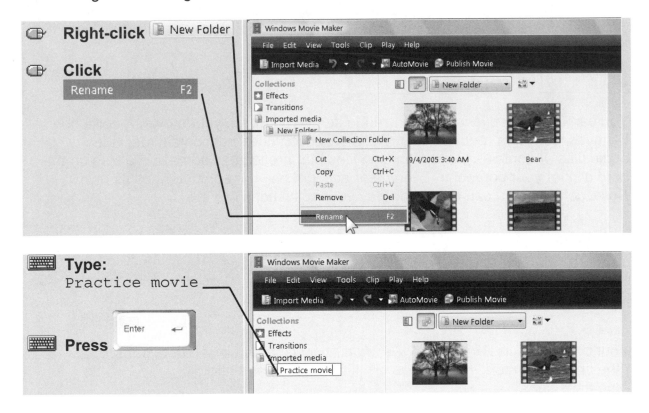

☞ **Right-click** New Folder

☞ **Click**
Rename   F2

⌨ **Type:**
Practice movie

⌨ **Press** Enter

To show the *Tasks* again:

☞ **Click** ▣

The *Tasks* are displayed again.

You see here that the collection ⊞ Practice movie is displayed in the *Contents pane*:

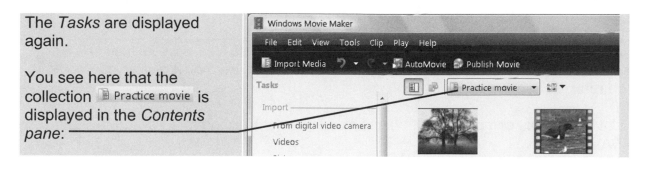

8.13 Adding Music

Video usually contains some sound that was recorded when the video was shot. But it is fun to add extra sound in the form of music. With music you can easily add a certain atmosphere to your movie. Before you can add music to the movie, you need to import a track into *Windows Movie Maker*.

💡 **Tip**

Do you see the right collection?
When you are going to import new audio or video clips after working with transitions or effects, you need to display the correct collection first. When you import something when the transitions or effects are displayed, a new collection is created for the imported item.
You can use the buttons

⭐ Effects ▼ or

▶ Transitions ▼ to quickly switch between the different parts of your collections:

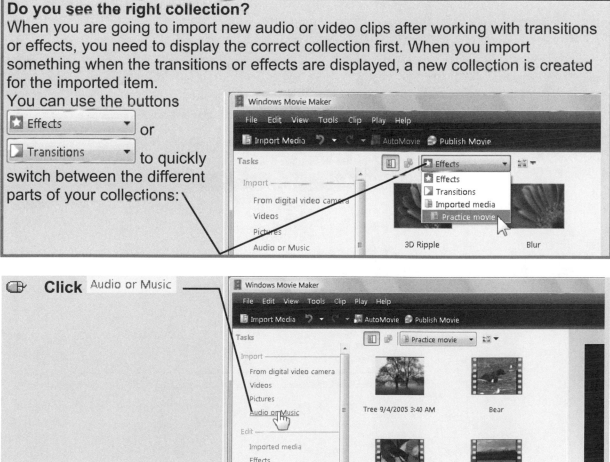

Click Audio or Music

⇨ **Please note:**

In the example, one of the *Windows Vista* sample music files is used. You can also use one of the MP3 tracks of the CD you copied to the hard disk of your computer in **chapter 2 Ripping a CD**.

Movie Maker is compatible with audio files in the familiar formats WMA, MP3 and WAV.

CDA files (the file format of tracks on an audio CD) are **not** supported. You need to rip your audio CD to MP3 or WMA format before you can use the music in a movie.

☞ **Double-click**

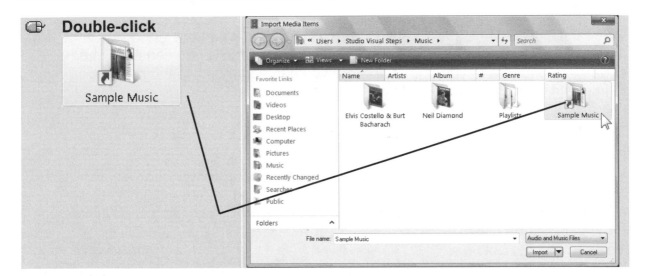

☞ **For example, click** ☐ Amanda

☞ **Click** [Import ▼]

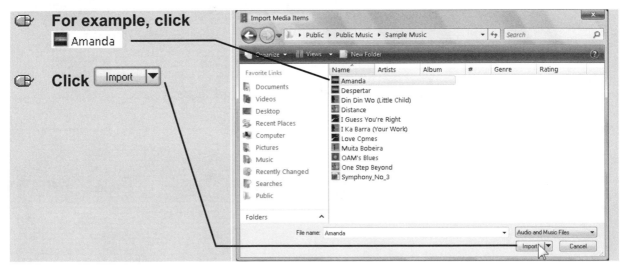

The audio track  has been added to the collection *Practice movie*:

Music can only be added in the *Timeline* view of *Movie Maker*:

👆 **Click** Storyboard ▼, Timeline

You add music to the movie by dragging the audio clip to the Audio/Music track:

👆 **Click** Amanda

👆 **Drag the audio clip to the beginning of the second clip**

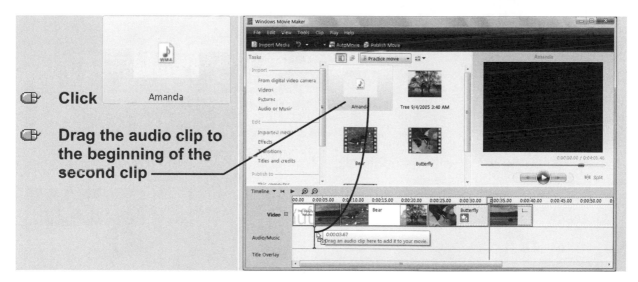

Now the timeline contains a video track as well as an audio track.

As you can see the audio track is much longer than the video track:

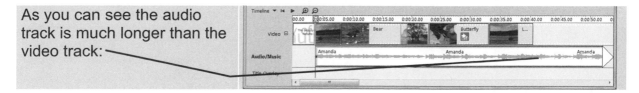

Just like you did with a video clip before, you can also trim an audio clip. You are going to try that:

☞ **Place the mouse pointer at the end of the audio track** ——

The mouse pointer changes into ⟷ :

☞ **Drag the mouse pointer to the left until the counter reads** 0:00:40.51 ——

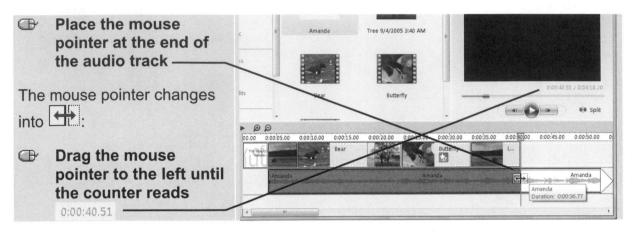

The audio tracks and the video track now have approximately the same length. Both picture and sound will end abruptly. It will be much nicer to gradually fade them out. You can arrange that like this:

☞ **Right-click the last video clip**

☞ **Click** Fade Out

At the end of the movie the image will slowly fade to black.

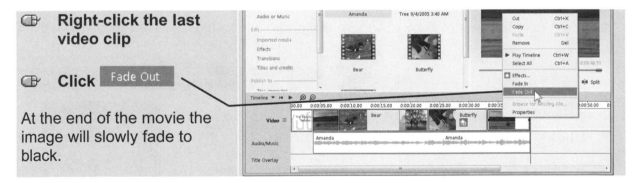

You do the same thing with the audio clip:

☞ **Right-click the audio track**

☞ **Click** Fade Out

You can also fade in the start of the music:

☞ **Right-click the audio track**

☞ **Click** Fade In

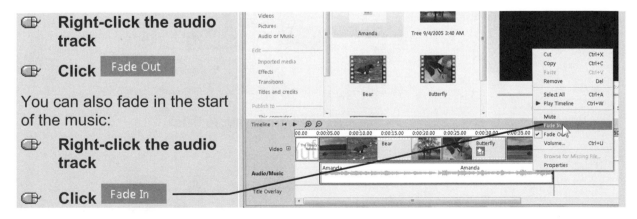

The music now starts softly and gradually becomes louder. At the end of the movie the music slowly fades away.

8.14 Adding a Narration

So far your movie contains the sound that was recorded with the video and music. You can also add a narration to the clips that do not contain music. This way you can describe what is shown in the movie.

 Please note:

You can only record a narration in the timeline view.

☞ **Connect a microphone to your computer**

💡 **Tip**

Connecting a microphone

On the back of the system case of your computer (sometimes also at the front) you find three ports for devices that have to do with sound: a microphone, headphones and extra speakers:

Next to the correct port you see a microphone

icon :

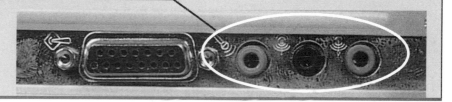

If you do not have a microphone you can just read through this section.

Click `Tools`

Click ✎ `Narrate Timeline...`

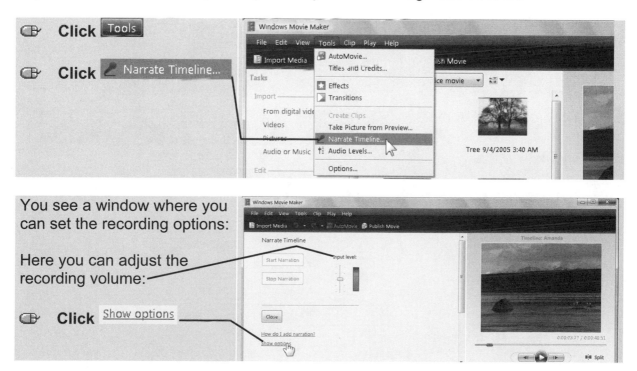

You see a window where you can set the recording options:

Here you can adjust the recording volume:

Click `Show options`

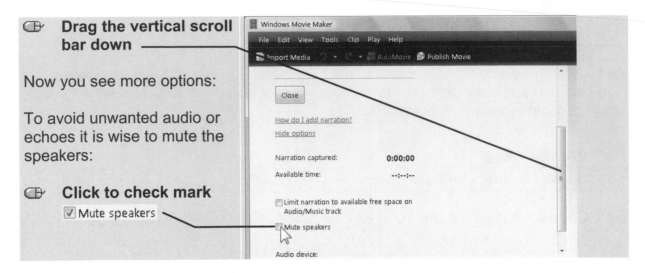

☞ **Drag the vertical scroll bar down**

Now you see more options:

To avoid unwanted audio or echoes it is wise to mute the speakers:

☞ **Click to check mark**
   ☑ Mute speakers

You are going to add a short narration to the title clip.

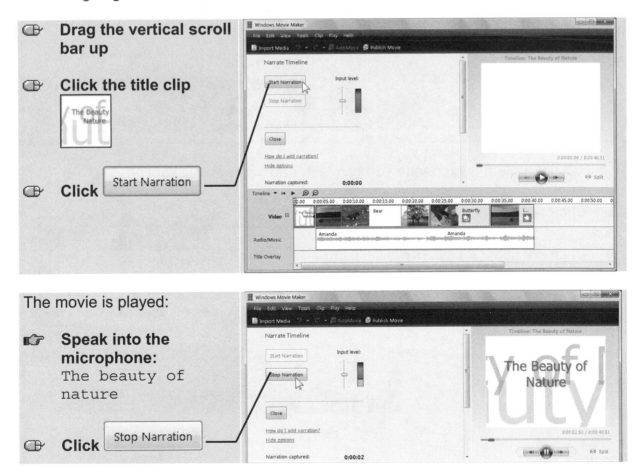

☞ **Drag the vertical scroll bar up**

☞ **Click the title clip**

☞ **Click** [Start Narration]

The movie is played:

☞ **Speak into the microphone:**
   The beauty of nature

☞ **Click** [Stop Narration]

You see the window where you can save the audio file:

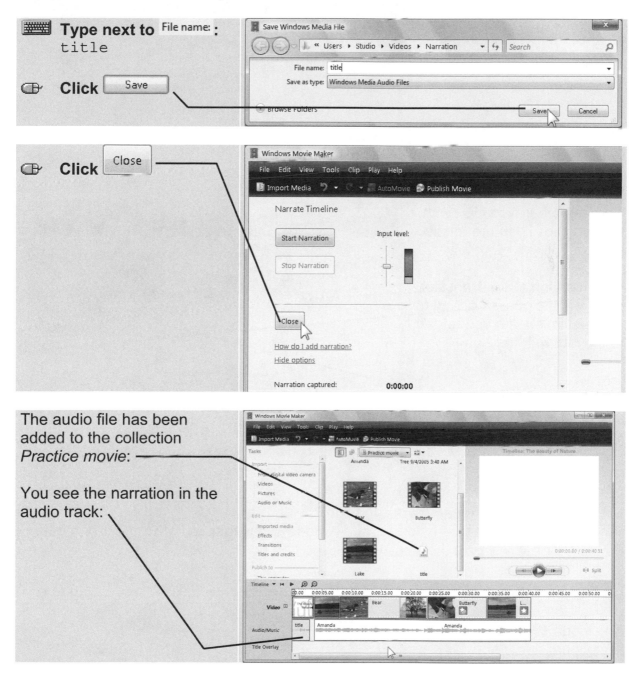

Type next to File name: :
title

Click Save

Click Close

The audio file has been added to the collection *Practice movie*:

You see the narration in the audio track:

Now you can play the complete edited movie:

☞ **Turn the computer speakers on**

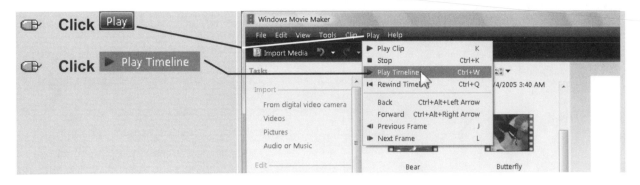

Click [Play]

Click ► Play Timeline

The movie is played:

You hear your narration with the title clip. Then the music starts.

Pay attention to the transition between clips 3 and 4, and to the special effects you added to the clip with the butterfly:

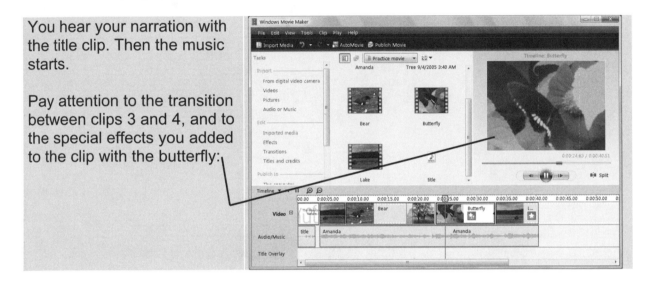

💡 Tip

Is the sound of the video track too loud?
When the sound that was recorded with a video clip is too loud or too soft, you can adjust it for each clip. In the timeline view you can do that like this:

☞ Click ⊞ next to Video

The video track is expanded. The video, audio and transitions of the video clips are displayed separately:

- Continue reading on the next page -

Right-click the audio of a video clip, for example

Butterfly

Click Volume...

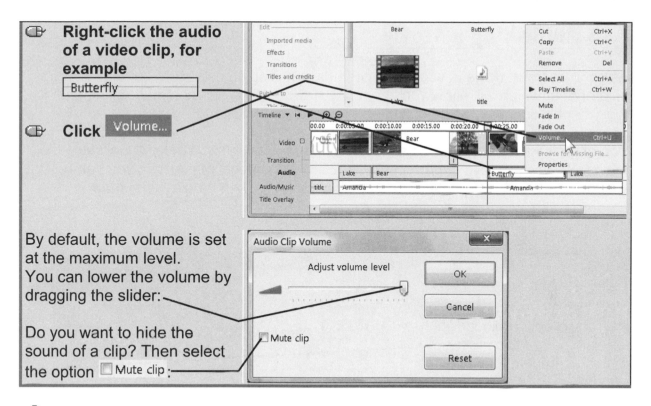

By default, the volume is set at the maximum level.
You can lower the volume by dragging the slider:

Do you want to hide the sound of a clip? Then select the option ☐ Mute clip :

💡 Tip

Music too loud?
You can also use the method described in the previous Tip to adjust the volume of the audio clips on the audio/music track.

💡 Tip

Adjust the balance between the audio/music track and the video track
You can adjust the balance between the volume level of the audio/music tracks and the original sound of the video clips:

Click Tools , Audio Levels...

The window *Audio Levels* appears:

Drag the slider more toward Audio from video **or to** Audio/Music

Click ✕

Please note: it is only possible to adjust the balance for the complete project, not for the separate clips.

8.15 Publishing a Movie

As soon as your movie is edited, you can save it. You can select to save all the clips as a project which will allow you to open it at a later time and continue working on it. But you can only watch and edit a project in *Movie Maker*.

You can also save the clips as a movie. In *Movie Maker* this is called *publishing* the movie. You can always import a published movie in *Movie Maker*, but you can no longer work on the separate parts. A published movie can be played in other programs like *Windows Media Player*.

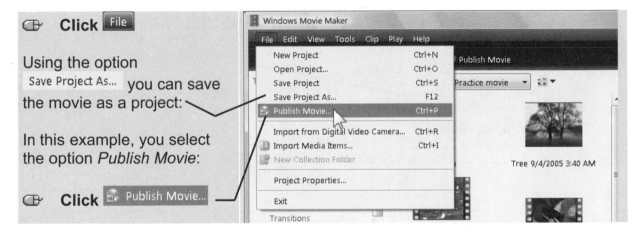

☞   **Click** `File`

Using the option
`Save Project As...` you can save
the movie as a project:

In this example, you select
the option *Publish Movie*:

☞   **Click** `Publish Movie...`

The wizard *Publish Movie* appears:

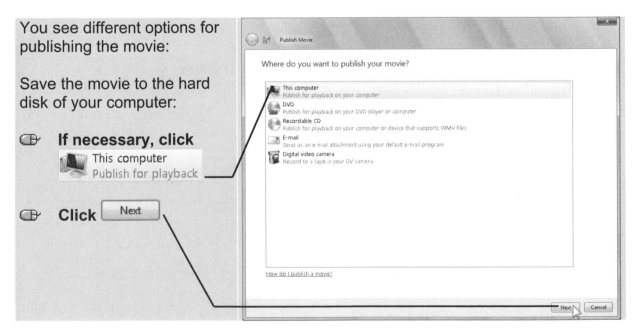

You see different options for
publishing the movie:

Save the movie to the hard
disk of your computer:

☞   **If necessary, click**
`This computer`
`Publish for playback`

☞   **Click** `Next`

You see a window where you can enter a name for your movie:

Type:
Practice movie

By default, the movie is stored in the folder 🖿 Videos :

Click [Next]

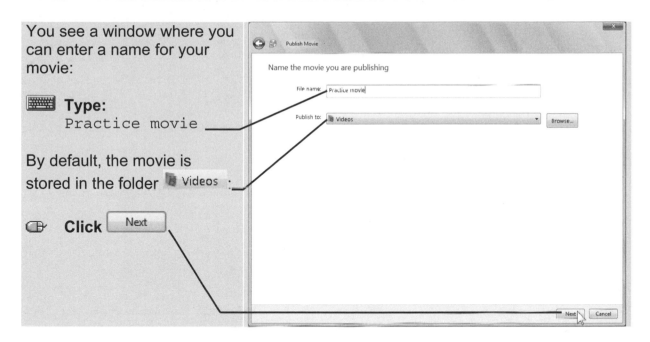

You see a window where you can view the settings of this movie and adjust them if necessary:

By default the best quality is selected:

If you want to view more options you can click
○ More settings: [DV-AVI (NTSC)] :

Here you see information about the movie:

Click [Publish]

The various components of the movie are now compiled. If you used a lot of clips, effects and music, this may take some time. Then the movie is saved to the folder *Videos*.

After the movie is published, you can watch the movie when you click | Finish |. You do not want to do that now:

☞ **Click to remove the check mark for**

☐ Play movie when I click Finish.

☞ **Click** | Finish |

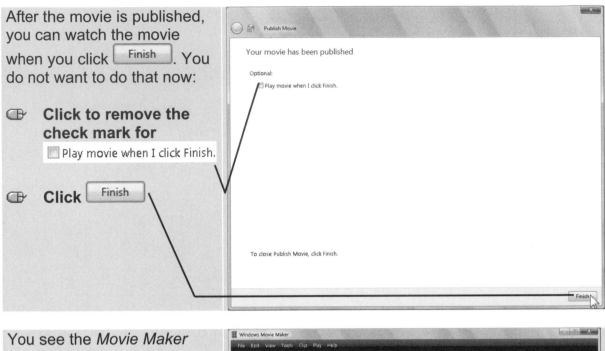

You see the *Movie Maker* window again:

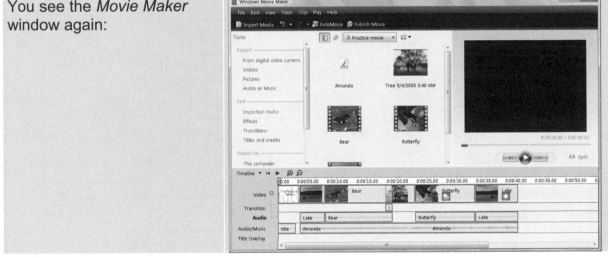

➡ **Please note:**

Even though you have published your movie, changes have not been made to your original project in *Windows Movie Maker*. A movie has been compiled from these project files and saved to the hard disk of your computer. But you can reopen the project, work further with it, or change it entirely. Then publish it again (under a different name and in a different location if you do not want to overwrite your first movie) using any of the other options available.

8.16 Sending a Movie by E-mail

Another way to publish is to send the movie by e-mail. Instead of using the wizard *Publish Movie*, you return to the *Tasks Pane* and select a different option:

☞ **If necessary, drag the vertical scroll bar down**

☞ **Click** `E-mail`

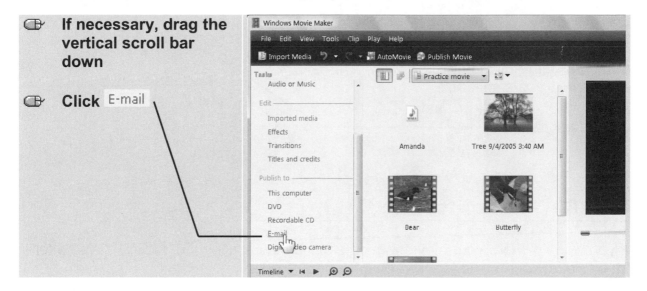

The movie is compiled again.

Now you have the option to play the movie, or save a copy of the movie to the hard disk of your computer. It is not necessary to do either of these when sending your movie in an e-mail:

☞ **Click** `Attach Movie`

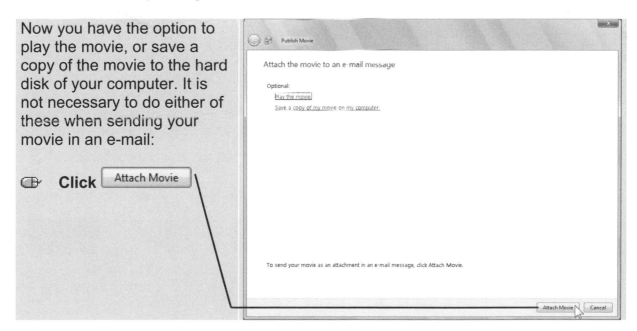

The movie is added as an attachment to a new e-mail message:

The size of the attachment containing this short movie is over 7 MB: ─────────

Sending and receiving this message will take a lot of time. It is better to send a message with a smaller file.

☞ **Click** ✖

8.17 Burning a Movie to DVD

If you want to share your movie with others and not sacrifice the quality, it is a better idea to burn your movie to a DVD.

⇨ **Please note:**

> To be able to burn a movie to DVD, you need to have the program *Windows DVD Maker*, a DVD writer and a writable DVD.
>
> The program *Windows DVD Maker* is **not** included in *Windows Vista Home Basic*. Only *Windows Vista Home Premium* and *Windows Vista Ultimate* users have *Windows DVD Maker* on their computer.
>
> If you use *Windows Vista Home Basic*, or you do not have a DVD writer or a writable DVD you can just read through this part of the chapter.

Go to the *Tasks Pane* again:

☞ **If necessary, drag the vertical scroll bar down**

☞ **Click** DVD

When you publish your movie to DVD, the project is saved, closed and then opened in *Windows DVD Maker*.

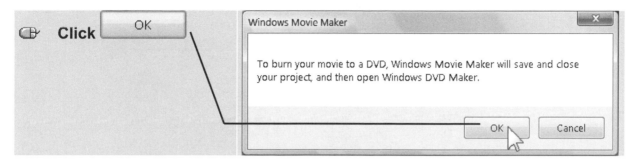

Click [OK]

> **Windows Movie Maker**
>
> To burn your movie to a DVD, Windows Movie Maker will save and close your project, and then open Windows DVD Maker.
>
> [OK] [Cancel]

You name the project:

Type:
Exercise project

Click [Save]

> **Save Project As**
> « Users ▸ Studio ▸ Videos ▸   Search
> File name: Exercise project
> Save as type: Windows Movie Maker Projects
> Browse Folders   [Save] [Cancel]

Windows DVD Maker opens:

The movie *Exercise project* is added to the DVD list:

You can also add the movie you published in the previous section to the DVD.

Click 📄 Add items

You see here that only a very small part of the available 150 minutes on the DVD is used:

> **Windows DVD Maker**
>
> Add pictures and video to the DVD
>
> File Add items Remove items ⬆ ⬇   DVD burner: E: ▼ ?
>
> | Order | Name | Duration | Status |
> |-------|------|----------|--------|
> | 1 | Exercise project | 0:00:40 | Ready |
>
> 1 of 150 minutes   Disc title: Exercise project   Options...
>
> [Next] [Cancel]

☞ **Click** Practice movie

☞ **Click** Add ▼

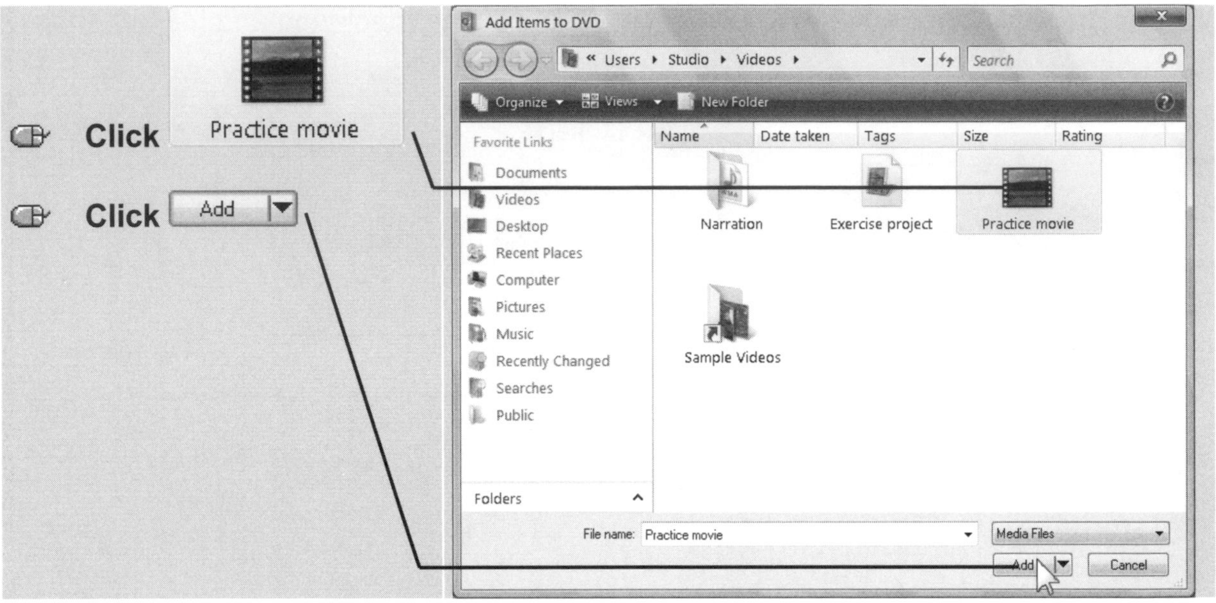

Both movies are now included in the DVD list. You can also add photos to the DVD. These are added to the DVD as a slide show. You do not have to do that now. **Chapter 9 Your Photos in Vista** contains more information about this subject.

☞ **Click** Next

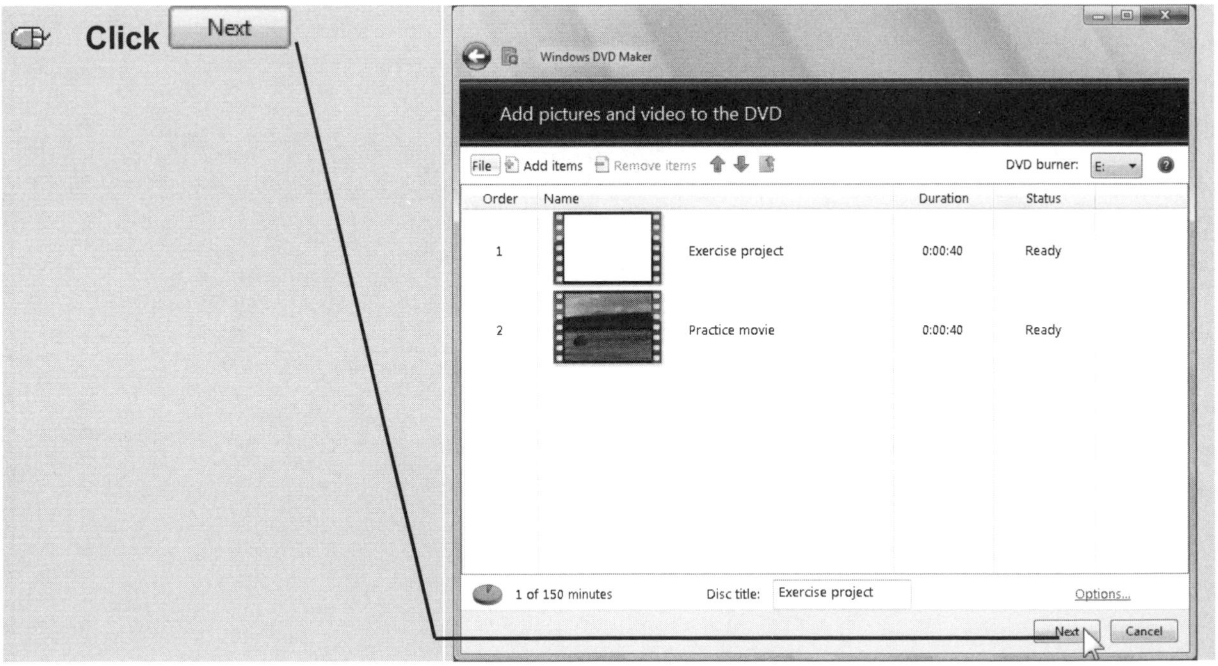

A DVD menu will be added to the DVD, just like the menu you know from professional DVDs you buy in the store. You can adjust this menu to your own preferences. You see a static preview of the menu in the *Preview pane*.

You can choose between different menu styles. For example, try the style *Reflections*:

☞ **Drag the vertical scroll bar down**

☞ **Click** Reflections

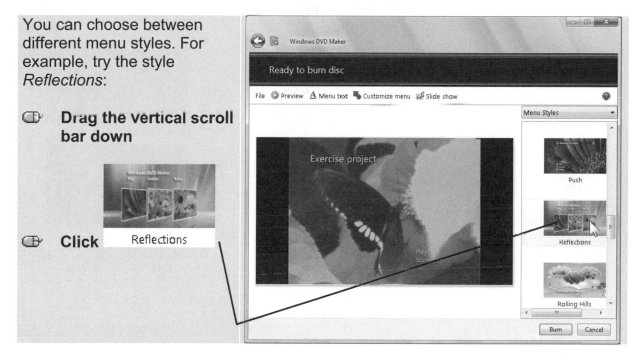

The *Preview Pane* is adapted to the new style immediately. The DVD is titled *Exercise project*. You can change the title like this:

☞ **Click** △ Menu text

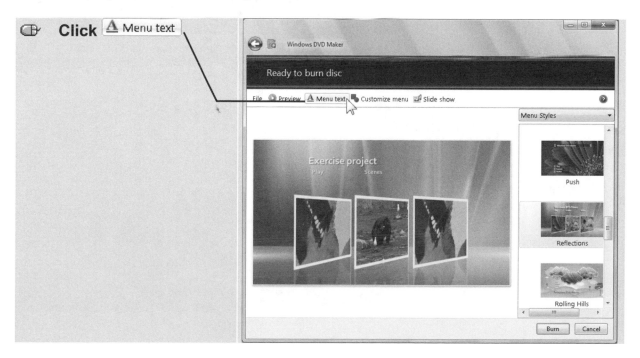

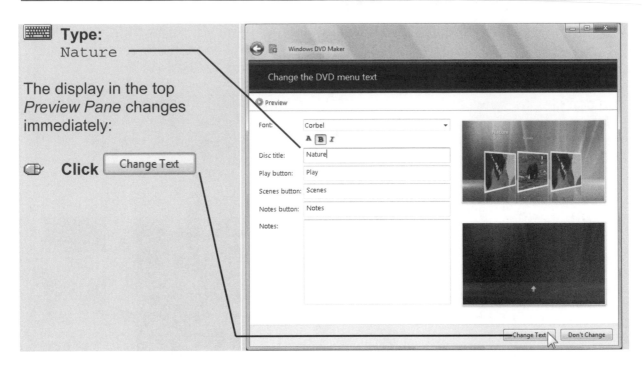

Type:
Nature

The display in the top *Preview Pane* changes immediately:

Click **Change Text**

Now you can take a look at a preview of what the finished DVD will look like.

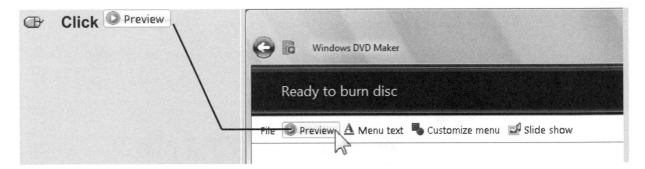

Click **Preview**

You see the opening sequence of the DVD. Then the DVD menu appears.

You can use the button **Play** to play all movies in a row. You can also check which movies are on the DVD:

Click **Scenes**

There are only two movies on the DVD. You can play them like this:

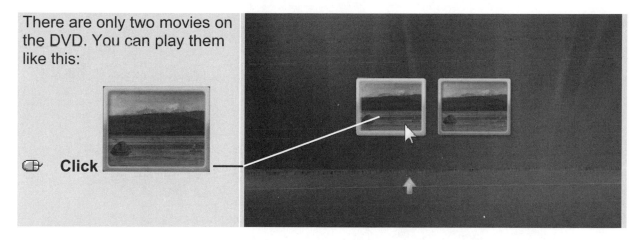

⊕ **Click**

The movies are played, one after the other. Then the menu appears again.

⊕ **Click** OK

Now you can burn the DVD.

⊕ **Click** Burn

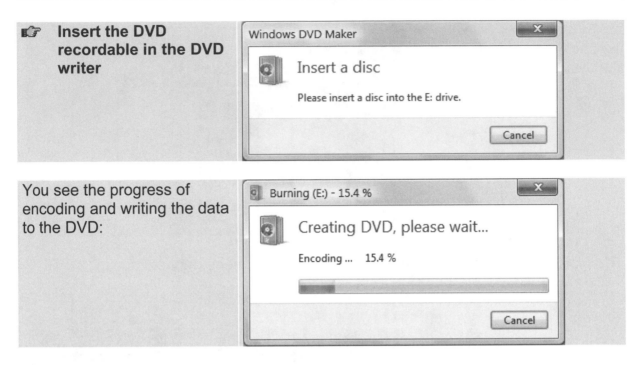

☞ **Insert the DVD recordable in the DVD writer**

Windows DVD Maker

Insert a disc

Please insert a disc into the E: drive.

Cancel

You see the progress of encoding and writing the data to the DVD:

Burning (E:) - 15.4 %

Creating DVD, please wait...

Encoding ...   15.4 %

Cancel

During the encoding process the DVD menu is created and the movies are converted to a format that can be played in a regular DVD player.

⇨ **Please note:**

Even though only a very small part of the DVD capacity is used, the encoding process will take a few minutes. When the full 150 minute capacity of the DVD is used, encoding will take much longer.
The process of encoding a DVD takes up a lot of memory capacity and computing power of your computer. It is better not to perform any other tasks on the computer during the encoding process. Otherwise there is a chance that the encoding will fail.

When the burning process has finished, the drawer of the DVD burner opens. *Windows DVD Maker* gives you the option to create a copy of the disk. You do not have to do that now.

☞ **Click** Close

Windows DVD Maker

Your disc is ready

➜ Make another copy of this disc

Close

You have created a simple movie using *Movie Maker*. Then you have written this movie to DVD using *DVD Maker*. You can now play the DVD in your regular DVD player.

☞ **Close the *Windows DVD Maker* window and do not save the changes to the project** $\ell\ell^{58}$

☞ **Close the *Windows Movie Maker* window** $\ell\ell^3$

☞ **Try to play the DVD in a regular DVD player**

💡 **Tip**

Opening Windows DVD Maker
In this chapter you have opened the program *Windows DVD Maker* from the program *Windows Movie Maker*. You can also open the program directly if you want to create a DVD:

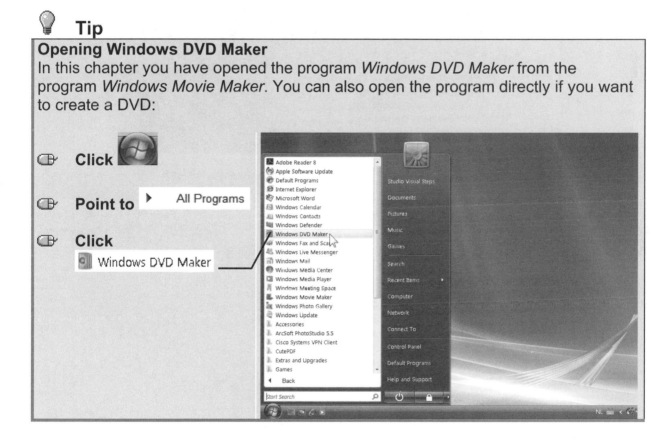

☞ **Click**

☞ **Point to** ▸ All Programs

☞ **Click**
📀 Windows DVD Maker

8.18 Importing Video from Your Digital Video Camera

In *Movie Maker* you can import video directly from your digital video camera.

If you do not have a digital video camera, you can just read through this section.

First you connect your digital video camera to your computer. You do that with a so called *FireWire*, *IEE1394 or i-link* connection. Your computer needs to have this type of port.

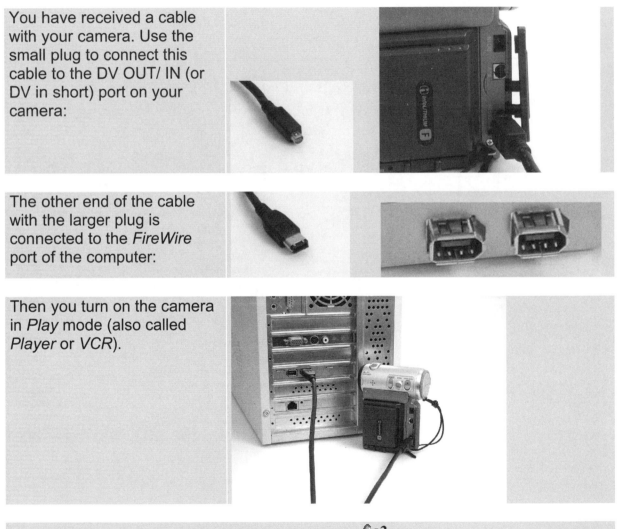

You have received a cable with your camera. Use the small plug to connect this cable to the DV OUT/ IN (or DV in short) port on your camera:

The other end of the cable with the larger plug is connected to the *FireWire* port of the computer:

Then you turn on the camera in *Play* mode (also called *Player* or *VCR*).

☞   **If necessary, close the *AutoPlay* window** 🦶³

☞   **Open *Windows Movie Maker*** 🦶⁵⁹

⇨ **Please note:**

Some digital video cameras have to be connected to the computer using a USB 2.0 connection. This type of connection is less common than the *FireWire* connection described before.

A camera with a USB connection has to support streaming over USB to be able to import video directly. This type of camera is also called a UVC camera (USB Video Class). In *Windows Vista* this camera is called a USB video device.

Refer to the documentation you received with your camera or the manufacturer's website to find out if your camera supports streaming over USB.

First you create a new folder in the *Collections Pane* for the videotape you are going to import.

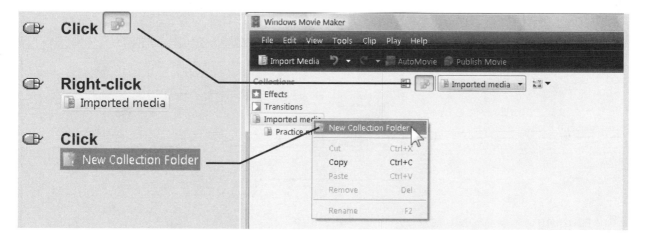

Then give a name to this folder:

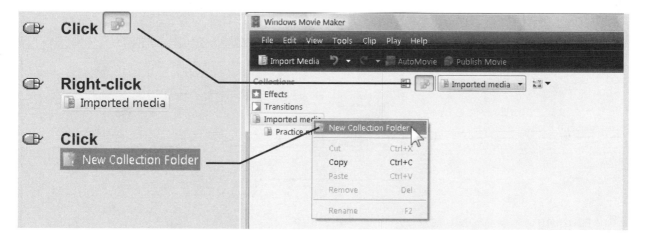

Now you can start importing from *Windows Movie Maker*:

☞ **Click** File

☞ **Click**
    Import from Digital Video Camera

HELP! I see an error message.

Do you see the message that no compatible video device can be found?

☞ **Click** OK

This problem may be caused by different things:
- Your digital video camera is not turned on.
- Your digital video camera went into standby mode. Some digital video cameras will go into standby mode if it is in the record (Camera) mode with a tape in it and no video or audio is being sent to or from the camera.

You can try a couple of things:
- Check if your digital video camera is connected properly to your computer with a *FireWire, IEE1394* or *i-link* connection.
- Check if your camera is turned on and in *Play* mode (also called *Player* or *VCR*).
- Turn your camera off and turn it on again in *Play* mode (also called *Player* or *VCR*)

☞ **Check to see if your digital video camera is recognized now**

Source: Windows Help and Support

The wizard *Importing Video* opens. First you enter a name for the videotape you are going to import:

Type a name for the videotape, for example:
The Netherlands

The videotape will be imported to the folder
Videos :

You can choose between three video file formats for the video you import:

- Audio Video Interleaved (single file): this is the file format your digital video camera uses by default. You can edit *AVI* files in *Windows Movie Maker*, but these files are quite large, up to 13 GB for every hour of video. When you have little disk space available, little internal memory or a slower processor, you may experience problems when importing video as an AVI file. Some frames of the video may be dropped and lost.
- Windows Media Video (single file): *WMV* files are much smaller than AVI files; they take up about 2 GB for each hour of video. When you import video as a WMV file, no frames will be lost. You can edit WMV files in *Windows Movie Maker*.
- Windows Media Video (one file per scene): you can also choose to have the video tape divided in separate scenes (clips) when it is imported. This is a convenient option when you plan to edit the video yourself. You can trim or split the scenes manually at another time.

Select the third option:

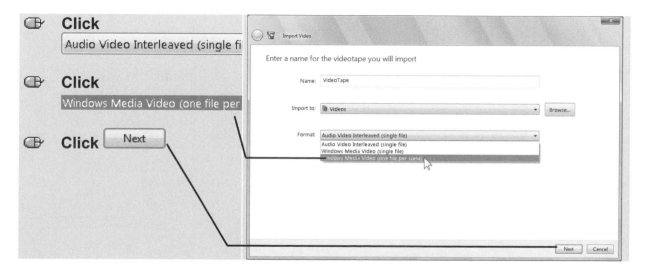

Click
Audio Video Interleaved (single fi

Click
Windows Media Video (one file per

Click Next

You are going to import the complete videotape:

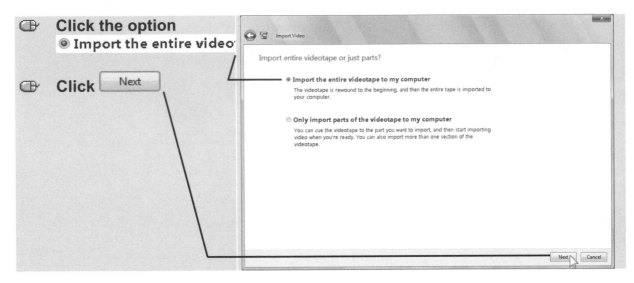

The videotape in your camera rewinds to the beginning.

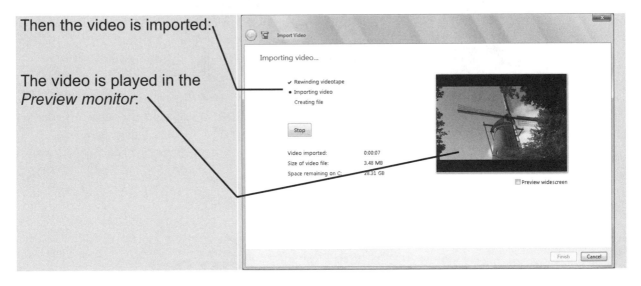

The wizard will 'look' at the complete videotape and import all available video footage. When your video does not fill the entire videotape, you do not have to be afraid that 'empty' frames are imported.

When you are certain that the still frame in the *Preview monitor* is the end of the video:

Click Stop

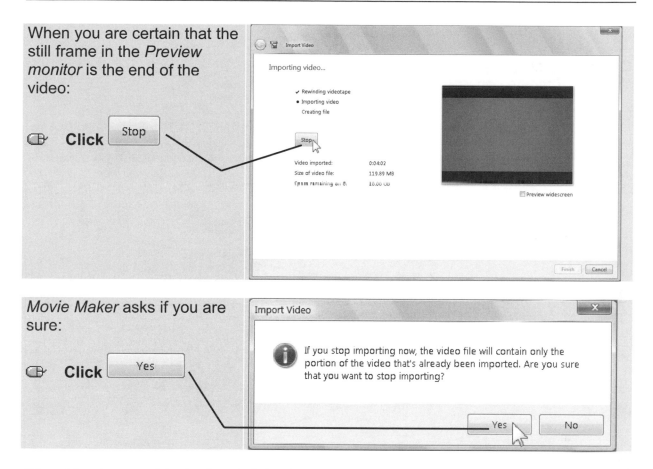

Movie Maker asks if you are sure:

Click Yes

The video is saved to the hard disk of your computer and imported in *Windows Movie Maker*.

In this example the video is divided into two clips:

If you have additional scenes in your video, then you will see more clips.

The clips have the name you entered, combined with the date, time and a number:

The Netherlands
2007_12_10_22_28_48 001

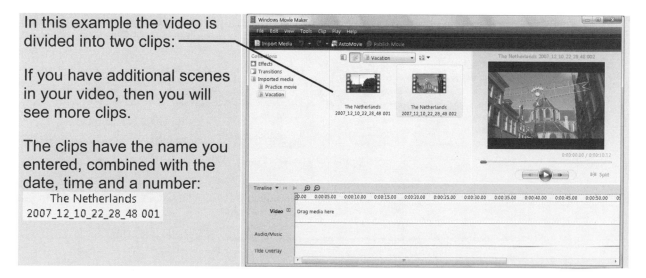

⚲ Tip

Combining clips

You can combine consecutive clips into one clip again. Like this:

☞ **Click the first clip**

⌨ **Hold down** `Shift`

☞ **Click the second clip**

⌨ **Release** `Shift`

Both clips are now selected.

☞ **Right-click the second clip**

☞ **Click** Combine

Now the consecutive clips are combined in one clip:

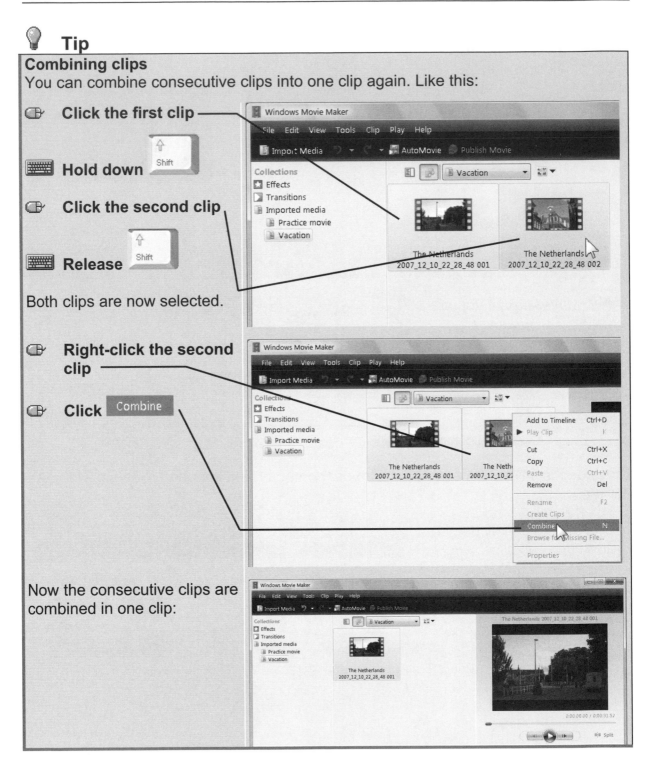

Even though the video you imported is divided in separate clips in *Movie Maker*, it is saved as one single video on the hard disk of your computer. You can verify that now. First open your *Personal folder*. Your *Personal folder* has the same name as your *Windows* user account. In this example the name is Studio Visual Steps.

The imported video is saved in the folder *Videos*:

The video is in a folder with the name you gave to the videotape in the previous section. You can open this folder:

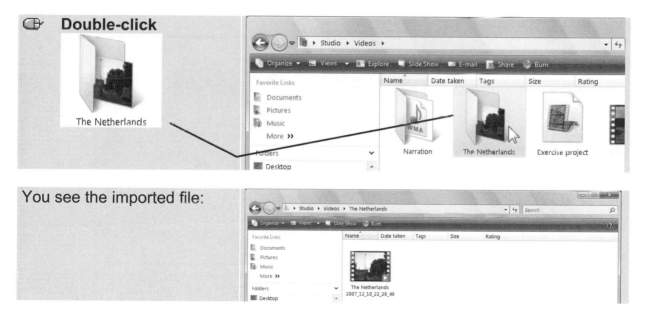

Windows Movie Maker only contains a shortcut to the original source file that is represented as two *clips* in *Windows Movie Maker*. As you can see, dividing the video in separate scenes when you import it does not affect the original file.

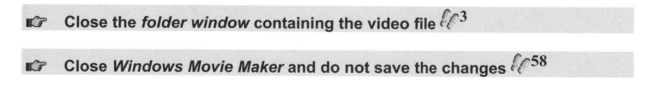

☞ **Close the *folder window* containing the video file** $\ell\ell^3$

☞ **Close *Windows Movie Maker* and do not save the changes** $\ell\ell^{58}$

Tip

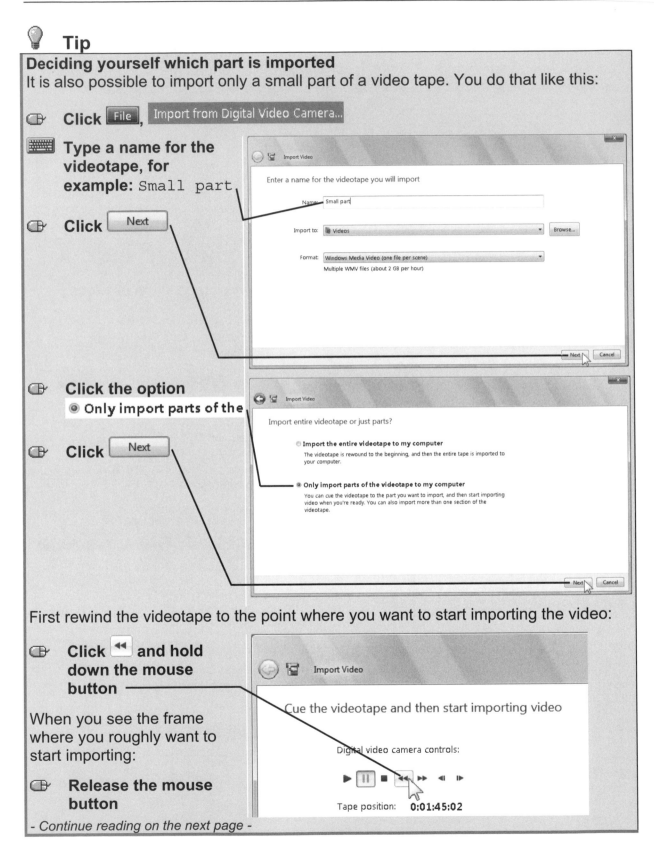

Deciding yourself which part is imported
It is also possible to import only a small part of a video tape. You do that like this:

👆 **Click File , Import from Digital Video Camera...**

⌨ **Type a name for the videotape, for example:** Small part

👆 **Click Next**

👆 **Click the option**
   ⦿ **Only import parts of the**

👆 **Click Next**

First rewind the videotape to the point where you want to start importing the video:

👆 **Click ◀◀ and hold down the mouse button**

When you see the frame where you roughly want to start importing:

👆 **Release the mouse button**

- Continue reading on the next page -

The video starts playing at that point. You can freeze the image with the button ■. With the buttons ◄| and |► you can take steps of 0.01 second to find the exact frame where you want to start importing. When you have found the correct spot:

👆 **Click** | Start Video Import |

When you have reached the end of the fragment you want to import:

👆 **Click** | Stop Video Import |

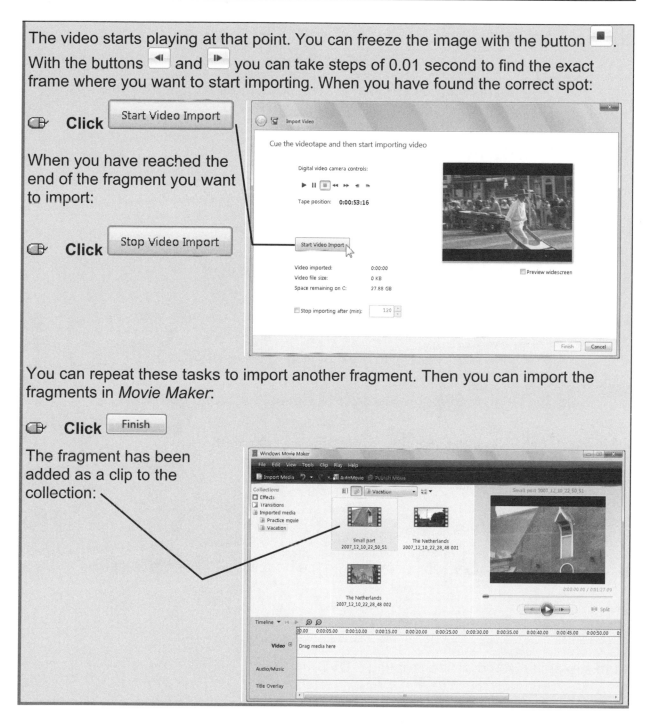

You can repeat these tasks to import another fragment. Then you can import the fragments in *Movie Maker*:

👆 **Click** | Finish |

The fragment has been added as a clip to the collection:

You can repeat the tasks you have practiced in this chapter using the exercises in the next section.

8.19 Exercises

🐾

Have you forgotten how to do something? Use the number beside the footsteps 🐾[1] to look it up in the appendix *How Do I Do That Again?*

Exercise: Editing a Movie

In this exercise you practice editing a movie.

✅   Open *Windows Movie Maker*. 🐾[59]

✅   If necessary, switch to *Storyboard* . 🐾[60]

✅   If necessary, display the collection *Practice movie* in the *Contents Pane*. 🐾[61]

✅   Copy the video clip *Butterfly* to the first slot on the *Storyboard*. 🐾[62]

✅   Copy the video clip *Bear* to the second slot on the *Storyboard*. 🐾[62]

✅   Place the transition *Dissolve, rough* between the clips. 🐾[63]

✅   Add the effect *Watercolor* to the video clip *Bear*. 🐾[64]

✅   Switch to *Timeline*.🐾[65]

✅   Trim approximately two seconds from the beginning of the clip *Butterfly*. 🐾[66]

Exercise: Creating a DVD

In this exercise you practice creating a DVD.

✅   Publish the movie to DVD, name the project *Exercise*. 🐾[67]

✅   Select menu style *Highlights*. 🐾[68]

✅   Cancel writing the DVD. 🐾[69]

✅   Close all open windows, do not save the changes. 🐾[58]

8.20 Background Information

Glossary

Audio/ Music track	In the *Timeline* view: shows which audio clips have been added to the project.
Clip	Imported video and audio files are displayed as clips in the *Contents Pane*. These are shortcuts to the original files on the hard disk of the computer.
Collection	A storage unit to organize clips in *Windows Movie Maker*.
Contents Pane	Shows clips, effects, or transitions you are working with while you create your movie.
Credits	Rolling text you see at the end of a movie.
Editing	Arranging and trimming clips in a project.
Effects	Special effects you can add to a video clip to change the way it is played.
Encoding	Compiling a DVD. During the encoding process the DVD menu is created and the movies are converted to a format that can be played in a regular DVD player.
Frame	Smallest unit that makes up a video clip.
Importing	Bringing digital media files into *Windows Movie Maker* so that you can work with them in different projects.
Preview monitor	Shows the clip or picture you are working on.
Project	Is created by adding (shortcuts to) clips, video files, audio files and photos to a folder in *Windows Movie Maker*. Contains information about the order and timing of clips, titles, transitions and effects on the *Storyboard* and the *Timeline*.
Publishing	Compile a movie from a project and then save it to the hard disk, write it to DVD or send it by e-mail.
Splitting	Divide a clip in two parts at the frame that is displayed in the *Preview monitor*.

- Continue reading on the next page -

Storyboard	Default view in *Windows Movie Maker*. Here you can view and change the order of the clips in your project. In this view you can also easily add effects and transitions.
Tasks Pane	Lists the common tasks you may need to perform when making a movie, including importing files, editing your movie, and publishing your movie.
Timeline	An editing view that shows a more detailed view of your movie project, where you can perform more detailed tasks. Like trimming video clips, viewing the audio track and check and adjust the timing of the clips in your project.
Transition	Effect that is shown when your movie plays from one video clip or picture to the next.
Video track	In the *Timeline* view: shows which video clips make up the project.
Windows DVD Maker	Program for creating and writing DVDs that comes packaged with *Windows Vista Ultimate* and *Windows Vista Home Premium*.
Windows Movie Maker	Program for video editing that comes packaged with *Windows Vista*.

Source: Windows Help and Support

File formats

In *Windows Movie Maker* you can import files with the following filename extensions for use in a project:

Video: ASF, AVI, DVR-MS, M1V, MP2, MP2V, MPE, MPEG, MPG, MPV2, WM, WMV

Audio: AIF, AIFC, AIFF, ASF, AU, MP2, MP3, MPA, SND, WAV and WMA

Images: BMP, DIB, EMF, GIF, JFIF, JPE, JPEG, JPG, PNG, TIF, TIFF, WMF

Video files

When you transfer video from your video camera to your computer, it is stored as a video file. There are different video file formats. Every format has its advantages and disadvantages. These are the most widely used video file formats:

AVI - Audio Video Interleaved. File format for video with sound, developed by *Microsoft*. Used frequently by *Windows*. You can play AVI video in *Windows Media Player*. The image quality can vary from fair to good, but good quality files take up a relatively large amount of space. AVI files can often be played on older computers.

MPG - (also called MPEG, *Motion Pictures Expert Group*). File format for video with sound that compresses video a lot without a lot of quality loss. This is the default file format for video files and the most frequently used. The quality is good, especially that of the second version: MPEG-2. This can be used to save image and sound with CD quality. The quality of MPEG-4 is even better.

WMV - Windows Media Video. File format developed by *Microsoft* to be played in *Windows Media Player*.

Deleting video files from the hard disk

When you are working on a project in *Windows Movie Maker*, never delete the original video files from the hard disk or move them to another folder. Keep in mind that a *Windows Movie Maker* project only contains shortcuts to the original files, and the editing you have done to this material. Only when the movie is compiled and published, the material and the editing is combined and saved in a new format. If you would delete or move the original files from the hard disk, the program can no longer find them. That means you have to start over again.

Only when you have finished your movie completely, can you delete the original files from the hard disk. This way you can free up space on the hard disk for a future project. Before you remove the files completely, consider keeping a backup of the original video files. If there is a chance you might want to use them again later, burn the original files to one or more DVDs using DVD burning software, or copy them to an external hard disk. After that you can delete the video files permanently from the hard disk in the same way you have become accustomed to in *Windows*: by selecting and deleting the files in the *Folder window* of the folder where they are stored.

8.21 Tips

💡 Tip

Automatically dividing a video file in clips
To make working on your project easier, you can divide one existing video clip in separate smaller clips.

When the source clip originates from a digital video camera, it is possible to divide it in clips automatically. These clips are made based on the time stamps added by the digital video camera when the video was filmed. Huge frame changes in the video are also taken into consideration.

Clips can be created automatically for WMV files (Windows Media Video) and AVI files (Audio-Video Interleaved) that uses the digital video codec.

In the *Contents Pane* you can divide a video into smaller clips like this:

☞ **Right-click the video clip**

☞ **Click** `Create Clips`

Now the divided video clip will be displayed as separate, numbered clips in the *Contents Pane*.

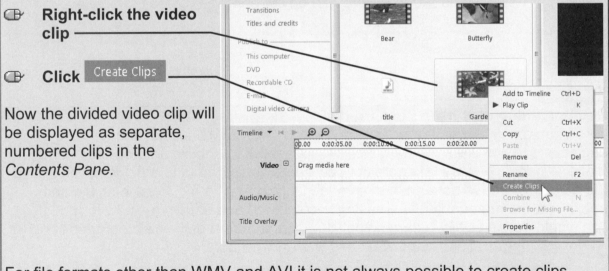

For file formats other than WMV and AVI it is not always possible to create clips automatically. Then the video file is displayed as one big video clip in *Windows Movie Maker*. Like you practiced before in this chapter, you can manually split a large video clip into smaller clips.

💡 Tip

Extra audio tracks

You have seen before that a narration can only be added to the audio/music track at locations where there was no music. You can use the following trick if you want to add background music as well as a narration for the whole movie.

☞ **Create a complete movie, including effects, transitions, titles, credits and music**

Make sure the movie is completely 'done' and you do not want to change anything else. The narration has to be the only thing that is missing.

☞ **Publish the movie to** *This computer / Publish for playback* **and name the movie** $\mathcal{U}^{70}$

☞ **Just to make sure, save the project you just published** $\mathcal{U}^{71}$

Now you open a new project in *Windows Movie Maker*:

👉 **Click** File

👉 **Click** New Project

☞ **Import the published movie** $\mathcal{U}^{57}$

☞ **If necessary, switch to the *Timeline* view** $\mathcal{U}^{65}$

👉 **Click the new movie**

👉 **Drag the movie to the video track**

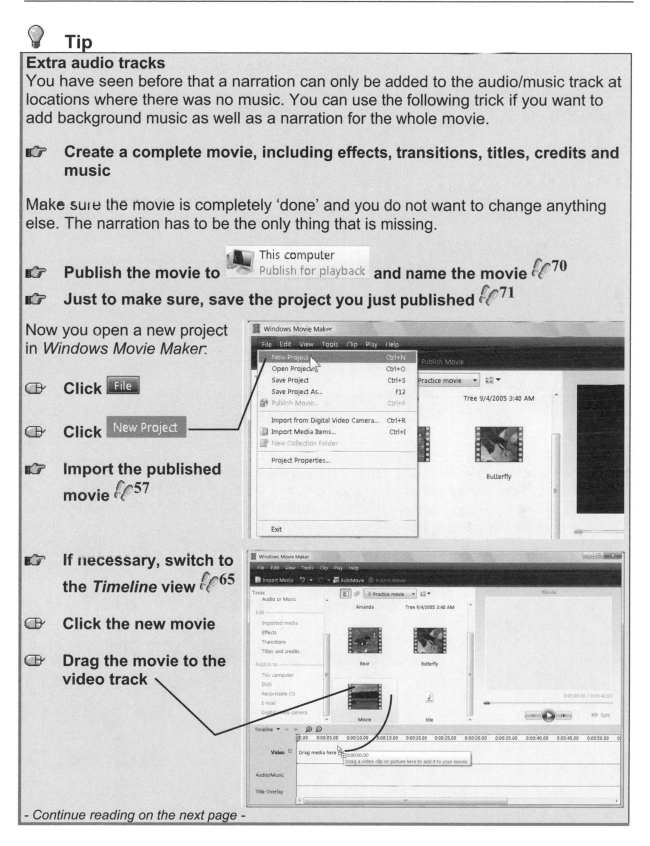

- Continue reading on the next page -

Now the entire movie is on the video track.
You see the video track:

The audio/music track is empty:

Now you can add a narration to the entire movie.

☞ **Click** Timeline ▼

☞ **Click** ✎ Narrate Timeline...

☞ **Connect a microphone to your computer**

☞ **Record your narration** 🐾72

💡 **Tip**

AutoMovie
Using the *AutoMovie* feature you can create a movie automatically in *Windows Movie Maker*. This can result in very funny movies. When an *AutoMovie* is created, every clip in the collection that is currently displayed in the *Contents Pane* is used. You can use the *AutoMovie* like this:

☞ **Click** 📹 AutoMovie

You can choose between different editing styles:

☞ **For example, click** Old Movie

Here you can also add a title for the movie and select the music:

- Continue reading on the next page -

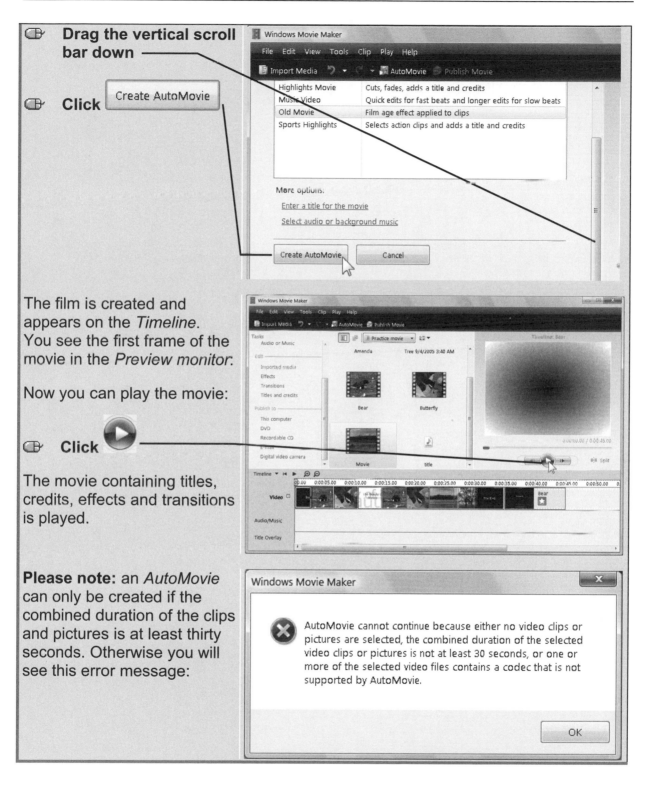

☞ **Drag the vertical scroll bar down**

☞ **Click** Create AutoMovie

The film is created and appears on the *Timeline*.
You see the first frame of the movie in the *Preview monitor*.

Now you can play the movie:

☞ **Click** ▶

The movie containing titles, credits, effects and transitions is played.

Please note: an *AutoMovie* can only be created if the combined duration of the clips and pictures is at least thirty seconds. Otherwise you will see this error message:

Notes

Write down your notes here.

9. Your Photos in Vista

Digital photography has become immensely popular in recent years. The camera with a roll of film has been pushed aside by the digital camera. Even regular printed photos are scanned nowadays to make them available in digital format.

In this manner, many people have amassed a large collection of digital photos on their computer. *Windows Photo Gallery* will help you organize your photo collection. You can add tags and ratings to the photos, making it a lot easier to quickly locate a specific photo or a group of them with similar characteristics. You can also easily assemble entertaining slide shows with *Photo Gallery* to share with friends or family.

But that is not all. With *Photo Gallery* you also have several tools on hand for basic photo editing. You can rotate and crop your photos, adjust the color and exposure or fix red eye. There are various options available to share your photos with others. You can print or e-mail your photos, or burn your photos as a slide show complete with background music on a video DVD.

In this chapter you learn how to:

- open *Windows Photo Gallery*;
- work with tags and ratings;
- add folders to *Windows Photo Gallery*;
- play a slide show;
- use tools for basic photo editing;
- print your photos;
- e-mail your photos;
- create a video DVD with a slide show of your photos;
- burn your photos to disc;
- do more photo editing with the program *Paint*;
- import photos from a digital camera;
- import photos from a scanner.

➡ **Please note:**

This chapter uses the practice photos from the CD-ROM you received with this book. To be able to work through this chapter, you need to copy these files to the hard disk of your computer. You can read how to do that in **Appendix A.**

9.1 Windows Photo Gallery

Windows Photo Gallery is a practical and easy-to-use program for managing, organizing and viewing your photos and videos. You can open *Windows Photo Gallery* like this:

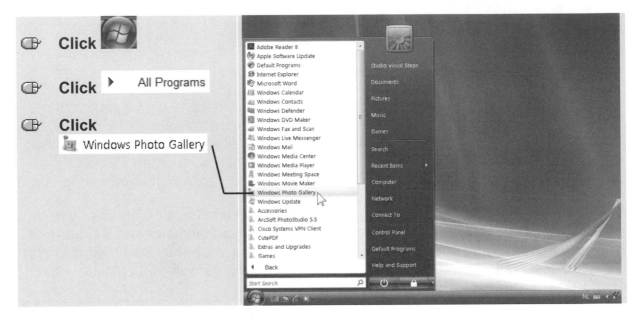

Click

Click ▶ All Programs

Click

Windows Photo Gallery

Windows Photo Gallery is opened. By default, the program displays the contents of your folders *Pictures* and *Videos*. If you did not store anything in these folders yet, they only contain the *Vista* sample photos and videos.

On the left side you see the *Navigation Pane*:

On the right you see the *Gallery* with thumbnails of the images and videos:

In this example the files are sorted by the year they were taken. That may be different on your computer.

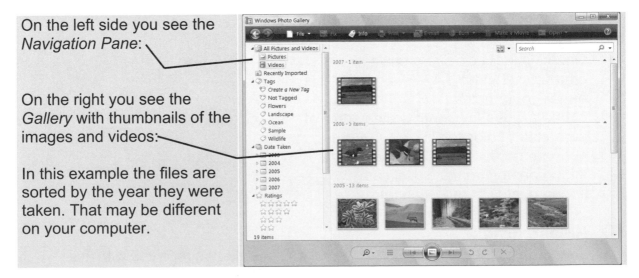

HELP! My Navigation Pane looks different.

Is the list in the *Navigation Pane* a lot shorter on your computer? Then all options are collapsed. You can expand everything like this:

- **Click the arrow ▷ next to** All Pictures and Videos
- **Click the arrow ▷ next to** Tags
- **Do the same for the other options**

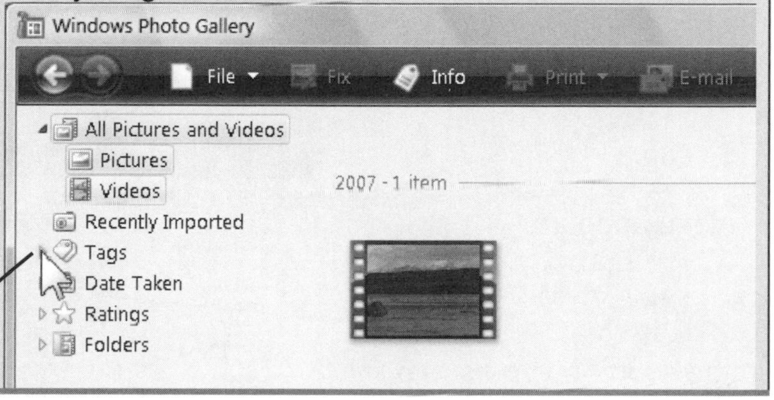

You can bring another pane into view:

- **Click** Info
- **Click a photo, for example**

Now the properties of the selected photo are displayed in the *Information Pane* on the right side:

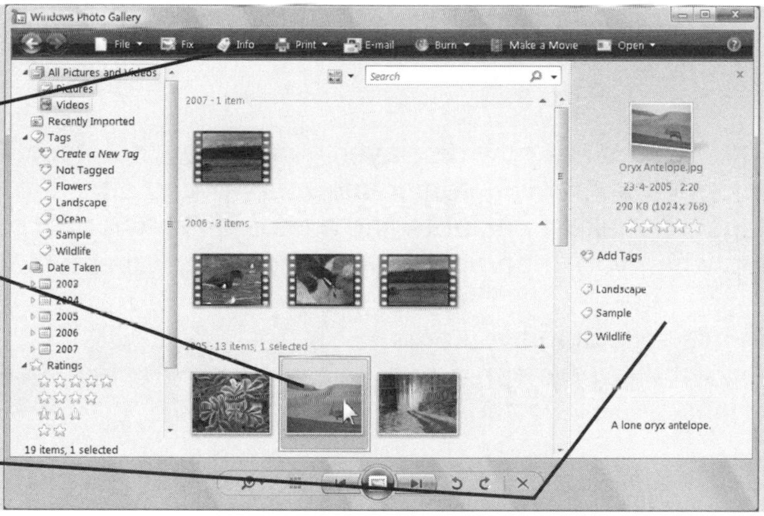

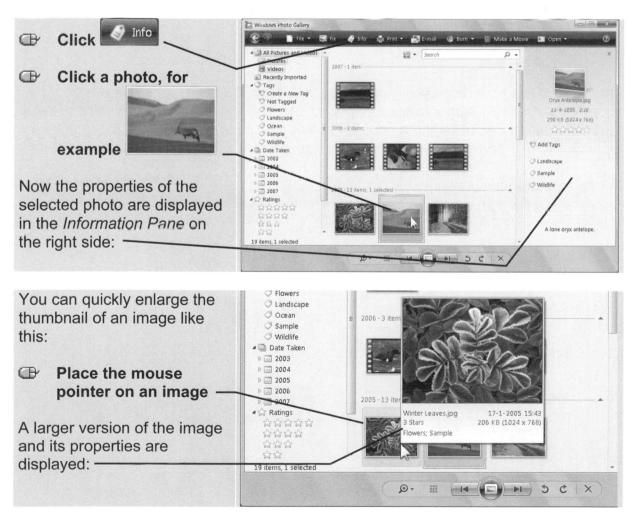

You can quickly enlarge the thumbnail of an image like this:

- **Place the mouse pointer on an image**

A larger version of the image and its properties are displayed:

9.2 Tags and Ratings

Finding a specific photo on your computer can be difficult when you have a large photo collection. *Windows Photo Gallery* offers useful tools to quickly find your photos:

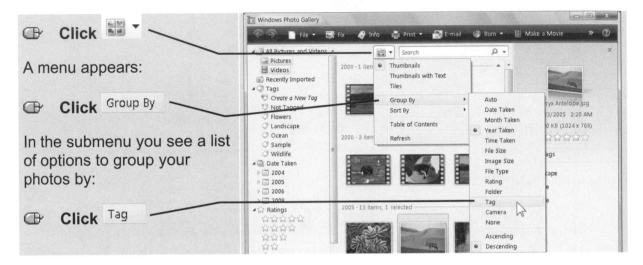

☞ **Click** ▦ ▾

A menu appears:

☞ **Click** Group By

In the submenu you see a list of options to group your photos by:

☞ **Click** Tag

The images are now displayed grouped by their tags. Tags are small pieces of information that you can create yourself and attach to your photos and videos. These tags will make it easier to find and organize your photos and videos. If you specify a tag when you import photos and videos, it will automatically be added to each file.

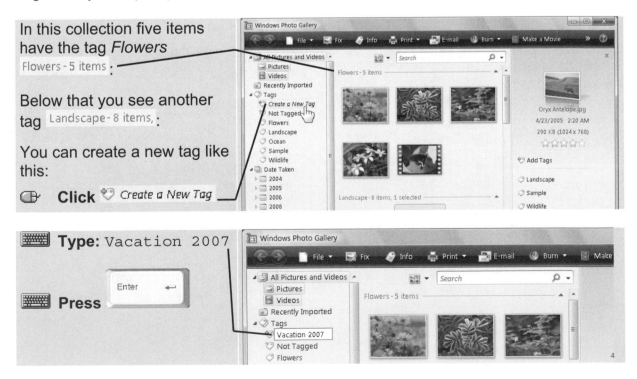

In this collection five items have the tag *Flowers* Flowers - 5 items :

Below that you see another tag Landscape - 8 items, :

You can create a new tag like this:

☞ **Click** ♡ Create a New Tag

⌨ **Type:** Vacation 2007

⌨ **Press** Enter ⏎

A new tag is created. Now you can add this tag to an image:

☞ **Click an image**

☞ **Drag the image to**
◌ Vacation 2007

☞ **Release the mouse button when you see**

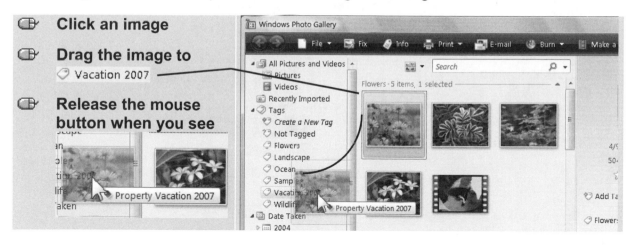

The tag is added to the image. You can do the same thing for a group of images: select the series and drag them all to ◌ Holiday 2007 in one go.

💡 **Tip**

Nesting tags
To keep the number of tags manageable, you can 'nest' groups of related tags. This means that you add multiple lower level tags to a top level tag.
You can add a lower level tag by right-clicking an existing tag and select Create Tag in the menu that appears. Here you see an example:

◀ ◌ Vacation 2007
  ◌ 2006
  ◌ 2007

You can also view images grouped by the date each photo was taken, or by its rating (the number of stars). You can add stars to your images in the *Information Pane* on the right side:

☞ **Click an image**

The properties of the image are displayed:

If you want to give the image a five-star rating:

☞ **Click the fifth star** ☆

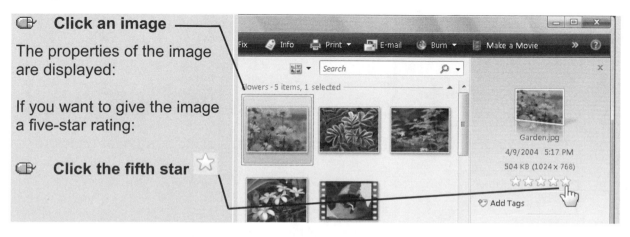

You can group the images by their rating like this:

☞ **Click** ⊞ ▾ , Group By , Rating

At the top you see all photos
and videos with rating 5 Stars:

Below you see the photos
and videos with rating 4 Stars:

☞ **Minimize the *Windows Photo Gallery* window** 👣⁹⁹

9.3 Search by Tag

When you consistently add one or more tags to each photo on the hard disk of your computer, you can quickly find a specific series of photos in a large collection. You can use the powerful search feature of *Windows Vista* to do this.

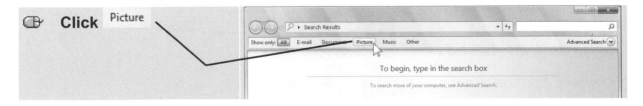

You see the search window. First you indicate that you want to search for a picture:

☞ **Click** Picture

You can type your search term in the *Search Box* [🔍] in the top right corner. For example, search for the tag *Vacation* you just created.

🖱️ **Click in the Search Box** ————

⌨️ **Type:** vac

As soon as you start typing the search results appear. The photo with the tag *Vacation* is found: ————

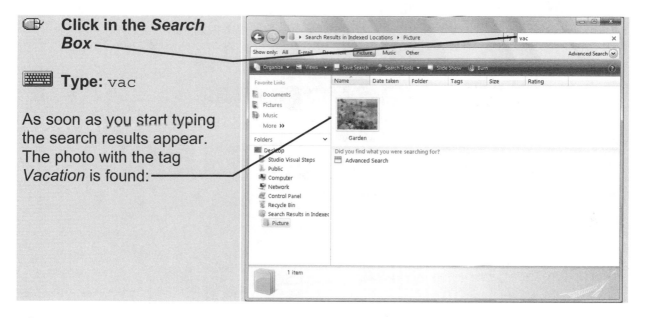

💡 **Tip**

Do not scrimp
Do not scrimp when you start assigning tags to your photos! It may seem logical to simply assign the tag *Vacation* to the photos of the summer vacation you spent with your (grand) children. But you can also assign the extra tag *Grandchildren* to the photos of your grandchildren. Do the same thing for the photos taken last Christmas: tag these with *Christmas* as well as *Grandchildren*.
Now you can easily find all photos of your grandchildren. If you tagged your whole collection this way, you will also find the photos you made of your grandchildren at other times.

👉 **Close the window with the search results** 👣³

👉 **Open the *Windows Photo Gallery* window from the taskbar** 👣¹⁰⁰

9.4 Playing a Slide Show

The *Windows Photo Gallery* slide show is a fun way to view a number of photos in a row. Your photos and videos will be displayed full screen. By default, your photos and videos are combined in a slide show. You can also choose to display just the images:

If necessary, drag the vertical scroll bar up

If necessary, click All Pictures and Videos

Click Pictures

You can start the slide show like this:

Click

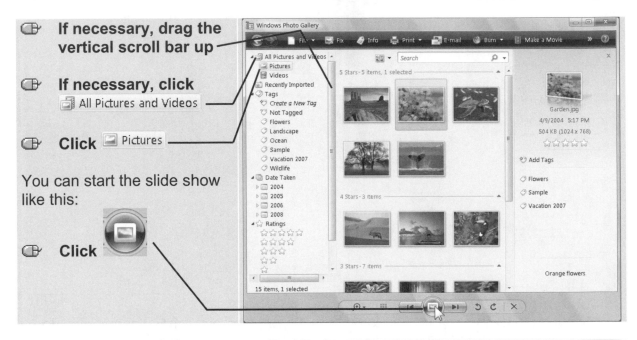

The screen goes dark for a moment, then the slide show starts:

At the bottom of the window you see several buttons you can use to adjust the settings for the slide show. For example, you can choose a different theme for the slide show:

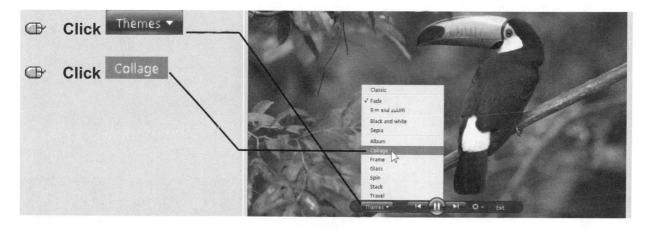

☞ **Click** `Themes ▼`

☞ **Click** `Collage`

✖ HELP! I do not see any buttons.

If you do not see the buttons in the slide show, your graphics card may not be powerful enough to handle the visual effects. Laptop users may also experience this same problem. If you do not see the buttons:

☞ **Right-click the photo**

Now you see the various options that you can use to adjust the settings for the slide show:

Unfortunately you can't make a collage.

Play
Pause
Next
Back

Shuffle
Loop

Slide Show Speed - Slow
◉ Slide Show Speed - Medium
Slide Show Speed - Fast

Exit

The slide show is now displayed as a changing collage:

You can adjust more settings for the slide show.

☞ **Click** [⚙ ▼]

Using these options you can
adjust the speed of the slide
show:

It is also possible to display
the photos in random order:

Now you can end the slide show:

☞ **Click** [Exit]

9.5 Adding Folders to Windows Photo Gallery

By default, *Photo Gallery* shows all photos and videos in the *Pictures* folder, but you
can add other folders to *Photo Gallery* as well. You can try that with the folder
containing the practice files.

➡️ **Please note:**

To be able to work through the rest of this chapter, the folder with the practice files
needs to be copied to the hard disk of your computer. You can find the practice files
on the CD-ROM you received with this book.
In **Appendix A** at the end of this book you can read how to copy the files.

You can add folders to *Photo Gallery* one at a time. Repeat the following steps for
each folder you want to add:

☞ **Click** [📄 File ▼]

☞ **Click** Add Folder to Gallery...

The folder with the practice files is stored in the folder *Documents* in your *Personal Folder*:

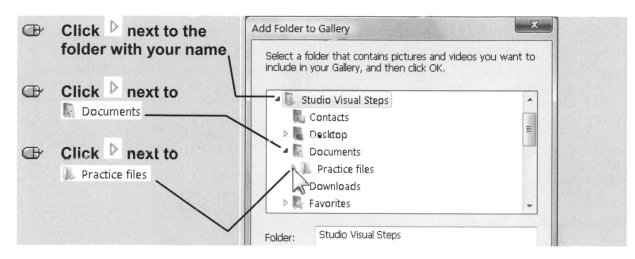

You add the folder containing the photos:

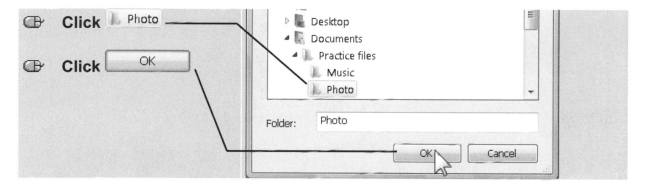

This folder is added very quickly. Adding folders with large numbers of files to *Photo Gallery* may take a little longer.

You see this window:

☞ **Click to check mark**
    ☑ Don't show this message again

☞ **Click** ❘ OK ❘

The message will not be displayed next time.

Add Folder to Gallery

This folder has been added to your Gallery.

It might take some time to add the files in this folder, and Photo Gallery might run slower while these files are being processed. When it's complete, you can view all the pictures and videos stored in this folder in your Gallery.

☑ Don't show this message again   ❘ OK ❘

How do I control which folders appear in the Gallery?

⇒ **Please note:**

You should avoid adding certain folders to *Photo Gallery*. The *Local Disk* folder ⬛ Local Disk (C:) below ⬛ Computer, for example, is called the root folder because it represents your entire hard disk. Adding this folder to *Photo Gallery* will make it run very slowly, because it possibly contains large numbers of images. For example images from websites you visited. You should avoid adding the *Windows* folder and other system locations to *Photo Gallery* for similar reasons.

You see the ten practice photos:

The order they are displayed in may be different on your computer.

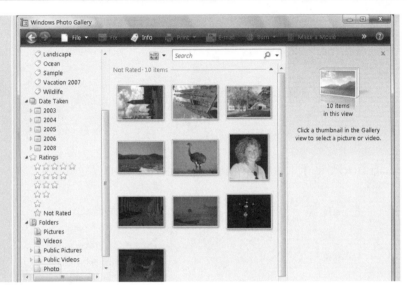

The folder *Photo* is displayed in the *Navigation Pane* as well:

Below ⊿ 🗐 Folders you see the folders that have been added to *Photo Gallery*. The folder 🗐 Photo is in this list as well:

💡 **Tip**

Removing a folder from Windows Photo Gallery

If you no longer want to display a folder in *Photo Gallery*, but you want to keep the photos on the hard disk of your computer, you do the following:

☞ **Right-click the folder**

☞ **Click** Remove from Gallery

Vista asks for a confirmation:

☞ **Click** ⬚ Yes ⬚

 **Please note!**

When you select `Delete` instead of `Remove from Gallery`, the folder is permanently deleted from the hard disk of your computer. The folders you see in the *Navigation pane* are not copies, but the original folders as they are stored on the hard disk of your computer.

9.6 Basic Photo Editing

You can perform a few basic photo editing tasks on your images in *Photo Gallery*. The following tasks are possible:

- rotate a photo;
- crop a photo;
- auto adjust a photo;
- adjust exposure;
- adjust color;
- fix red eyes.

Each action is explained in the next section.

9.7 Rotating a Photo

Often photos from your digital camera or scanner are not displayed in the correct position. It is very easy to fix this problem:

☞ **Click the photo of Big Ben**

At the bottom of the *Photo Gallery* window you find two buttons to rotate your photos:

☞ **Click** 🔄

The photo is rotated 45 degrees clockwise. You see that the thumbnail of the image is displayed in the correct position right away:

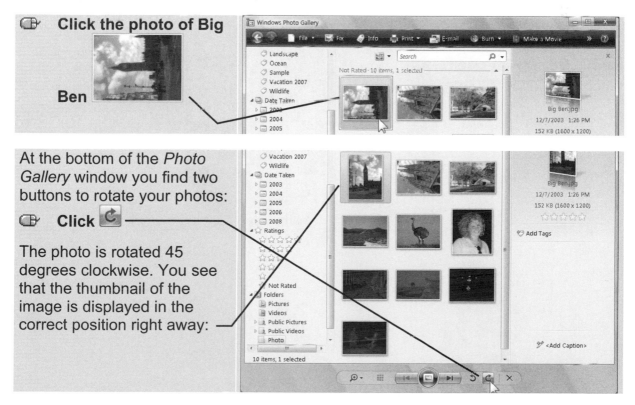

9.8 Cropping a Photo

Often photos contain unimportant items that nobody really looks at. That is also the case in the photo of the Big Ben. When you switch to the view where you can edit the photo, you can see that clearly.

Click [Fix]

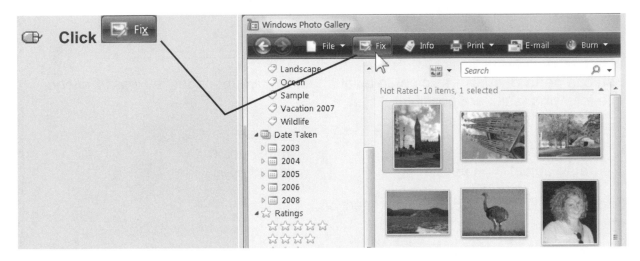

The *Edit Pane* is opened and the photo is displayed in a larger size.

In this photo the building on the left and the road in front take the attention away from the real subject of the photo: the Big Ben and the Houses of Parliament in London.

Click

[Crop Picture]

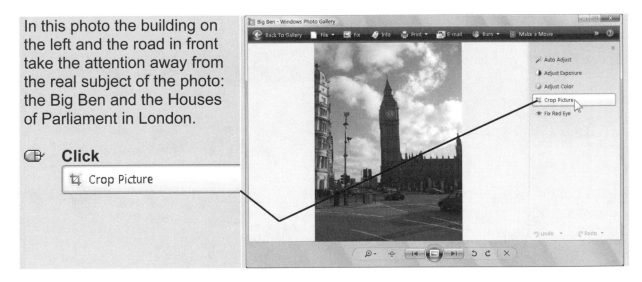

You can easily crop a picture in *Photo Gallery*. The program shows a crop frame that you can drag to the most important part of the photo:

☞ **Click in the crop frame**

The mouse pointer changes into ⬦:

☞ **Drag the crop frame to the top right corner of the photo**

You can increase or decrease the size of the crop frame by dragging the corners:

☞ **Place the mouse pointer on the bottom left corner**

The mouse pointer changes into ⬋:

☞ **Drag the corner to the bottom of the fence**

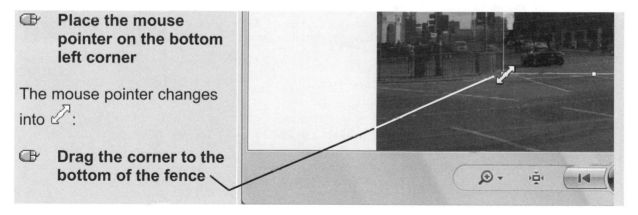

The most important part of the photo is inside the crop frame. Now you can trim the photo:

☞ **Click** [Apply]

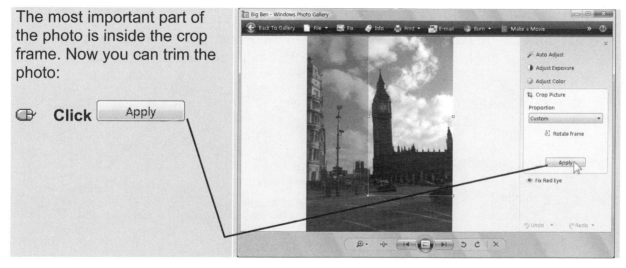

The less important parts are eliminated and the photo becomes smaller:

You have finished editing this photo. If you want to keep the original photo as well as the cropped version, you need to take a detour in *Photo Gallery*. First you save a copy of the cropped photo:

Click File ▼

Click Make a Copy...

Type next to File name: :
Big Ben cropped

Click Save

Now the copy of the cropped photo is saved. In the *Photo Gallery* window you still see the cropped photo. You are going to restore this photo to its original state:

Click next to
Undo

The menu has three options:

Click Undo All

Now you see the original version of the photo once again.

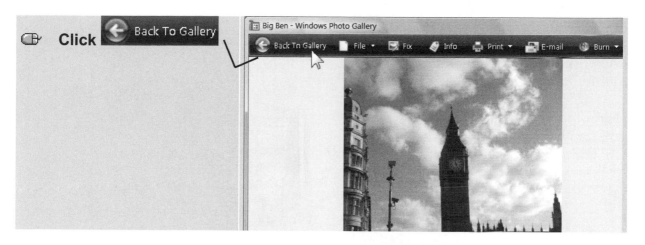

There are now two versions of the photo of the Big Ben on the hard disk of your computer: the original and the cropped version.

💡 Tip

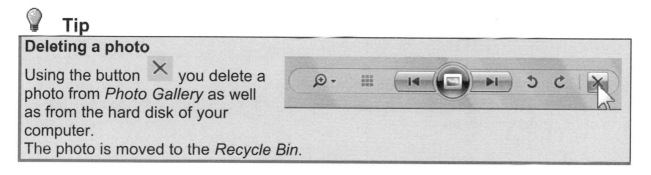

Deleting a photo

Using the button ✕ you delete a photo from *Photo Gallery* as well as from the hard disk of your computer.
The photo is moved to the *Recycle Bin*.

9.9 Adjusting the View of the Gallery

To edit the next photo, you need to change the view of the photos in the *Gallery*:

Now the photos are displayed in a list, with the name of each photo next to the thumbnail:

Using the vertical scroll bar you can take a look at the whole list:

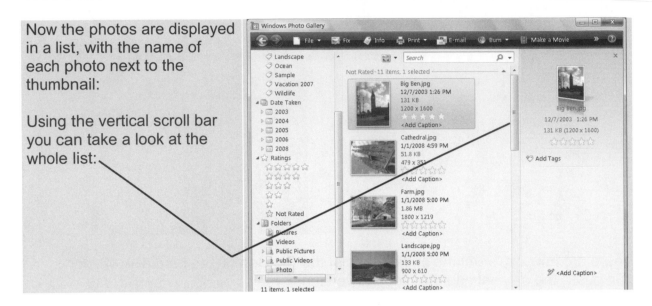

9.10 Auto Adjust

Windows Photo Gallery contains another useful feature that can be used to improve some of your photos surprisingly quickly: *Auto Adjust*. You can see for yourself with one of the practice photos.

☞ **Select the photo *Rome pillars*** 🦶🏻73

☞ **Open the *Edit Pane*** 🦶🏻74

You see this dark photo:

🖱 **Click**

     🪄 Auto Adjust

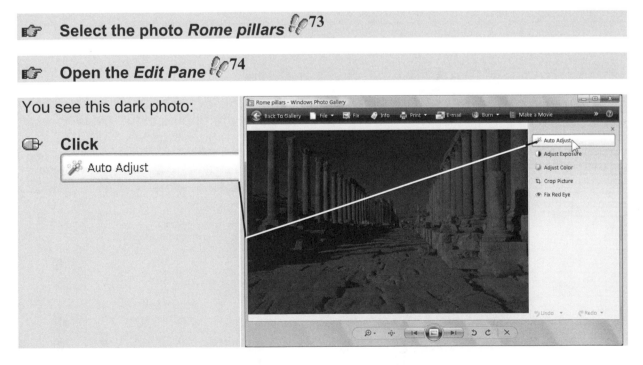

The *Auto Adjust* feature adjusts the brightness, the contrast and the colors of the photo.

The photo has become a lot clearer:

☞ **Click** Back To Gallery

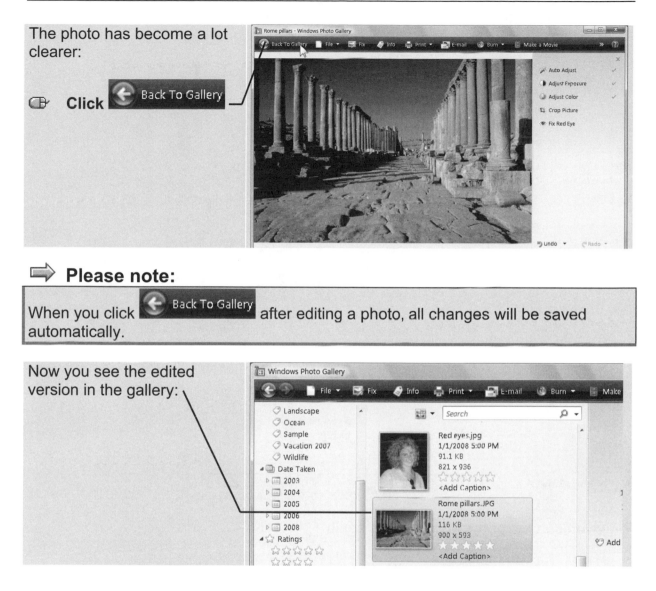

➡ **Please note:**

When you click Back To Gallery after editing a photo, all changes will be saved automatically.

Now you see the edited version in the gallery:

9.11 Reverting a Photo to the Original Version

If you still are not satisfied with the edited version, *Windows Photo Gallery* lets you revert back to the original photo. You can restore the original version like this:

☞ **Click the photo you want to restore**

☞ **Click** Fix

You see the *Edit Pane* again.

☞ **Click** 🔲 Revert

Crop Picture
Fix Red Eye

Revert ▾   Redo ▾

Photo Gallery asks if you are sure:

☞ **Click** Revert

Revert to Original   ✕

❓ Are you sure you want to revert to the original version of this picture?

If you revert, all changes you have made to this picture will be lost.

Revert   Cancel

Now you see the original, dark photo again.

☞ **Click** ⬅ Back To Gallery

Rome pillars - Windows Photo Gallery

⬅ Back To Gallery   📄 File ▾   🖼 Fix   ✏ Info   🖨 Print ▾   ✉ E-mail   💿 Burn ▾   Mak

By default, *Windows Photo Gallery* saves a copy of your original photo. This way you can always revert back to the original version of your photo, even after editing and saving it. Take a look at the setting that allows this.

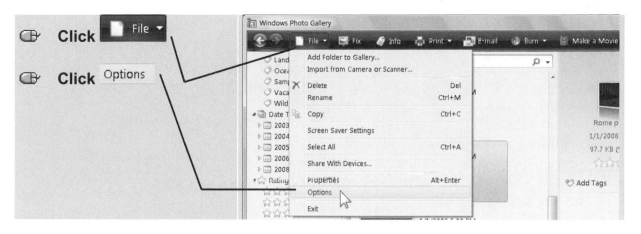

The *Windows Photo Gallery Options* window is opened.

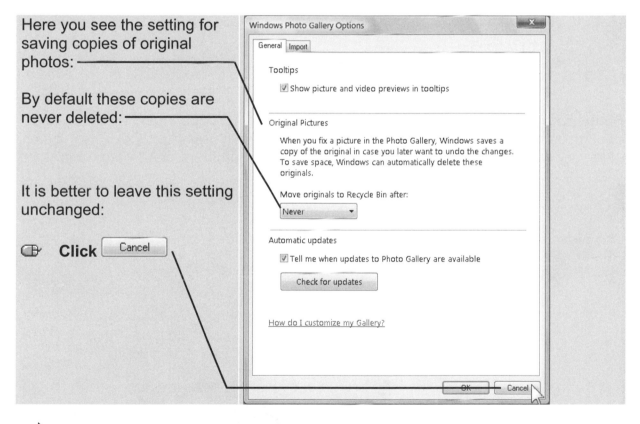

⇨ **Please note:**

You may want to change the setting for saving copies of original photos in order to save disk space. If you do, always make sure that you safeguard your original photos in some other way. For example, you can burn a DVD containing your original photos. In **section 9.18 Burning Photos to disc** you can read how to do that.

♀ Tip

Safety first

Even the most stable computer may experience hardware and/or software problems. If your photo archive is stored only in one place (the hard disk of your computer), you risk losing everything in a hard disk crash!

To safeguard your original photos:
- always make a copy of the original photo you are going to edit and
- create a backup of your photos on an external medium, like a writable DVD or an external hard disk.

This way you know for sure that you still have your original photos, even when you have computer problems or when edited photos can no longer be reverted to the original version.

9.12 Adjusting Exposure

Sometimes photos are too dark or too light. Photos may become too dark when not enough light is available or when a flash fill is not used in bright sunlight. The subject of the photo is then underexposed. You can solve this problem with *Photo Gallery*.

☞ **Select the photo *Statues* $\ell\ell^{73}$ and open the *Edit Pane* $\ell\ell^{74}$**

The photo is very dark, making it difficult to see the statues.

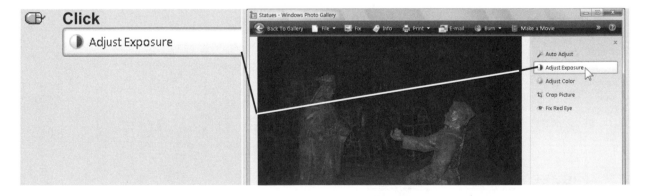

When you increase the brightness, the image becomes clearer.

Drag the slider below Brightness **to the right**

In the image below you can see how far the slider was moved in the example:

Now you can see the statues in the background:

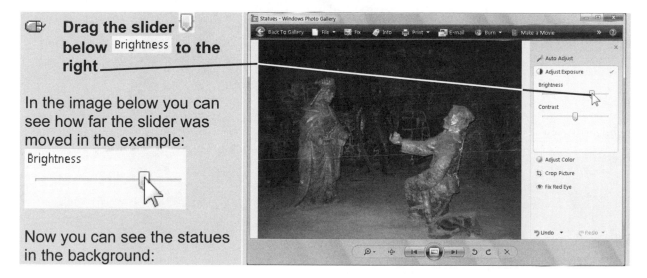

When you increase or decrease the brightness, you should also increase or decrease the contrast with a lower value to make the photo appear properly exposed.

Drag the slider below Contrast **a little bit to the right**

The image is improved a little.

The image still has a reddish glow. Perhaps the *Auto Adjust* feature gives you an even better result:

Click Auto Adjust

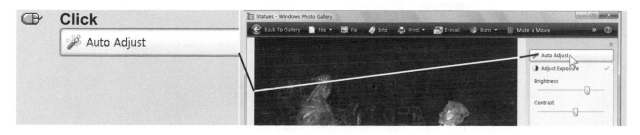

The photo has improved. The scene on the photo is now clearly visible, even though the statue in the foreground is a little overexposed:

⇨ **Please note:**

When you apply a strong correction to the exposure of a photo, the end result will not always be perfect. Specks of dust, stains or spheres may appear which were invisible in the darkened version of the photo. There is nothing you can do about this.

☞ **Undo all changes** $\ell\ell^{75}$ **and go back to the *Gallery*** $\ell\ell^{76}$

9.13 Adjusting Colors

Sometimes photos have a color cast problem. The photo may be too red, too green or too blue. In *Windows Photo Gallery* you can adjust the colors of a photo.

☞ **Select the photo *Landscape*** $\ell\ell^{73}$ **and open the *Edit Pane*** $\ell\ell^{74}$

This photo has a strong red color cast. Try the *Auto Adjust* feature first:

⊞ **Click**

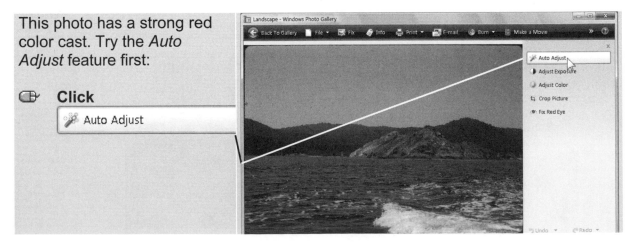

The photo has improved a bit, but is still too red:

☞ **Click**

Adjust Color

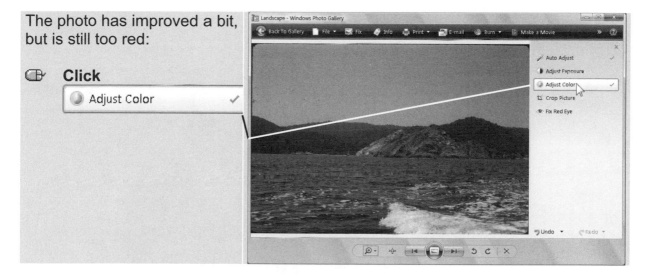

In *Photo Gallery* you can adjust three color settings:

Color Temperature : affects the overall tone of a picture by making it appear warmer (red) or cooler (blue).

Tint : removes the color cast from a picture by adding or removing green.

Saturation : adjusts the vividness of colors in a picture.

First you remove some red from the photo:

☞ **Drag the slider below** Color Temperature **to the left**

In the image below you can see how far the slider was moved in the example:

Color Temperature

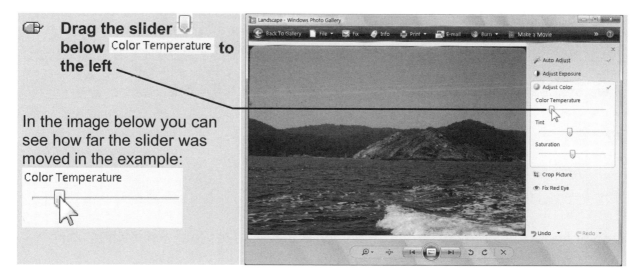

The photo has become bluer, but the tint is becoming purpler now. You can solve that by adding some green.

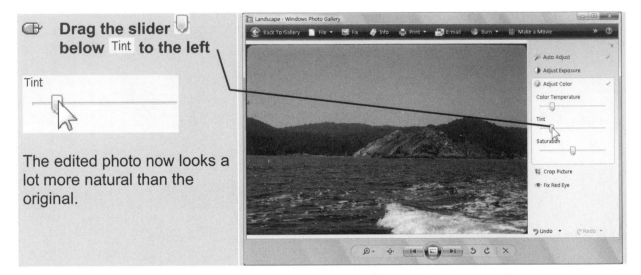

☞ **Drag the slider below Tint to the left**

Tint

The edited photo now looks a lot more natural than the original.

As you can see, when you start editing your own photos, you will probably have to experiment a little before achieving a result that satisfies you.

⇨ **Please note:**

Keep in mind that a photo that looks good on your screen may still have a color cast problem or may be too dark or too light when you print it. The color settings of your monitor and your printer are not always in sync with one another. You may need to make a larger or smaller correction to your photo to get a better quality print.

Save the changes you made to this photo:

☞ **Go back to the *Gallery* ℓℓ⁷⁶**

9.14 Fixing Red Eyes

One of the most common 'errors' on photos is the red eyes that occur when using a flash. *Photo Gallery* contains a tool that you can use to fix red eyes.

☞ **Select the photo *Red eyes* ℓℓ⁷³**

☞ **Open the *Edit Pane* ℓℓ⁷⁴**

You see this photo. It is really unfortunate that the girl in this otherwise charming picture has red eyes:

☞ **Click**

    👁 Fix Red Eye

The red eye removal tool is very easy to use: all you need to do is to draw a rectangle around the red eye with the mouse.

🖱 **Place the mouse pointer above the left eye on the left side**

🖱 **Drag a rectangle around the eye**

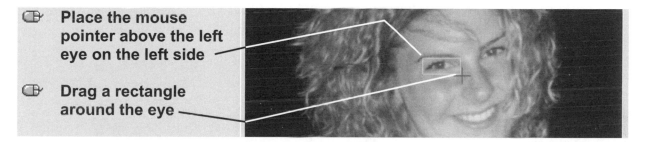

As soon as you release the mouse button, the red eye is fixed:

Now the girl only has one red eye:

👉 **Do the same thing with the other red eye**

The photo now looks a lot better. You can save this change:

☞ **Click** Back To Gallery

You have been introduced to the different photo editing tools available in *Windows Photo Gallery*. The next section highlights the methods to use for printing your photos.

💡 Tip

Following the workflow in Photo Gallery

Digital workflow is a term used by digital photographers to refer to the order in which pictures are edited. Following the correct digital workflow can make a big difference in the quality of your edited pictures.

The *Edit Pane* in *Windows Photo Gallery* shows you the various changes you can make in the best order, starting with exposure adjustments and ending with red eye removal.

It is advisable to edit your photos in this order. Imagine, for example, that you want to correct the color balance in your picture. If the overall exposure is wrong (the picture is too dark or too light), it will be difficult to identify the correct color balance. Only by correcting the exposure first, you can be sure the colors also look right when you reach that step.

(Source: Windows Help and Support)

9.15 Printing Photos

Windows Vista contains a convenient printing wizard that you can use to print your photos in different sizes. First you use the *Navigation Pane* to display all images in *Photo Gallery*:

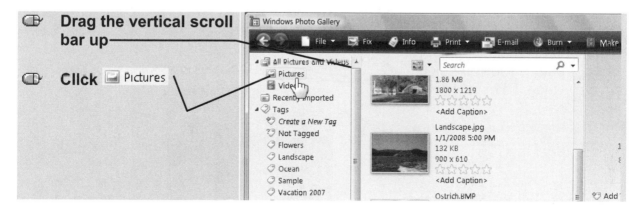

Now you can select the photos you want to print. In this example, choose the first and the third photo:

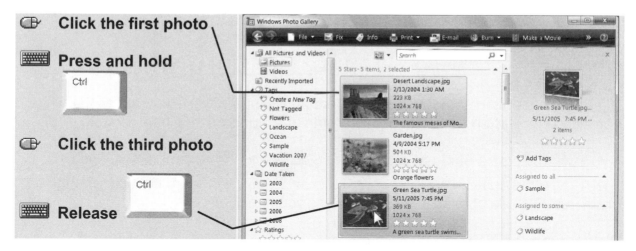

You can open the window *Print Pictures* like this:

In this window you can adjust several settings for printing photos. Depending on your printer, the available options on your computer may be different from what you see in the example.

In this bar you see the settings of your default printer:

When you use special paper for your prints, you can select the type and size here:

You can also choose the print quality yourself:

Here you can choose the number of copies you want to print:

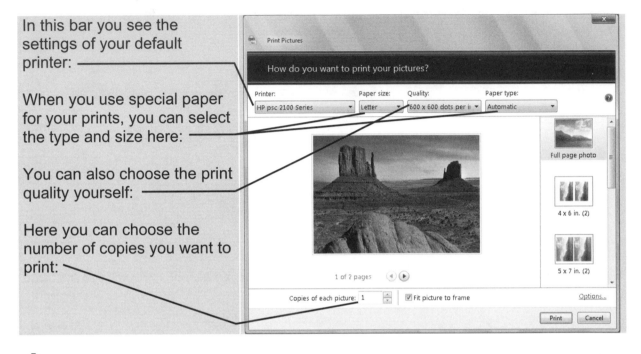

💡 Tip

Fit picture to frame
Digital pictures often do not match standard print proportions. That causes the white border you see when you try to put the photo in a standard size photo frame.

If you want to print a photo at exactly the selected size (for example 4 x 6 inch), check mark the option ☑ Fit picture to frame . Then *Vista* will enlarge the print enough to make sure it prints at exactly the proportions you specified.

Please note: because the photo is enlarged, a small amount of the photo extends outside the printable area. This means a border of the photo will not be printed.

Try printing both photos in the 3.5 x 5 inch size:

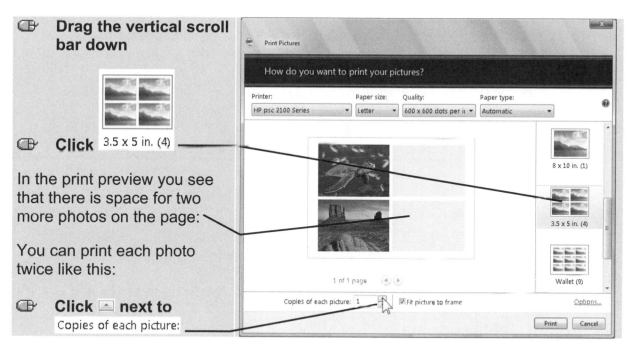

Drag the vertical scroll bar down

Click 3.5 x 5 in. (4)

In the print preview you see that there is space for two more photos on the page:

You can print each photo twice like this:

Click ⬆ next to
Copies of each picture:

The print preview updates immediately. Now you can print the photos.

☞ Check if your printer is turned on

Click Print

The photos are printed.

⇨ **Please note:**

The quality of the prints depends on a number of factors. The most important one is the quality and resolution of the photo itself. The number of pixels determines the quality of your photo. The higher the number, the clearer your photo. When you try to print a lower resolution photo in a larger size format, the print will look grainy. That is not caused by the type of paper or the ink, but by the lack of pixels in the photo.

In that case, try to print the photo in a smaller size format. You will see that the print looks better that way. The resolution of a photo is fixed, you cannot change it.

💡 **Tip**

Contact sheet
A convenient feature in *Vista* is printing a *contact sheet.* A contact sheet is a page with 35 thumbnail images of selected photos. Below the thumbnails the file names are displayed.
To create a contact sheet with all photos in *Photo Gallery* you do the following:

👆 **Click** ▮ File ▼ , Select All

👆 **Click** 🖶 Print ▼ , 🖶 Print...

👆 **Drag the vertical scroll bar down**

👆 **Click** Contact sheet (35)

You see the thumbnail images of the photos in the example:

👆 **Click** Print

When you have large numbers of digital photos, it is advisable to log them on contact sheets. That will make it easier to find the photo you are looking for.

9.16 E-mailing Photos

You can quickly share your photos with others by sending them by e-mail. You can do that directly from *Photo Gallery*. Try that with the two photos you just printed:

The two photos are still selected:

👉 **Click** E-mail

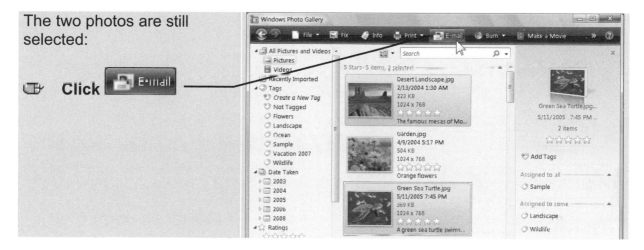

The window *Attach Files* appears:

In this window you see the total estimated size of the e-mail attachment:

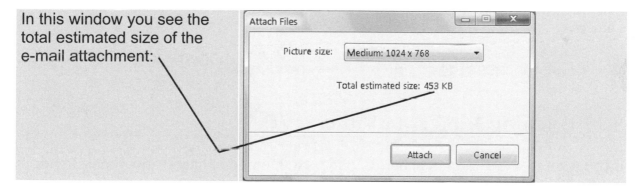

When the attachment is too large, you can adjust the size of the attached images.

You can choose a smaller size, or send the images in their original size:

Now you can attach the files to the e-mail message:

☞ **Click** ⬛ Attach

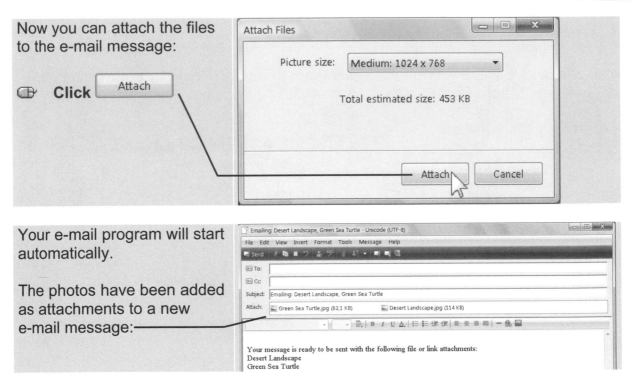

Your e-mail program will start automatically.

The photos have been added as attachments to a new e-mail message:——————

Now you can choose an addressee, type a message and send the e-mail. If you do not want to do that:

☞ **Close the message and do not save the changes** 👣**58**

9.17 Burning Images to Video DVD

If you want to share large numbers of photos with others, printing and e-mailing are not really convenient options. *Vista* offers an entertaining alternative. You can burn a video DVD with a slide show of your photos in the program *Windows DVD Maker*. A video DVD can be played on your computer and in the DVD player hooked up to your television.

⇨ **Please note:**

To be able to burn your images to video DVD, you need to have the program *Windows DVD Maker*, a DVD burner and a writable DVD.

The program *Windows DVD Maker* is **not** included in *Windows Vista Home Basic*. Only *Windows Vista Home Premium* and *Windows Vista Ultimate* users have *Windows DVD Maker* on their computer.

If you use *Windows Vista Home Basic*, or you do not have a DVD burner or a writable DVD, you can just read through this part of the chapter.

First you select all images in *Photo Gallery*:

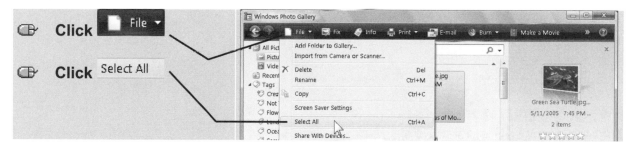

All files are selected. Now you can compile the video DVD.

☞ **Insert the writeable DVD in the DVD burner**

☞ **If necessary, close the *AutoPlay* window**

The program *Windows DVD Maker* is opened automatically.
In **chapter 8 Windows Movie Maker and DVD Maker** you have seen how you can use *Windows DVD Maker* to create a video DVD in a few easy steps. You can create a video DVD with a slide show the same way.

In the *Windows DVD Maker* window you see the images you selected:

You can change the order of the photos by selecting a photo and using the buttons ⬆⬇.

You can add other images or video files to this project by clicking ⊞ Add items :

☞ **Click** Options...

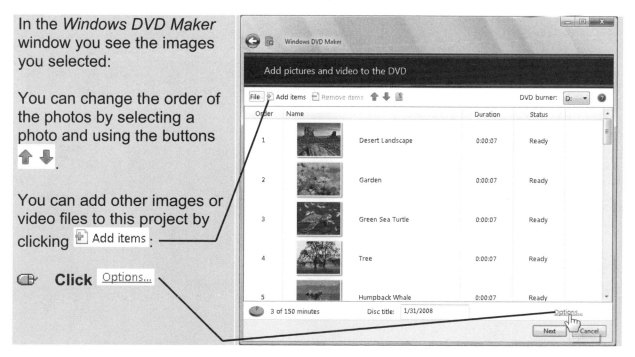

In the window *DVD Options* you can select the DVD playback settings.

Here you choose the preferred DVD aspect ratio (normal 4:3 or wide screen 16:9):——

To play the DVD in the format for American or Canadian DVD players choose video format ⊙ NTSC :——

☞ **Click** OK

You see the previous window again. Here:

☞ **Click** Next

In the next window of the wizard you can adjust the DVD menu. You do not need to do that now. In **section 8.17 Burning a Movie to DVD** you can read how to make adjustments to the DVD menu to suit your particular requirements.

The preview may look different on your computer. By default, *DVD Maker* uses the menu style you selected the last time you burned a DVD:

You can adjust the settings of the slide show here:

☞ **Click** 📄 Slide show ——

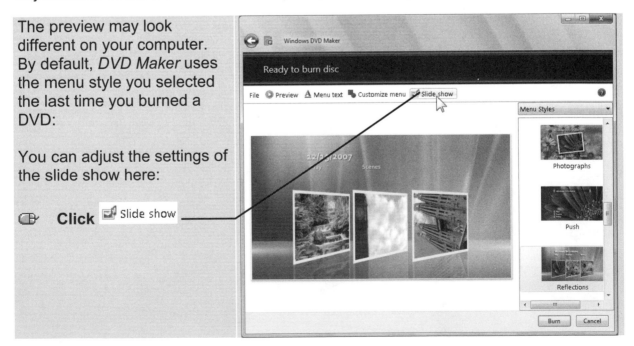

You can add music to the images like this:

⊞ **Click** Add Music...

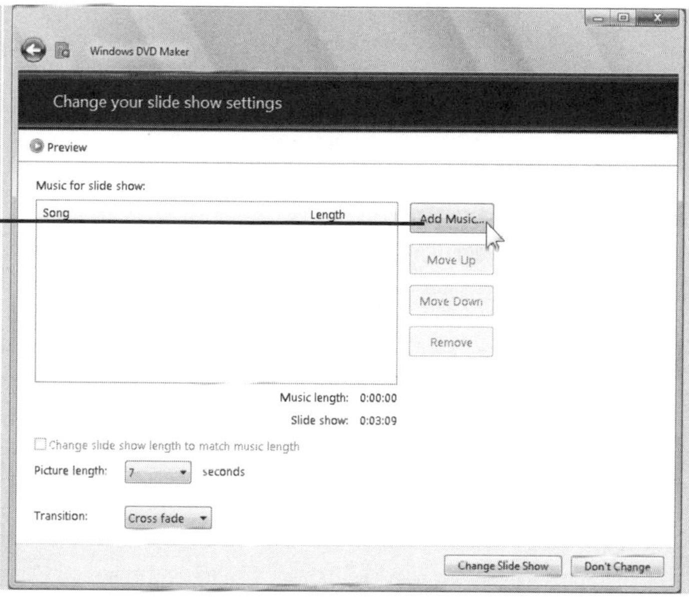

You see the contents of your *Music* folder. In this example one of the *Vista* sample files is used. You can also use a track from the CD you ripped in **chapter 2 Ripping a CD**.

⊞ **Double-click** Sample Music

You see the *Windows Vista* sample files. Choose one of the tracks:

⊞ **Click** Muita Bobeira

⊞ **Click** Add ▼

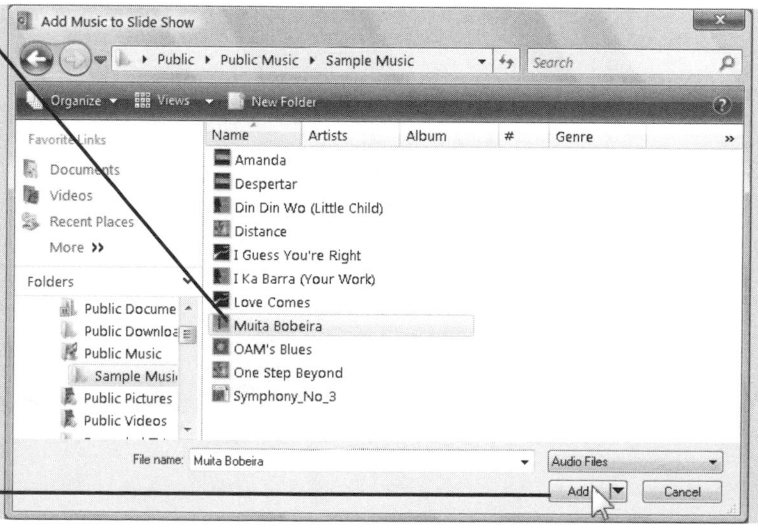

Here you see how long the music and the slide show lasts: ―――

This setting will display each photo for seven seconds: ―――

You can adjust the length of the slide show so it matches the duration of the music you have added:

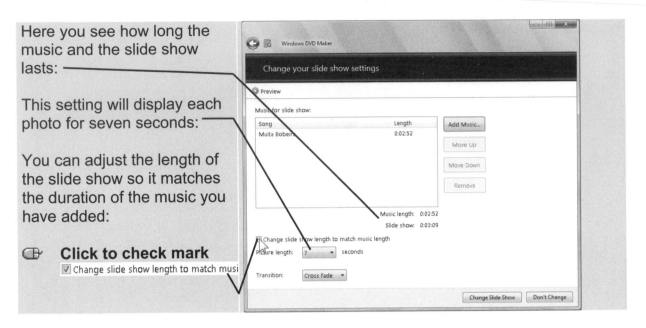

Click to check mark

☑ Change slide show length to match musi

Now the photos are displayed for a shorter time, so the slide show and the music end at the same time.

You can also choose a transition for the slide show. A transition is the effect that appears between each *slide* in your slide show, in other words how one slide is removed from the screen and another slide takes its place.

Click `Cross fade  ▼`

Click `Random`

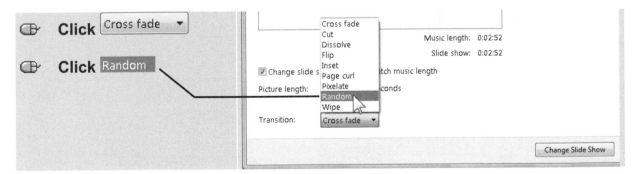

Now you can preview what the DVD will look like:

Click ⊙ Preview

☞ **Turn on the speakers of your computer**

You see the opening
sequence of the DVD. Then
the DVD menu appears.

Click Play ——————

The slide show starts and you hear the accompanying music. You see different
transitions between the photos. The music ends at the same time the last photo is
displayed. Then the DVD menu appears again.

Click OK

If you are happy with the slide show as previewed you can apply the changes:

Click Change Slide Show

Now you can burn the DVD.

Click Burn

You see the progress of encoding and burning the data to the DVD:

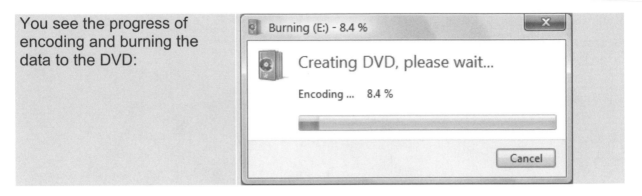

During the encoding process the DVD menu is created and the slide show is converted to a format that can be played in a regular DVD player.

 Please note:

Even though only a very small part of the DVD capacity is used, the encoding process will take a few minutes. When the full 150 minutes capacity of the DVD is used, encoding will take much longer.

The process of encoding a DVD takes up a lot of memory capacity and computing power of your computer. It is better not to perform any other tasks on the computer during the encoding process. Otherwise there is a chance that the encoding will fail.

When the burning process has finished, the drawer of the DVD burner opens. *Windows DVD Maker* gives you the option to create a copy of the disk. You do not have to do that now.

Click [Close]

☞ Close the *Windows DVD Maker* window and do not save the project ℓℓ⁵⁸

☞ **Try to play the DVD in a regular DVD player**

Most modern DVD players will be able to play a video DVD.

Tip

Creating a movie with your photos *DVD Maker* has limited options for creating a slide show. When you want to have more control over the transitions and other effects in your slide show, you can use the program *Windows Movie Maker* to create the slide show from scratch. In **chapter 8 Windows Movie Maker and DVD Maker** you learned how to create a movie in which video clips and images were combined. You can use the same method to create a movie containing a collection of images. You can select different transitions for each photo. You can also add special effects to the photos. Here you see an example of a slide show under construction in the *Storyboard* of *Movie Maker*. In the *Timeline* view you can add music and a narration to the slide show. **In chapter 8 Windows Movie Maker and DVD Maker** you can read more about this topic.

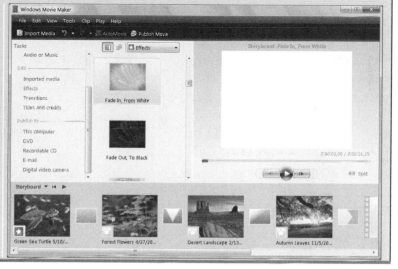

9.18 Burning Photos to Disc

You can also burn your photos as a data disc with files. You can use both blank CDs and DVDs for that. This is not only useful as a means of exchanging photos with other people, but is also a good way of storing your original files in an additional location.

⇨ **Please note:**

To be able to burn your images to a data disc, you need to have a CD or DVD burner and a writeable CD or DVD. If you do not have a burner or a writeable CD or DVD, you can just read through this part of the chapter.

☞ **Select all images** *ℓℓ*77

You can burn a data disc with your images like this:

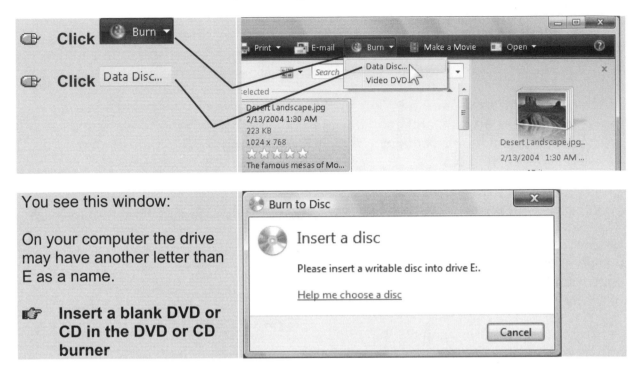

You see this window:

On your computer the drive may have another letter than E as a name.

☞ **Insert a blank DVD or CD in the DVD or CD burner**

Now you can give the disc a name:

⌨ **Type:**
Practice Photos

🖰 **Click** ⊗

You see the formatting options for the disc. You can choose between:
- *Live File System*: this option allows you to copy files to disc immediately without having to burn them all at the same time.
- *Mastered*: with this option files are not copied right away. This means you have to select the complete collection of files you want to copy to the disc and then burn them all at the same time.

⇨ **Please note:**

Live File System may not function properly on computers with operating systems older than *Windows XP*.

Live File System is selected by default:

☞ **Click** Next

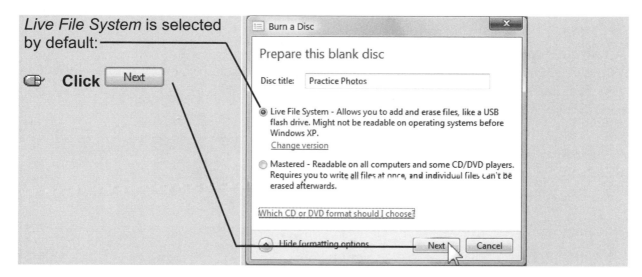

The disc is formatted first.

Then the files are copied:

When the copying process has finished you see this *Folder window*:

At the top you see that the contents of the disc
▸ DVD RW Drive (D:) Practice Photos
are displayed: ────────

All files appear on the disc:───

You can close this window:

☞ **Click** X ────────

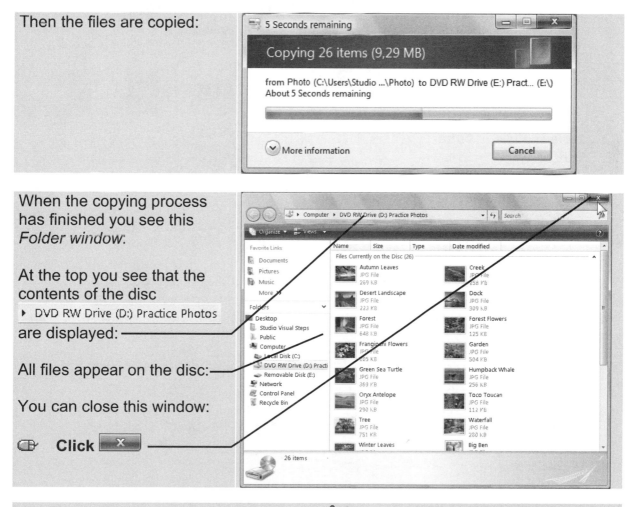

☞ **Close the *AutoPlay* window as well** $\mathcal{E}^3$

💡 Tip

Adding more files to the disc

You can always add more files to a *Live File System* disc later. From *Photo Gallery* you can do that like this:

☞ **Make sure the CD or DVD is in the burner**

👉 **Select the photos you want to copy**

👉 **Click** Burn ▾

👉 **Click** Data Disc...

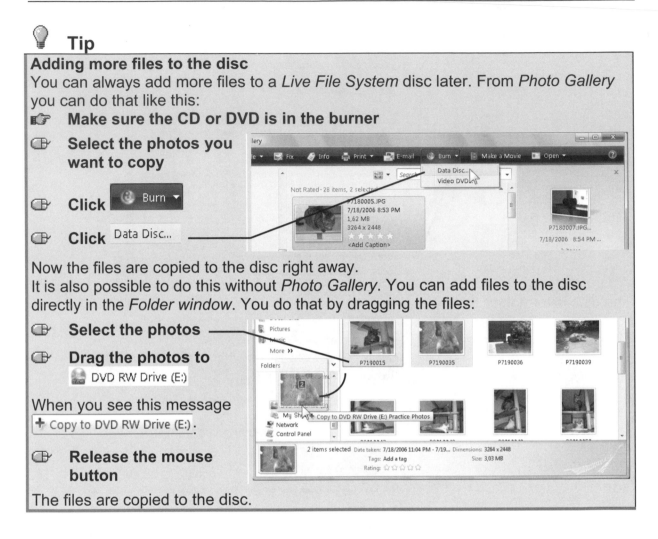

Now the files are copied to the disc right away.
It is also possible to do this without *Photo Gallery*. You can add files to the disc directly in the *Folder window*. You do that by dragging the files:

👉 **Select the photos**

👉 **Drag the photos to**
    DVD RW Drive (E:)

When you see this message
✚ Copy to DVD RW Drive (E:).

👉 **Release the mouse button**

The files are copied to the disc.

9.19 Photo Editing with Paint

You have already been introduced to the options available for photo editing in *Windows Photo Gallery*. Using the program *Paint* you can edit your photos in other ways. You can zoom in and out on a photo for example, or make different selections and add text to a photo.

You can open the program *Paint* from *Photo Gallery*. First you use the *Search Box* to find the photo you are going to edit in *Paint*:

👉 **Click in the Search Box**

⌨ **Type:** ostr

You see the photo of an ostrich:

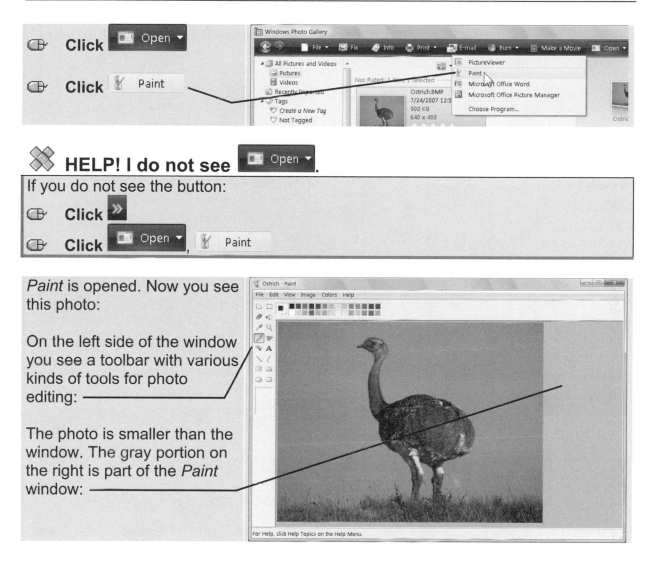

Click [Open ▾]

Click [✗ Paint]

✂ HELP! I do not see [Open ▾].

If you do not see the button:

Click [»]

Click [Open ▾] , [✗ Paint]

Paint is opened. Now you see this photo:

On the left side of the window you see a toolbar with various kinds of tools for photo editing: —

The photo is smaller than the window. The gray portion on the right is part of the *Paint* window: —

9.20 Zooming In and Out

Paint has a magnifier you can use to zoom in on the photo. The *Magnifying Glass*, or *Zoom* tool, can be used to get a closer, more detailed view of an image:

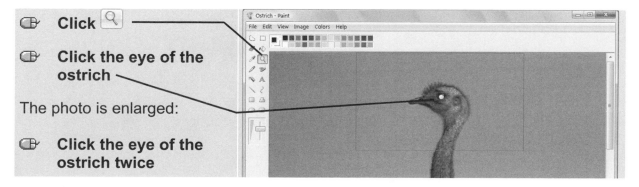

Click [🔍]

Click the eye of the ostrich

The photo is enlarged:

Click the eye of the ostrich twice

Zooming in and out does not affect the actual image in any way, just how it appears on your screen.

You cannot zoom in any further. You can see that the photo is made up of rows of pixels (small dots of colors):

Now you can zoom out on the photo again:

☞ **Drag the slider all the way down**

Now the size of the photo is decreased as far as it will go:

Now you can go back to display the photo at its original size:

☞ **Drag the slider half way**

Now the photo is displayed at the normal size.

You can turn the magnifier off like this:

⌨ **Press** Esc

9.21 Selecting

Paint contains two selection tools that can be used to select a rectangular or free-form portion of a photo. First try to select the entire ostrich by using the rectangle:

Click the selection tool

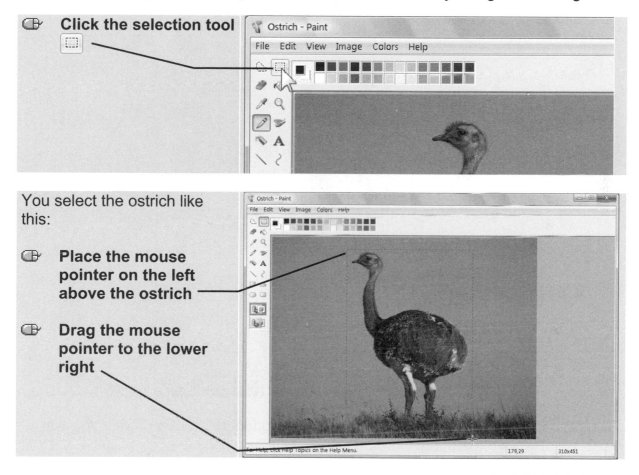

You select the ostrich like this:

Place the mouse pointer on the left above the ostrich

Drag the mouse pointer to the lower right

Now you see a dotted rectangle around the selection:

Now you can move this selection:

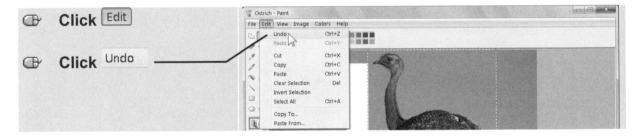

Place the mouse pointer in the rectangle

The mouse pointer changes into ✛:

Drag the selection up and to the right

You see that the selection is moved:

You can quickly undo this change:

Click Edit

Click Undo

The photo is restored to its original state. Using the tool *Free-Form Select* you can select an object on the photo more precisely:

Click ⬭

Now you select the whole ostrich again:

☞ **Drag the mouse carefully around the outer edges of the ostrich**

You can go a bit wider around the head and the top of the neck. When you have reached the starting point again:

☞ **Release the mouse button**

Now it looks like a rectangular selection has been made. You will see later that that is not the case. First you need to copy the selection:

☞ **Right-click the selection**

☞ **Click** Copy

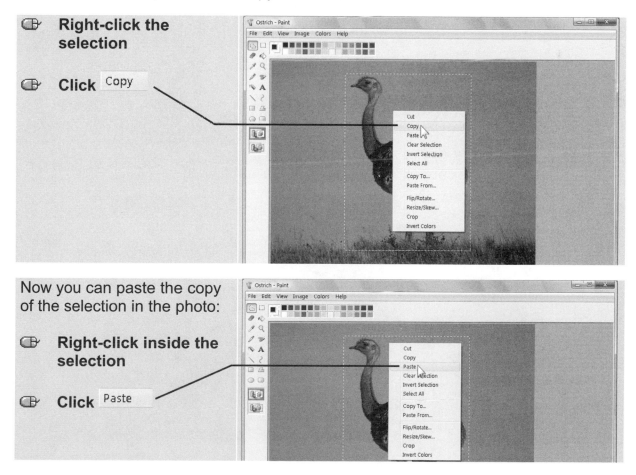

Now you can paste the copy of the selection in the photo:

☞ **Right-click inside the selection**

☞ **Click** Paste

The cut-out ostrich is placed in the photo:

When you make the white background transparent, the photo will look a little better:

Click

Now you can move the copy to the right side of the first ostrich:

Click the copied ostrich

Drag the copy next to the other bird

When you place the second ostrich a bit lower, the boundary portion of the legs, which may not have been cut precisely, will disappear gracefully in the grass.

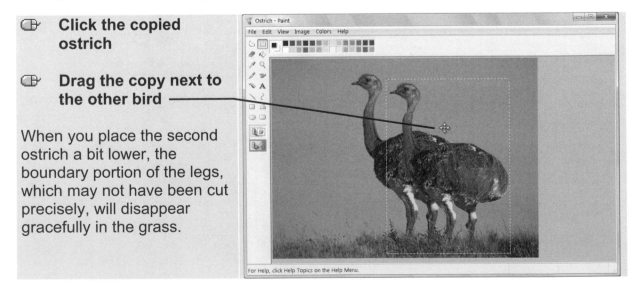

Now you can fix the copied ostrich in your trick photo:

☞ **Click somewhere outside the dotted frame**

The frame has now disappeared:

9.22 Adding Text to a Photo

By adding some text you can quickly turn your photo into a postcard. In *Paint* you can easily add text to a photo:

☞ **Click the text tool** 🅰

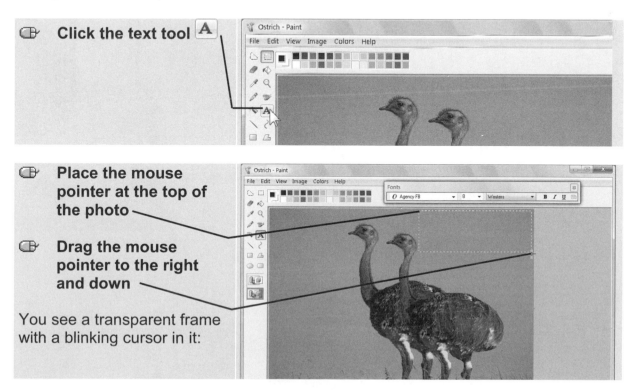

☞ **Place the mouse pointer at the top of the photo**

☞ **Drag the mouse pointer to the right and down**

You see a transparent frame with a blinking cursor in it:

A toolbar for text formatting has appeared as well:

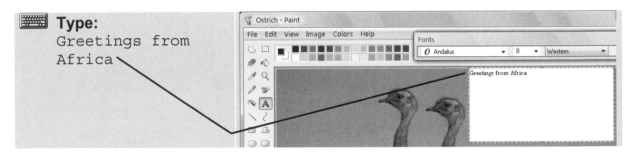

The text will be more visible when the frame is no longer transparent:

⊕ **Click** [icon]

The text frame is now white. You can type your text in the white frame:

⌨ **Type:**
Greetings from
Africa

You can use the toolbar to select a particular font, for example *Comic Sans MS*:

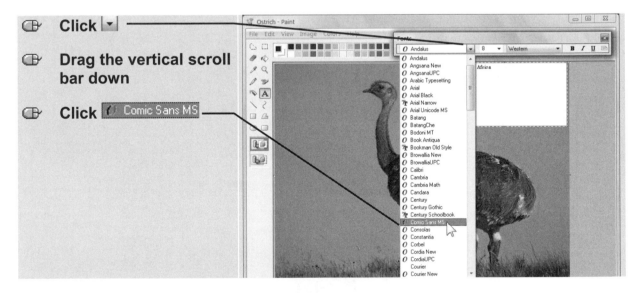

⊕ **Click** [▼]

⊕ **Drag the vertical scroll
bar down**

⊕ **Click** *O* Comic Sans MS

The letters are still small. You can adjust them:

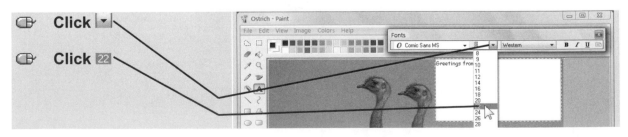

⊕ **Click** [▼]

⊕ **Click** 22

The letters are now clearly readable. If black is not the color you want for your text, you can also change the color.

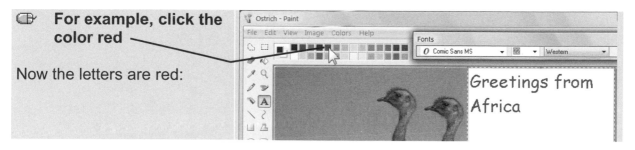

☞ **For example, click the color red**

Now the letters are red:

You can make the white text frame transparent again:

☞ **Click**

You see that the white text frame is now transparent:

🩹 HELP! The text does not fit inside the frame.

Then the frame is too small for the letters. You can make it wider like this:

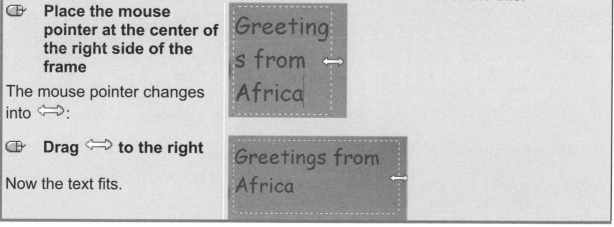

☞ **Place the mouse pointer at the center of the right side of the frame**

The mouse pointer changes into ⟺:

☞ **Drag ⟺ to the right**

Now the text fits.

When you are satisfied with the format of the letters, you can stop editing the text.

⇨ Please note:

When you stop editing the text, you can no longer make any new changes to the text. You can remove the text by clicking Edit, Undo.

☞ **Click outside the text frame** ─────

The dotted frame and the toolbar *Fonts* have disappeared:

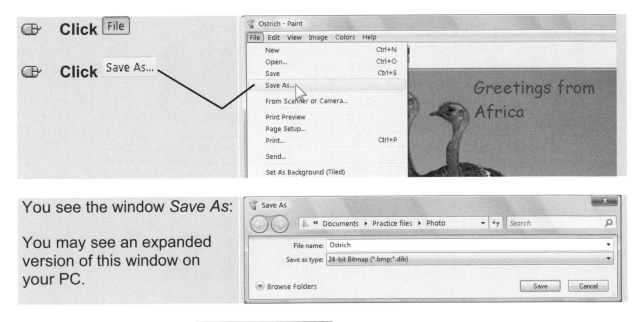

9.23 Saving a File

Paint has a clear advantage over *Photo Gallery*. In *Paint* you can save a file in different file formats. You can try that now:

☞ **Click** File

☞ **Click** Save As...

You see the window *Save As*:

You may see an expanded version of this window on your PC.

The image file format is 24-bit Bitmap (*.bmp;*.dib). A BMP file has a high resolution with many colors, but it is a large file. A disadvantage of BMP files is that you cannot edit them in *Windows Photo Gallery*.

It is better to choose a different file type. Aside from BMP, you can choose JPG, TIF (also called TIFF), GIF and PNG in *Paint*.

JPG is the most common file format used for photos. It is also the default file format of *Windows Photo Gallery*. Photos imported from your digital camera will most likely be JPEGs. JPG is a compressed file format that limits the size of the file. A disadvantage of JPG is that the compression slightly reduces the quality of a photo every time you edit and save a photo. Usually this quality loss is hardly visible, but when you keep changing the same photo and save it at an average quality level it may result in loss of sharpness and color.

TIF files are also compressed, but the quality does not diminish with repeated editing. A TIF file can also be edited in *Windows Photo Gallery*.

GIF is used often on the Internet and is good for line art and simple graphic illustrations such as a logo. The moving images you see on many websites are made in this format, as well as low resolution video clips. GIF files cannot be imported and edited in *Windows Photo Gallery*.

PNG: this strongly compressed file type is also used on websites. PNG can be imported, but cannot be edited in *Windows Photo Gallery*.

HELP! Which file type should I choose.

Usually JPG is the best file type because it creates high quality photos with a small file size. This is done by compressing the data. This file type is perfect for storing and saving your photos.

If you need a higher quality (for example when printing 8 x 10 enlargements), you should save your photos as TIF files or save your JPG photo with the least compression level possible. This is done automatically when you save a JPG using *Windows Photo Gallery* or *Paint*.

HELP! My digital camera creates RAW files.

You cannot open photos in RAW format in *Paint* and in *Windows Photo Gallery*. For file types that are not supported by *Paint*, you need to use a more extensive photo editing program like *Paint Shop Pro* or *Adobe Photoshop*. These programs are able to convert RAW files to file formats *Paint* and *Photo Gallery* can use.

You can save your edited photo with a different name like this:

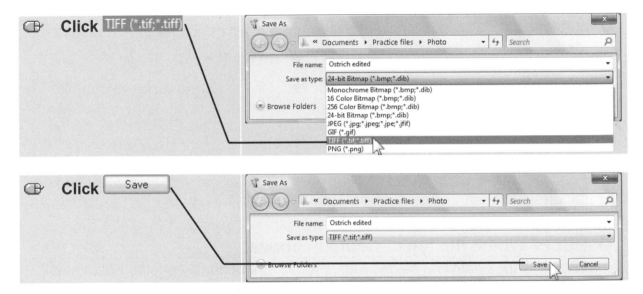

Type:
Ostrich edited

Click
24-bit Bitmap (*.bmp;*.dib)

In this example, select the TIF file format:

Click TIFF (*.tif;*.tiff)

Click Save

The photo is now saved as a TIF file. You can verify this in *Windows Photo Gallery*.

☞ **Close the *Paint* window** $\ell\ell^3$

Next, clear the search results from the previous search in *Photo Gallery*:

Click ✕

You see all of the photos in *Photo Gallery* again:

👆 **Drag the vertical scroll bar down**

👆 **Click**

In the *Information Pane* on the right side you see the properties of the selected photo Ostrich edited.tif :

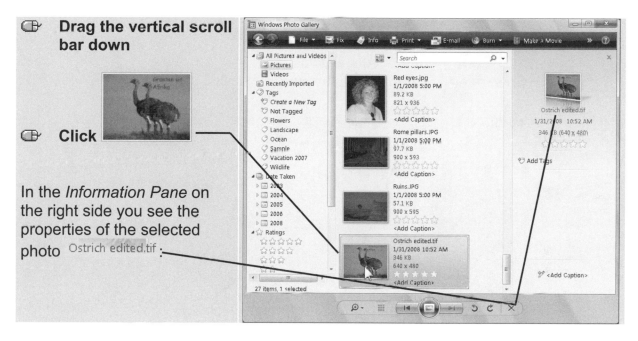

You have seen how to manage and edit your photos using *Photo Gallery* and *Paint*. The next section will give you more information on how to get your images from your digital camera into your computer.

9.24 Importing Photos from Your Digital Camera

In *Photo Gallery* you can directly import photos from your digital camera.

If you do not have a digital camera you can just read through this section.

👉 **Connect your digital camera to your computer and turn the camera on**

⇨ **Please note:**

Digital cameras can be connected to the computer in different ways. Please refer to the manual of your digital camera for more information.

When you connect and turn on your camera, *Vista* will recognize it right away and install the correct driver automatically.

If that is not the case for your camera, you can use the *Scanner and camera Installation* wizard. This wizard helps you to install drivers for older scanners and cameras that are not recognized by *Vista* automatically.

You can open the *Scanner and camera Installation* wizard like this:

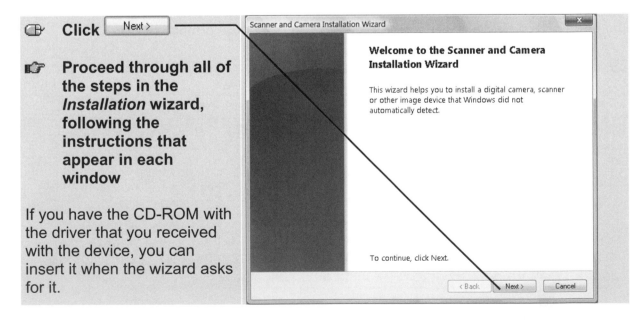

☞ **Click** 🪟 , **Control Panel**

☞ **Click** Hardware and Sound , Scanners and Cameras

☞ **Click** 🔳 Add Device...

Scanners and Cameras

If you do not see your device in the list, make sure it is connected to the computer and turned on, then choose Refresh.

Scanners and Cameras

Refresh | Add Device... | Scan Profiles | Properties

Do I need to use this to install my scanner or camera?

Close

Your screen goes dark and you need to give your permission to continue. Then you see the next window:

☞ **Click** Next >

☞ **Proceed through all of the steps in the Installation wizard, following the instructions that appear in each window**

If you have the CD-ROM with the driver that you received with the device, you can insert it when the wizard asks for it.

Scanner and Camera Installation Wizard

Welcome to the Scanner and Camera Installation Wizard

This wizard helps you to install a digital camera, scanner or other image device that Windows did not automatically detect.

To continue, click Next.

< Back | Next > | Cancel

As soon as your camera is detected by *Vista*, you see the *AutoPlay* window.

You are going to import the photos using *Photo Gallery*, so just close this window:

☞ **Click**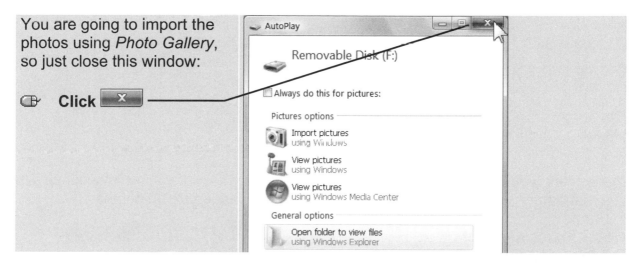

In *Photo Gallery* you can start importing like this:

☞ **Click** [File ▾]

☞ **Click**
Import from Camera or Scanner..

The *Wizard Import Pictures and Videos* searches for a camera that is connected to the computer. Then the next window appears:

This camera is displayed as

Removable Disk (F:) .

You may see the actual name of your camera, for example

Canon PowerShot A70 .

☞ **Click** [Import]

The wizard first determines how many photos are on the camera:

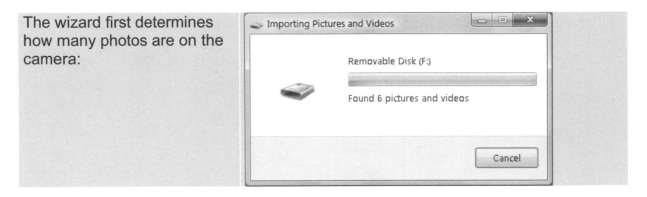

If you want, you can add tags that apply to the photos you import. This is optional, not mandatory. In this example, the tag *cats* has been added to the photos:

Type a tag in this window, for example: `cats`

Click [Import]

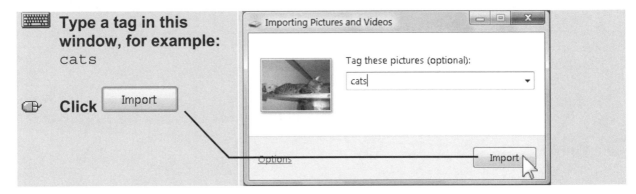

The photos are imported.

The colored green bar indicates the import is in progress:

![Importing Pictures and Videos window showing Removable Disk (F:), Importing item 2 of 6, Erase after importing checkbox, Cancel button]

HELP! Is it possible to manually select the photos to import?

No. *Vista* always checks which photos you took last. Older photos that were already copied to the computer are not copied again. This allows you to import photos in one easy step to your *Pictures* folder.

After that you can check the imported photos in *Photo Gallery*. You see the thumbnail images, enabling you to quickly decide which imported photos you want to remove.

The photos have now been added to *Windows Photo Gallery*. You can quickly find them using the tag you added to the photos:

☞ **Click the tag, for example** 🏷 cats

You see the photos you just imported:

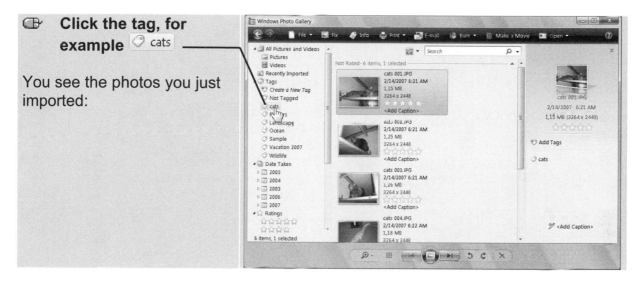

The photos are stored in the *Pictures* folder of your computer. You can verify this:

☞ **Click** 🪟, Pictures

The photos have been stored in a separate folder inside the *Pictures* folder:

The name of the folder is made by combining today's date with the tag you applied to the photos:

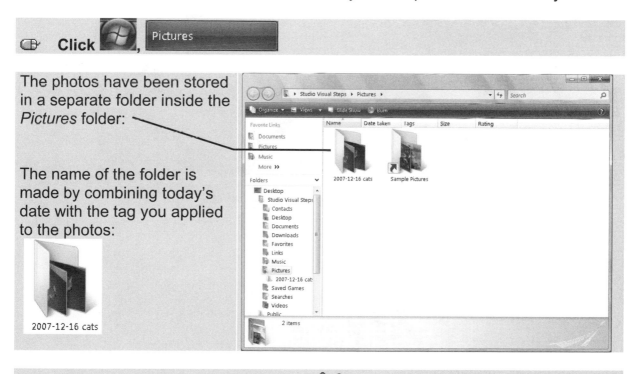

2007-12-16 cats

☞ **Close the *Folder window Pictures*** 🖐³

Now you know how to import files using the *Wizard Import Pictures and Videos*.

💡 Tip

Importing photos from CD or DVD
When you exchange photos with others, the photos may be saved on a disc. You can import these photos to your computer in the same easy way as described previously.

☞ **Insert the CD or DVD in your CD or DVD drive**

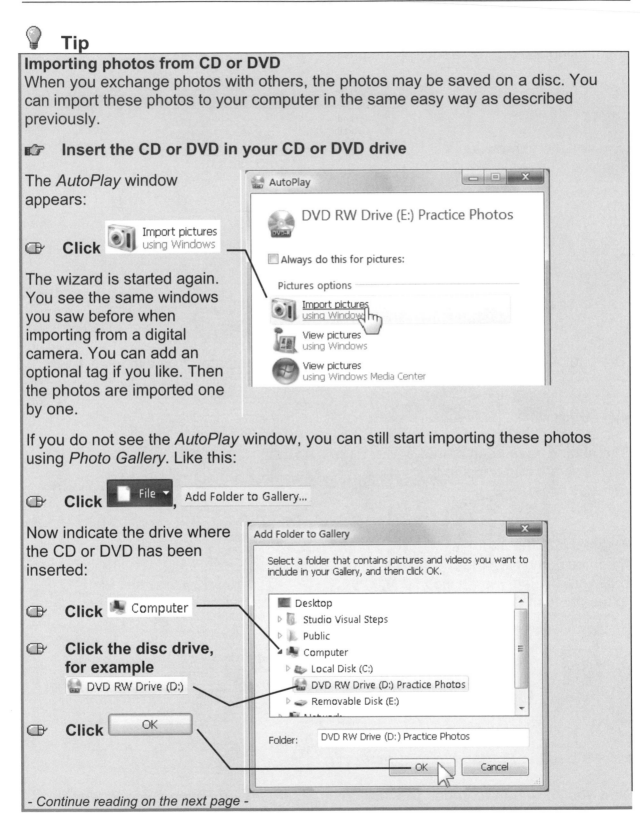

The *AutoPlay* window appears:

☞ **Click** Import pictures using Windows

The wizard is started again. You see the same windows you saw before when importing from a digital camera. You can add an optional tag if you like. Then the photos are imported one by one.

If you do not see the *AutoPlay* window, you can still start importing these photos using *Photo Gallery*. Like this:

☞ **Click** File ▼ , Add Folder to Gallery...

Now indicate the drive where the CD or DVD has been inserted:

☞ **Click** 🖥 Computer

☞ **Click the disc drive, for example**
🖴 DVD RW Drive (D:)

☞ **Click** OK

- Continue reading on the next page -

Next *Vista* asks if you want to start the wizard:

☞ **Click** Import

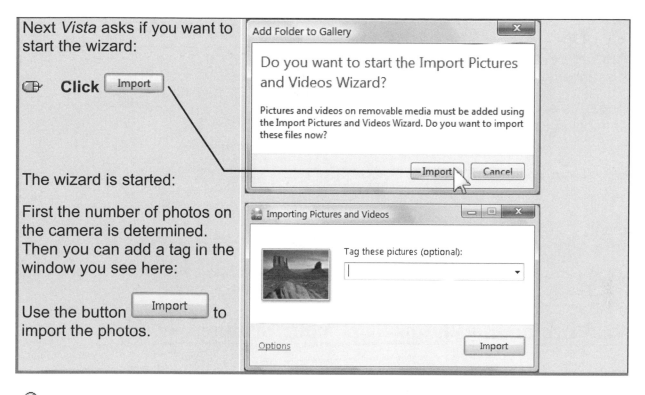

The wizard is started:

First the number of photos on the camera is determined.
Then you can add a tag in the window you see here:

Use the button Import to import the photos.

💡 **Tip**

Changing the file location
You can always select a different location to store your photos rather than *Pictures*.

☞ **Click** Options **in the window** *Importing Pictures and Videos*

Next to Import to: you can change the file location:

Next to Folder name: you can change the name of the folder where the photos will be stored:

When you click How do I change my Import Settings? , the *Windows Help and Support* window appears and you see several articles about *Windows Photo Gallery*.

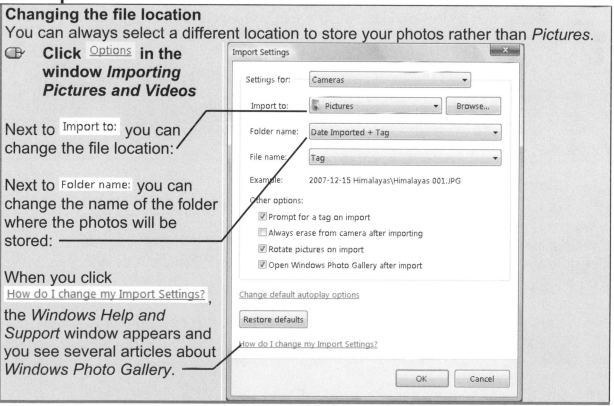

⚲ Tip

Adding several tags when importing
If you want to, you can add more than one tag when you import photos.

Separate each tag by typing a semicolon (;) after each word:

☞ **Then click** ⌷ Import ⌷

Importing Pictures and Videos

Tag these pictures (optional):

test;exercise;Visual Steps

Options　　　　　　　　　　　　　　　Import

9.25 Importing Photos from Your Scanner

In the following example, you can read how to scan a photo from *Photo Gallery*.

⇨ Please note:

If your scanner has a USB connection, you can connect it to your computer. Usually *Vista* will install the correct driver for your device automatically.

However, for some scanners you need to install the driver first, before you connect the scanner to the USB port, while other scanners may need to be turned on before or during the installation. It is important to check the manual of your scanner to make sure you connect it in the proper way. You can also use the *Scanner and Camera Installation* wizard (see **section 9.24**).

✖ HELP! My scanner is still not recognized.

If your scanner is not recognized in *Windows Vista* when you use the *Scanner and Camera Installation* wizard, you can check the website of the manufacturer. It may be possible to download a driver from the website that is compatible with *Windows Vista*. You can also ask your hardware supplier for advice.

If you do not have a scanner you can just read through this section.

☞ **Make sure the scanner is installed correctly**

☞ **Make sure the scanner is turned on**

Some scanners automatically start a scanning program that belongs to the scanner itself. If that is the case with your scanner:

☞ **Close the scanning program**

☞ **Place a photo in the scanner with the print side of the photo on the glass**

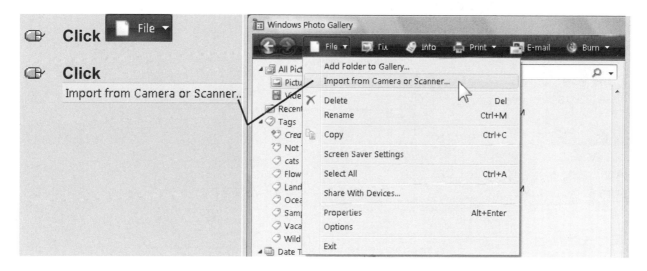

The *Wizard Import Pictures and Videos* searches for scanners and cameras that are connected to the computer. Then the next window appears:

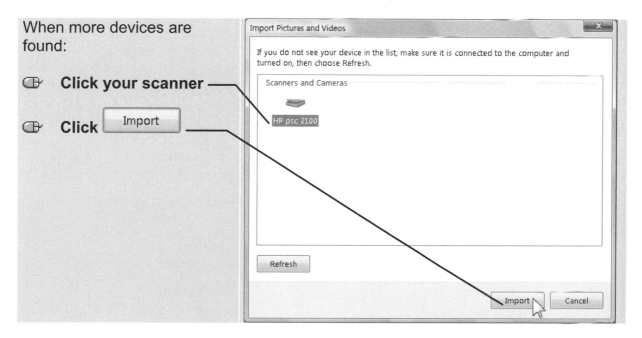

The *New Scan* window appears:

By default, the program
assumes you want to scan a
photo: ————————

Here you can select to scan
the photo in color, black and
white, or grayscale: ————

Here you can select which file
type to use: ————————

With `Resolution (DPI):` you can
set how many pixels (Dots
Per Inch) to be used for the
scan.

New Scan	
Scanner: HP psc 2100	Change...
Profile:	Photo (Default) ▼
Source:	Flatbed ▼
Paper size:	▼
Color format:	Color ▼
File type:	JPG (JPEG Image) ▼
Resolution (DPI):	200
Brightness:	0
Contrast:	0

☐ Preview or scan images as separate files

See how to scan a picture   Preview   Scan   Cancel

☞ **Click** [Preview] ———————————

💡 **Tip**

Scan quality and DPI
Scan quality is expressed in DPI: *Dots per Inch*. This is also called the *resolution*.
The DPI setting ranges from 75 to a maximum of 2400. How to decide on the right
setting depends on what you want to do with the photo after it is scanned.
If you want to use your photo on a website, it does not need to be high quality.
75 DPI is sufficient. If you want to print a photo after scanning it, you can choose a
higher resolution, such as one that matches the maximum resolution of your printer.
If you want to edit a photo first, you should select the highest possible resolution.

Bear in mind that selecting a resolution of 1200 DPI or higher results in a larger file.

A test scan is made, so you can preview the photo first and make any necessary
adjustments before you actually carry out the scan.

You see the test scan:

A dotted frame indicates which surface is going to be scanned. As you can see, a large part of the white space will be scanned as well:

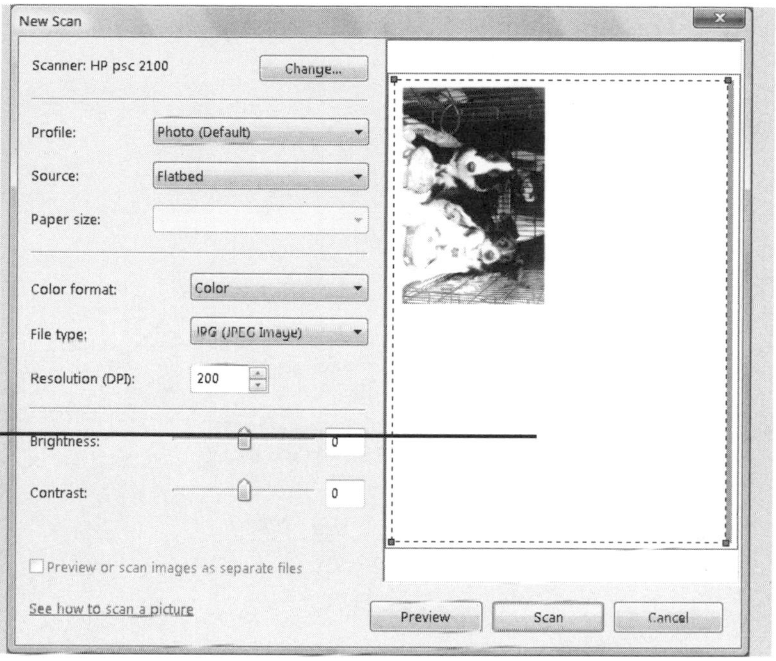

You can adjust the scan surface:

Place the mouse pointer on a corner of the dotted frame

Drag the corner grip until you have reached the correct size

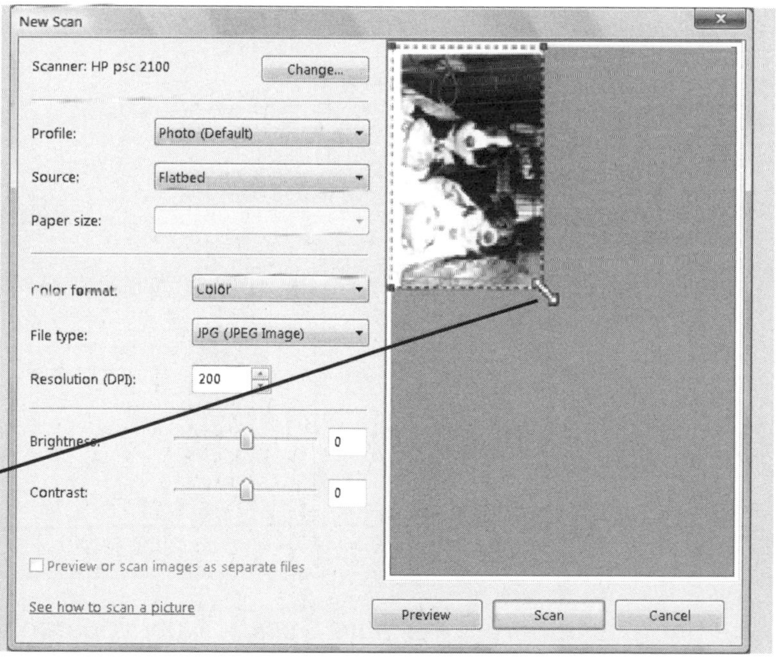

When you are satisfied with the settings, you can start the scan:

Click [Scan]

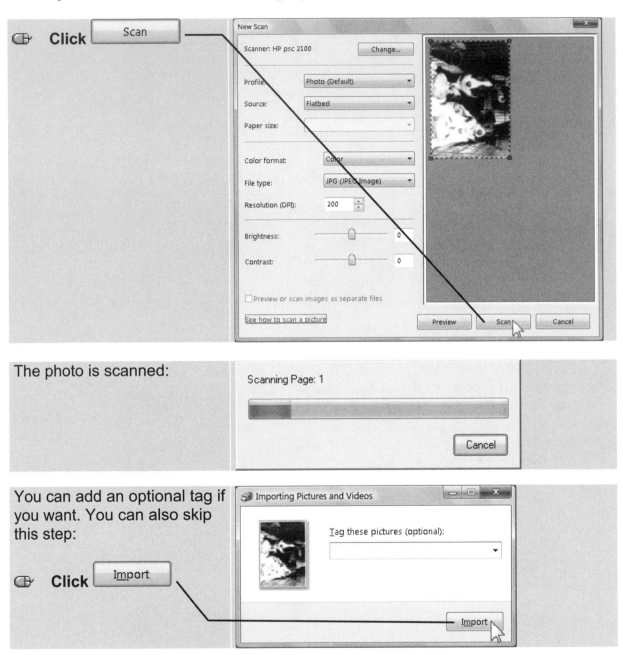

The photo is scanned:

You can add an optional tag if you want. You can also skip this step:

Click [Import]

The photo is imported in *Photo Gallery*. Now you can view the photo and edit it if necessary, the way you practiced earlier in this chapter. If you prefer to do that at another time:

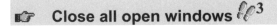

Close all open windows $\ell\ell^3$

In the next exercises you can repeat what you have learned in this chapter.

9.26 Exercises

Have you forgotten how to do something? Use the number beside the footsteps ₰1
to look it up in the appendix *How Do I Do That Again?*

Exercise: Tags and Ratings

Use this exercise to practice working with tags and ratings.

✔ Open *Windows Photo Gallery*. ₰78

✔ Display all images in the *Gallery*. ₰79

✔ Group the images by tag. ₰80

✔ Add the tag *landscape* to the photo *landscape*. ₰81

✔ Give the photo *ostrich* a four-star rating. ₰82

✔ Close *Windows Photo Gallery*. ₰3

Exercise: Slide Show

In this exercise you play and adjust a slide show.

✔ Open *Windows Photo Gallery*. ₰78

✔ Start the slide show. ₰83

✔ Select the theme *Pan and zoom*. ₰84

✔ Exit the slide show. ₰85

✔ Close *Windows Photo Gallery*. ₰3

Exercise: Photo Editing

In this exercise you practice using the different options available for photo editing in *Windows Photo Gallery*.

✔️ Open *Windows Photo Gallery*. $\ell\ell^{78}$

✔️ Select the photo *cathedral*. $\ell\ell^{73}$

✔️ Rotate the thumbnail 45 degrees to make it stand up. $\ell\ell^{86}$

✔️ Select the photo *ruins*. $\ell\ell^{73}$

✔️ Open the *Edit Pane*. $\ell\ell^{74}$

✔️ Apply the *Auto Adjust* feature. $\ell\ell^{87}$

✔️ Adjust the exposure of the photo. $\ell\ell^{88}$

✔️ Adjust the color of the photo. $\ell\ell^{89}$

✔️ Go back to the *Gallery*. $\ell\ell^{76}$

✔️ Revert the photo *ruins* back to its original state. $\ell\ell^{90}$

✔️ Close *Windows Photo Gallery*. $\ell\ell^{3}$

Exercise: Printing

In this exercise you practice printing your photos.

✔️ Open *Windows Photo Gallery*. $\ell\ell^{78}$

✔️ Select the photo *red eyes*. $\ell\ell^{73}$

✔️ Print the photo in size 5 x 7 inch. $\ell\ell^{91}$

✔️ Close *Windows Photo Gallery*. $\ell\ell^{3}$

Exercise: Burning a Video DVD

In this exercise you create a video DVD with a slide show of your photos.

✓   Open *Windows Photo Gallery*. $\ell\ell^{78}$

✓   Select all images. $\ell\ell^{77}$

✓   Insert a blank DVD in your DVD burner.

✓   Start compiling a video DVD. $\ell\ell^{92}$

✓   Select menu style *Photos*. $\ell\ell^{93}$

✓   Add the track *Amanda* to the slide show. $\ell\ell^{94}$

✓   Adapt the length of the slide show to the music. $\ell\ell^{95}$

✓   Apply the changes in the slide show. $\ell\ell^{96}$

✓   Watch the video DVD preview. $\ell\ell^{97}$

✓   Cancel burning the video DVD and do not save the project. $\ell\ell^{98}$

✓   Remove the blank DVD from your DVD burner.

✓   Close *Windows Photo Gallery*. $\ell\ell^{3}$

9.27 Background Information

Glossary

Auto Adjust	Feature in *Photo Gallery* that automatically corrects the brightness, contrast and colors of a photo.
BMP	File extension for bitmap files. A BMP file has high quality with many colors, but is very large. BMP files cannot be edited in *Photo Gallery*.
Brightness	The amount of light that is emitted by a photo. Forms the exposure of a photo together with the contrast.
Color temperature	Feature in *Photo Gallery* that allows you to make adjustments to the overall tone of a picture by making it appear warmer (red) or cooler (blue).
Contact sheet	Sheet with 35 thumbnail images of photos. Below the photos the file names are displayed.
Contrast	The difference between the brightest and darkest parts of an image. Forms the exposure of a photo together with the brightness.
DPI	The standard used to measure screen and printer resolution, expressed as the number of dots that a device can display or print per linear inch. The greater the number of dots per inch, the better the resolution.
Encoding	Compiling a DVD. During the encoding process the DVD menu is created and the movies are converted to a format that can be played in most regular DVD players.
Exposure	Brightness and contrast of a photo.
GIF	File format that is used often for drawings on the Internet. GIF files cannot be imported and edited in *Photo Gallery*.
Importing	Transferring digital photos from your digital camera or scanner to the hard disk of your computer, so you can organize and edit them in *Photo Gallery*.

- Continue reading on the next page -

Information Pane	Area in *Windows Photo Gallery* where more information about a selected photo or video is displayed.
JPG	File format commonly used for photos. This is the default file type in *Windows Photo Gallery*. JPG is a compressed file format that reduces the size of the image files.
Live File System	A file system that can be used to create CDs and DVDs. Discs formatted with *Live File System* allow you to copy files to the disc at any time, instead of having to burn all files at once.
Mastered	A file system used to create CDs and DVDs. Discs created using the *Mastered* format are more likely to be compatible with computers with operating systems older than *Windows XP*. In this file system you can only copy files to the disc one time. You first need to select all the files you want to burn and then they are burned to the disc all at once.
Navigation Pane	Area in *Photo Gallery* where folders, tags and ratings are displayed.
Paint	Program you can use to edit digital photos and add text. *Paint* can also be used to make drawings.
Pixel	The smallest element used to form the composition of a digital image.
PNG	Strongly compressed file type that is frequently used on websites. PNG can be imported but cannot be edited in *Windows Photo Gallery*.
Rating	Another way of helping you organize your photo collection by using stars to express how well you like a particular photo. You can choose from zero to five stars.
RAW	Uncompressed file type used by some digital cameras. Cannot be imported or edited in *Photo Gallery*.
Red eyes	Phenomenon caused by the camera flash bouncing off of the person's retina. Can be adjusted in *Photo Gallery* using the *Fix Red Eye* tool.
Resolution	The amount of fine detail in a photo, determined by the number of pixels in the image.

- Continue reading on the next page -

Saturation	Feature in *Photo Gallery* that allows you to make adjustments in how vivid the colors appear in a picture.
Scanner	Device you can use to digitize an image or document. By saving it to your computer, you can use it for other purposes.
Slide show	Automatic full screen display of images, with selected transitions between the photos.
Tag	Words that can be added to your photos and videos. Another way of helping you locate and organize your photo collection.
Thumbnail image	Reduced image of a photo that is used as a preview of the complete version.
TIF / TIFF	Compressed file format. Has the distinct advantage that high image quality is maintained even after repeated editing and saving. TIF files can be imported and edited in *Photo Gallery*.
Tint	Feature in *Photo Gallery* that removes the color cast from a picture by adding or removing green.
Video DVD	DVD you can play in your regular DVD player on your television.
Windows DVD Maker	Program for burning DVDs in *Windows Vista*. Not available in *Windows Vista Home Basic*.
Windows Movie Maker	Program for video editing in *Windows Vista*.
Windows Photo Gallery	Program for viewing, managing and editing photos in *Windows Vista*.
Zooming in	Enlarge the display of a photo.
Zooming out	Reduce the display of a photo.

Source: Windows Help and Support

Why some files cannot be edited

Sometimes you cannot edit a photo or change its file properties (like tags, ratings or captions) using *Photo Gallery*. If this is the case, you may see a message indicating that the file cannot be changed.

You will be unable to edit the picture if any of the following conditions apply:

- *The photo is read-only.*
  If a picture is read-only, you cannot edit the picture or change its file properties. You can correct this problem by changing the picture's read-only setting. In the Tip **Turning off read-only** at the end of this chapter you can read how to do that.

- *The photo is stored in a read-only location.*
  If your pictures are stored on a CD, DVD, or a portable media player, for example, you cannot edit them or change file properties. You can correct this problem by copying the pictures you want to change to a folder on the hard disk of your computer.

- *The photo is saved in an unsupported file format.*
  Photo Gallery cannot open or edit some photo file formats, such as BMP, PNG, RAW or GIF. If you want to edit a picture that is saved in one of these file formats, you first need to convert it to a compatible file format like JPG.

- *The photo is in an offline location.*
  If you are trying to change a picture that is stored on a network location or on removable media, it is possible that the location is not currently connected to your computer or the media is not currently inserted in your computer. You can correct this problem by re-establishing a network connection or inserting the media that contains your photo.

- *The photo is deleted or moved.*
  It is possible that the picture was moved or deleted after you selected it for editing. When *Photo Gallery* tried to access the file, it was no longer there.

Source: Windows Help and Support

9.28 Tips

💡 Tip

Slide show with your own photos in Windows Sidebar
By default, the gadget *Slide Show* in *Windows Sidebar* uses the folder *Sample Pictures*. You can select your own photo collection for this slide show. Like this:

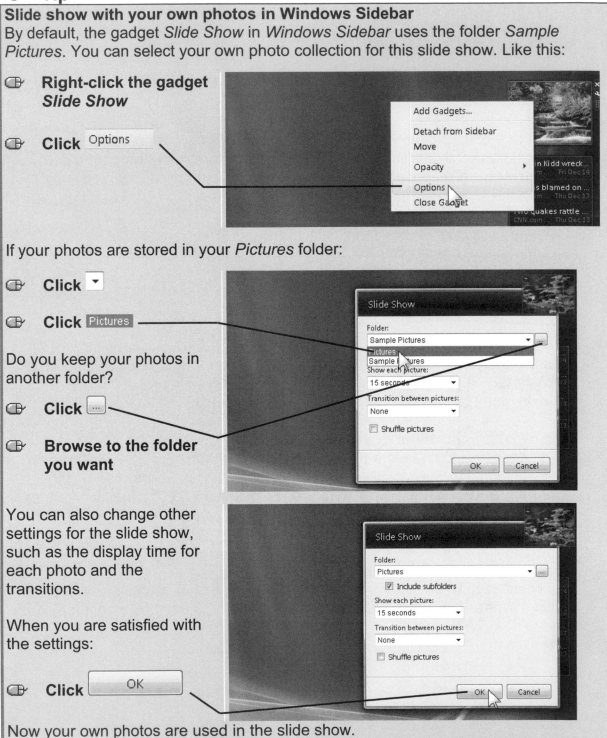

👆 **Right-click the gadget** *Slide Show*

👆 **Click** Options

If your photos are stored in your *Pictures* folder:

👆 **Click** ▼

👆 **Click** Pictures

Do you keep your photos in another folder?

👆 **Click** ...

👆 **Browse to the folder you want**

You can also change other settings for the slide show, such as the display time for each photo and the transitions.

When you are satisfied with the settings:

👆 **Click** OK

Now your own photos are used in the slide show.

💡 Tip

Cropping in fixed proportions
Sometimes it is useful to crop a photo using fixed proportions. For example if you want to print part of a photo to place it in a frame with a specific size.

👆 **Click**

    🔲 Crop Picture

👆 **Click**

    Custom ▾

👆 **Click** 4 x 6

Now the frame has the selected 4 x 6 proportion.

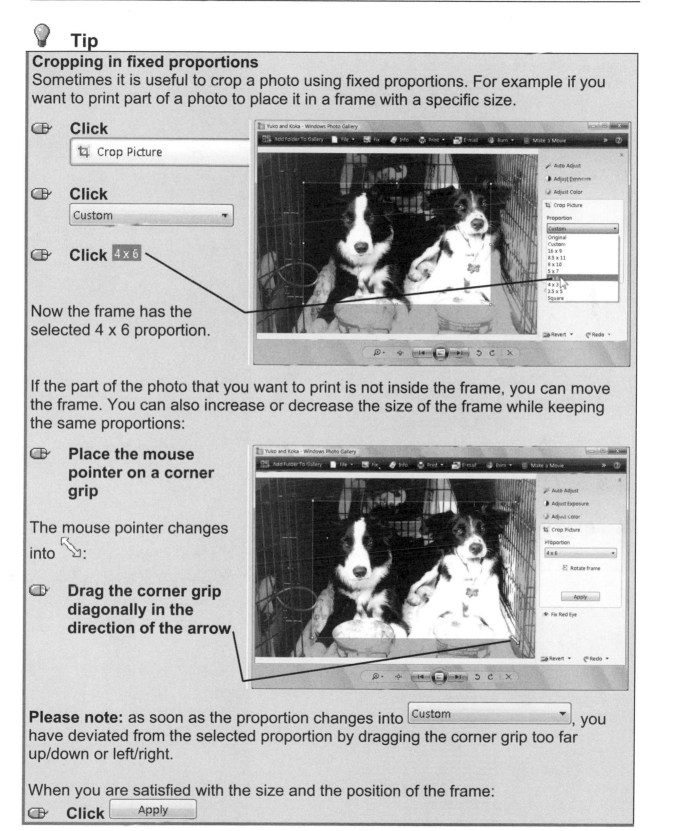

If the part of the photo that you want to print is not inside the frame, you can move the frame. You can also increase or decrease the size of the frame while keeping the same proportions:

👆 **Place the mouse pointer on a corner grip**

The mouse pointer changes into 🖱:

👆 **Drag the corner grip diagonally in the direction of the arrow**

Please note: as soon as the proportion changes into Custom ▾ , you have deviated from the selected proportion by dragging the corner grip too far up/down or left/right.

When you are satisfied with the size and the position of the frame:

👆 **Click** Apply

💡 Tip

Turning off read-only

When a photo has the property *Read-only*, you will not be able to edit it in *Photo Gallery*. You can turn this property off by doing the following:

👉 **Right-click the photo**

👉 **Click** Properties

You see the *Properties* window:

👉 **Click the tab** General

👉 **Click to remove the check mark for**
☐ Read-only

👉 **Click** OK

Now you can edit the photo in *Photo Gallery*.

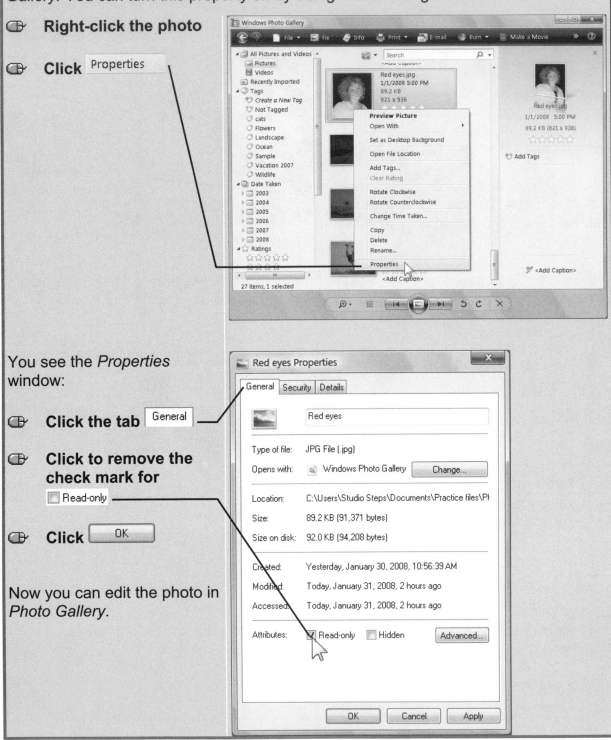

10. Windows Media Center

The owners of *Windows Vista Home Premium* and *Windows Vista Ultimate* have the extensive program *Windows Media Center* at their disposal. This program is the center for all your digital entertainment. You can use *Media Center* to view your photos, watch videos and DVDs and listen to music. Furthermore, you can view many different types of online media. For example, you can download and play music videos, watch live sports or news broadcasts, and even movies or television.

When your computer is equipped with an analog or digital TV tuner, you can use *Windows Media Center* to watch and record television shows on your PC. A TV tuner is a video card that can receive TV signals through your cable connection.

Using the convenient Electronic Programming Guide (the Guide) in *Windows Media Center,* you can record your favorite TV show in just a few mouse clicks. You can watch the recording in *Media Center.* If you would like to save a recording for later, you can use *Media* Center to copy it to a video DVD. This DVD can be played on your computer and also in the regular DVD player connected to your television.

In this chapter you will learn how to:

- open *Windows Media Center;*
- explore *Windows Media Center;*
- play a slide show of your photos;
- play a video;
- view online media;
- set up *Windows Media Center* to enable TV broadcasts on your PC;
- watch live television using *Media Center;*
- record live television;
- use the *Guide;*
- program a TV show recording in advance;
- view planned TV recordings;
- watch a TV recording;
- use *SportsLounge;*
- create a video DVD in *Windows Media Center;*
- watch a DVD in *Windows Media Center;*
- remove a TV recording.

10.1 Opening Windows Media Center

Windows Media Center is the center for viewing digital media in *Windows Vista*.

⇨ **Please note:**

Windows Media Center is only available in the editions *Windows Vista Home Premium* and *Ultimate*.

Do you use *Windows Vista Home Basic*? Then you can just read through this chapter.

When you start *Windows Media Center* for the first time, you will need to configure some initial settings for the program. You can always change these settings later in *Windows Media Center*.

The most convenient choice is the default setup option 'Express setup' that allows information for your media and improvements to the program to be downloaded:

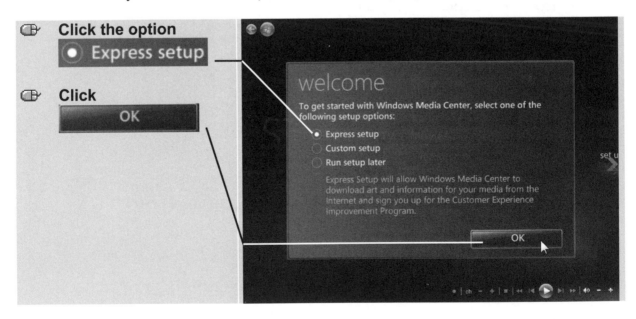

The settings have been applied:

You see the media menu of
Windows Media Center:

10.2 Exploring Windows Media Center

When compared to other familiar *Windows* programs, *Windows Media Center*
appears very different. By default, *Windows Media Center* is displayed full-screen
instead of in a window. This Is because the program can also be used on a television.
In that case, *Media Center* can be operated by a special remote control. That is why
the program looks a lot like a DVD menu:

Media menu:

Options for media type:

Player and settings:

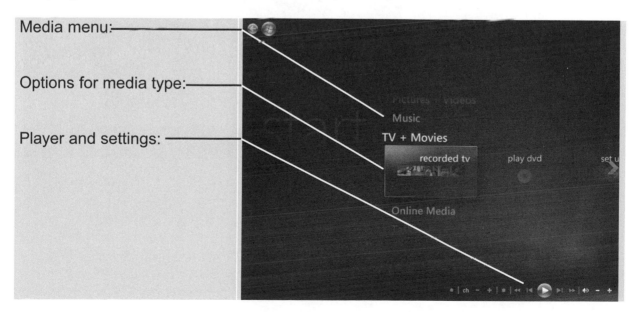

You can scroll through the different media types like this:

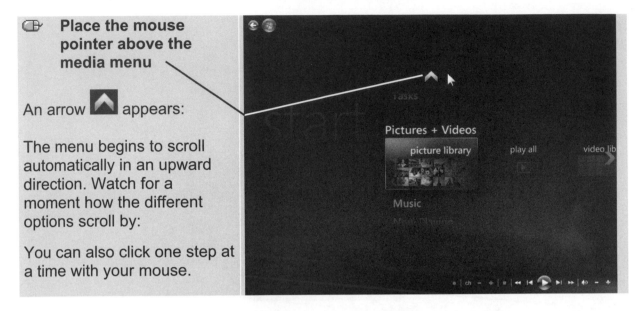

Place the mouse pointer above the media menu

An arrow appears:

The menu begins to scroll automatically in an upward direction. Watch for a moment how the different options scroll by:

You can also click one step at a time with your mouse.

The menu goes round, so you always end up at the first option again.

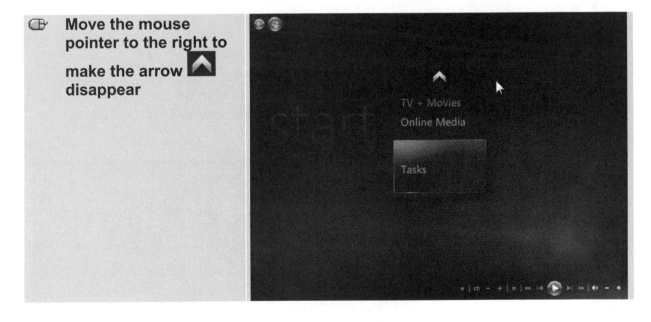

Move the mouse pointer to the right to make the arrow disappear

If the scrolling has not already stopped, it will now:

Another media type has been selected: ─────────

When you place the mouse pointer below the menu, you can scroll in the other direction: ─────────

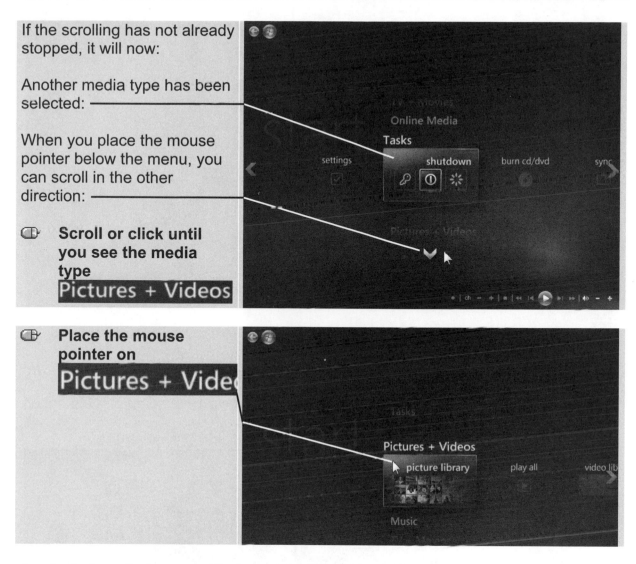

☞ **Scroll or click until you see the media type**
Pictures + Videos

☞ **Place the mouse pointer on**
Pictures + Vide

A selected media type usually has options of its own. These are found on the left and right side of the media type. You can scroll through these options as well:

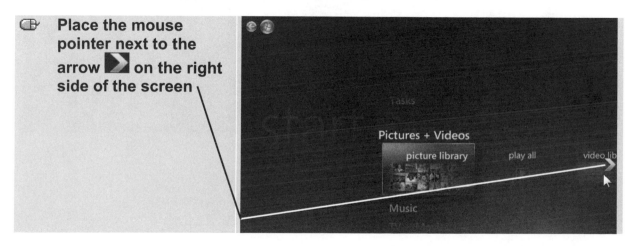

☞ **Place the mouse pointer next to the arrow ▶ on the right side of the screen**

You see the other options:

When you place the mouse pointer next to the other arrow, you scroll in the opposite direction:

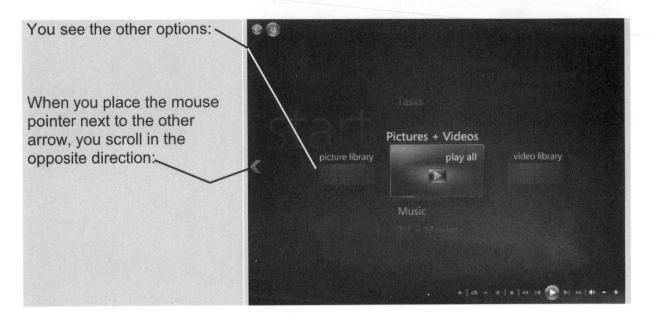

10.3 Playing a Slide Show

You can work with many different media types in *Windows Media Center*. One option is to view a slide show of the photos on your computer:

picture library

Click

When you open the page *Picture Library* for the first time, the *Picture Library* is created automatically:

You can choose to have other folders checked for images:

☞ **Click**

> No

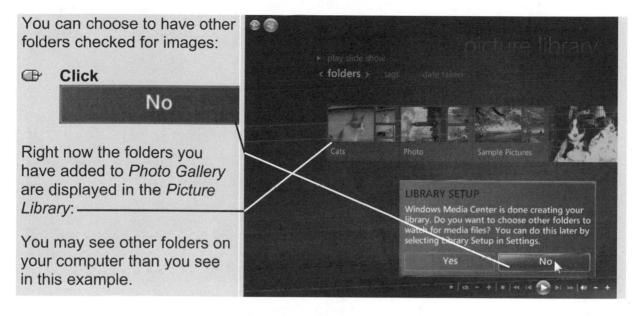

Right now the folders you have added to *Photo Gallery* are displayed in the *Picture Library*: ————

You may see other folders on your computer than you see in this example.

Now you can view your photos in a slide show:

☞ **Click**
> ► play slide show

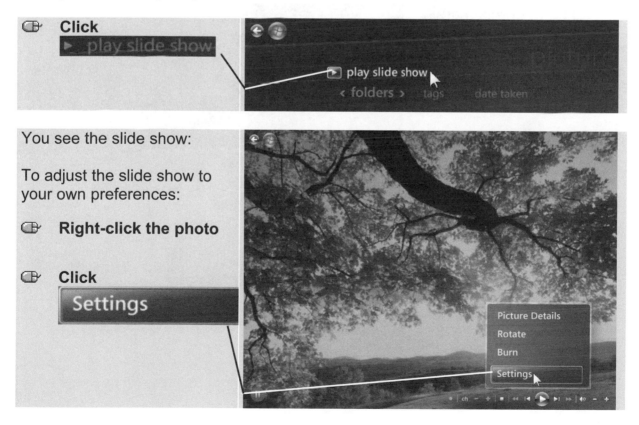

You see the slide show:

To adjust the slide show to your own preferences:

☞ **Right-click the photo**

☞ **Click**
> Settings

You see the page *settings*. To access the slide show settings you do the following:

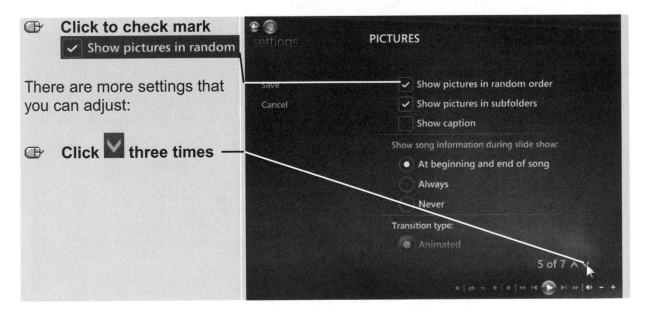

For example, you can show the photos in random order during the slide show:

You see that the transition type 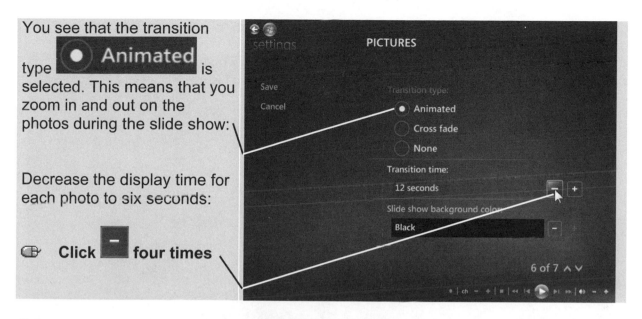 is selected. This means that you zoom in and out on the photos during the slide show:

Decrease the display time for each photo to six seconds:

☞ **Click** [–] **four times**

When you are satisfied with the changes you made, you can save the settings:

☞ **Click** Save

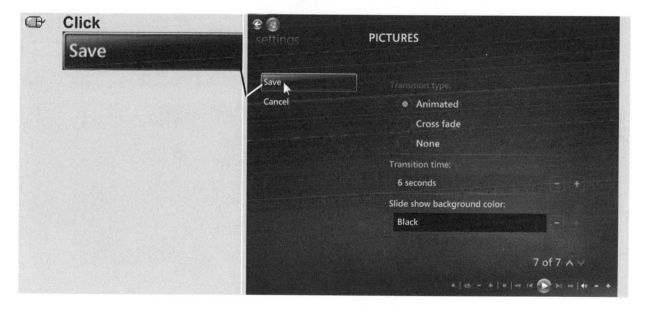

You see the *settings* page again. This is how you return to your slide show:

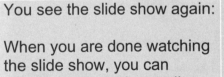 **Click**

General

TV

Pictures

Music

DVD

Extender

Library Setup

💡 Tip

You can create your own slide show, with customized transitions and background music, and save it to DVD. See **chapter 8 Windows Movie Maker and DVD Maker**.

You see the slide show again:

When you are done watching the slide show, you can quickly return to the media menu of *Windows Media Center*:

 **Click**

10.4 Playing a Video

You can also play videos in *Windows Media Center*. For example, the home videos you have made yourself.

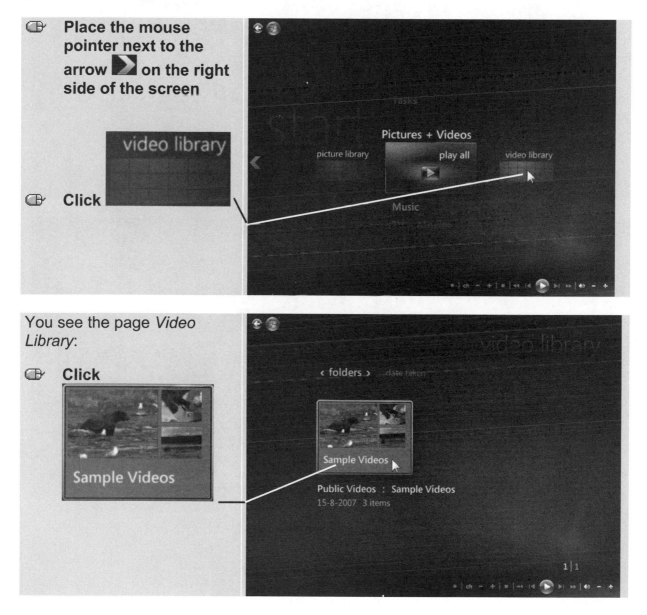

Place the mouse pointer next to the arrow ▶▶ on the right side of the screen

video library

Click

You see the page *Video Library*:

Click

Sample Videos

You see the sample videos
that are included in *Vista*:

☞ **Click**

The video is played:

As soon as the video has finished playing you see this window:

You do not have to use the buttons you see here. You can go straight back to the media menu instead:

Bear

■ Finished

Done
Restart
Delete

☞ **Click**

Is the button invisible? Move the mouse pointer to its location and the button will appear.

10.5 Viewing Online Services

Windows Media Center is not limited to playing the content residing on your computer. You can also use *Media Center* to play media hosted from the Internet and perform all kinds of tasks online. For example, you can play music videos, watch sports or the news, download and watch movies or watch Internet television.

⇨ **Please note:**

In order to watch online video you will need a high-speed Internet connection such as DSL or cable. If you have that kind of connection, but are unable to connect to the Internet in *Windows Media Center*, check the settings of your firewall program. It is possible that *Windows Media Center* is being blocked by your firewall.

☞ **Select the media type**
Online Media

explore

☞ **Click**

start

TV + Movies
Sports
Online Media

program library   what's new   explore

Tasks

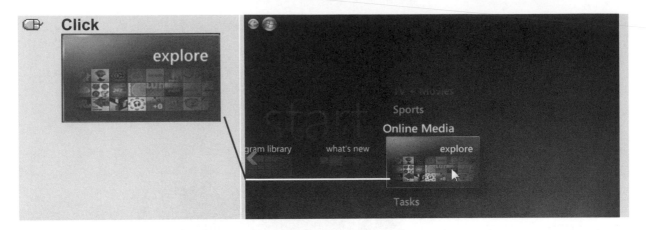

Now you can choose an online option:

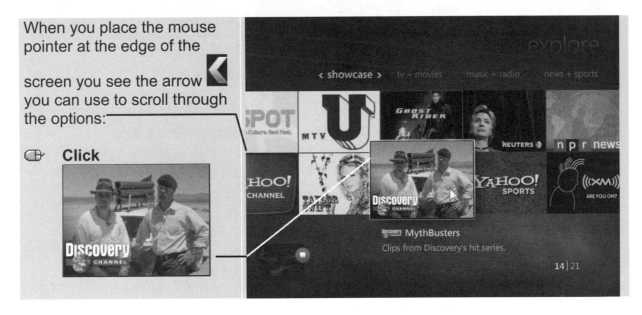

You can choose video previews from several TV programs broadcasted by Discovery Channel, Animal Planet, TLC and Travel Channel. In this example, you can try one of the video previews offered by Discovery Channel:

Click the video preview you want to see

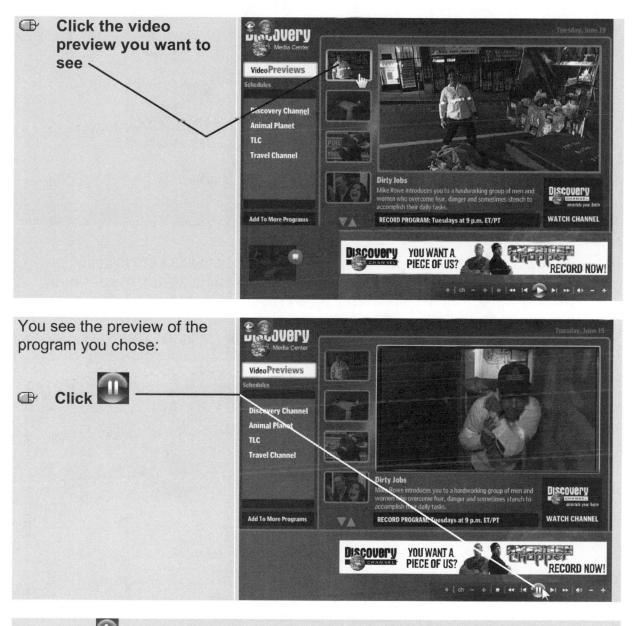

You see the preview of the program you chose:

Click

Click in the top left corner of your screen

You see the online options again:

You can use the category titles above to jump to the category of your interest:

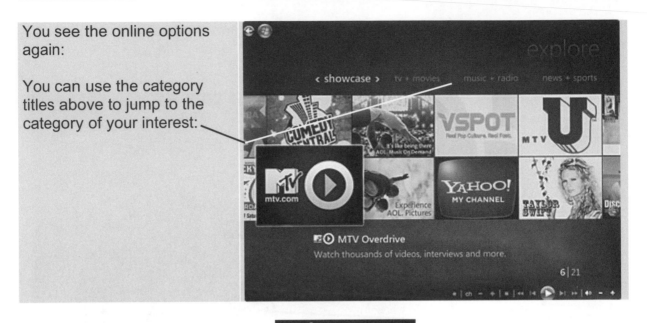

In the example above the category < showcase > is selected. This category contains all available online media from all categories. Some services are currently only available in the U.S. Additional content and useful plug-ins will be coming soon.

You probably see many familiar names among the online options. There are too many options to be able to discuss them all in this book. A couple of highlights:

Take a look at NPR news. **NPR** delivers its content through a clean, easy interface.

Morning Edition, All Things Considered, Fresh Air and other NPR favorites are featured.

It is easy to find what you want: just click and listen.

Watch, subscribe and manage video podcasts in **TVTonic**. TVTonic allows you to subscribe to any RSS 2.0 feed with video enclosures. It is a small software program that can be downloaded directly from ***Online Media*** in *Windows Media Center*. The installation only takes a few minutes. Once you have installed the TVTonic software, you can access TVTonic with the icon in the program library. Then simply subscribe to channels via the TVTonic *Add Channels* section. The channels are categorized into genres like news, music, and cartoons:

TVTonic:
Choose from easy-to-navigate categories containing over 300 channels.

Here is an example from the popular U.S. morning news show the *Today Show*.

TVTonic:

Here is an example from the *Weather Channel*.

Windows Media Center also contains links to two online video stores: *Vongo* and *Movielink*. These services offer thousands of titles around the clock, from recent blockbusters to Hollywood classics. When you select either one for the first time, you are prompted to download a small software program. You need that program to be able to watch the movies you can purchase or rent from these services.

Vongo:
Vongo is a subscription service. For about ten dollars a month, you get unlimited downloads from its rotating library of more than 2,500 titles.

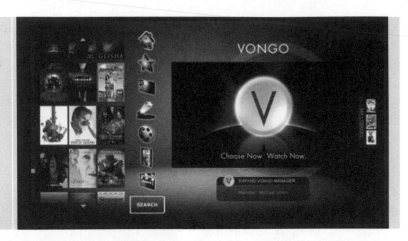

Vongo also offers 400 titles as pay-per-view movies. These range in price from one to four dollars and expire 24 hours after you first click *Play*. During that time, you can watch it as many times as you want.

To protect your (grand)children, *Vongo* offers the option to block movies rated PG-13 or R.

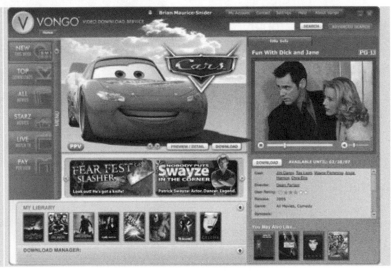

Even with a fast Internet connection, it will take at least 45 minutes to download a 105-minute movie. However, you can already start watching the movie a few minutes after the download starts.

Movielink:
This is a service (owned by Blockbuster) for viewing movies. *Movielink* sells or rents its movies.

Most movies cost between one and five dollars to rent and twenty dollars or less to buy. Once you click *Play*, you have 24 hours to watch your movie. During that time, you can watch it as many times as you want.

Movielink has a broad selection of films from most of the major studios: Fox, MGM, Sony, Universal and more. Once you buy a *Movielink* movie, it is yours forever. *Vongo* movies expire after several weeks or months after you download them to make space for more titles.

In the *News + Sports* category you can find several news and sports channels.

Here you can watch or listen to news from Reuters, NPR, (mentioned earlier) Yahoo! Sports and Fox Sports.

When you are looking for entertainment instead of news, choose the category *TV + Movies* in the *Explore* page. In addition to the Discovery Channel clips or the video podcasts from TVTonic, you can also find shows from Comedy Central and children's shows on the Nickelodeon channel TurboNick.

TurboNick:
Here children can choose from hundreds of video clips, play games and take trivia challenges.

10.6 Internet TV

Even if you do not have a TV tuner installed in your computer, you can watch *Internet TV*. This feature allows you to enjoy free streaming video content on demand. Choose from more than 100 hours of TV entertainment, music concerts, movie trailers, news, and sports content from MSN Video.

Internet TV is currently only available in the U.S.

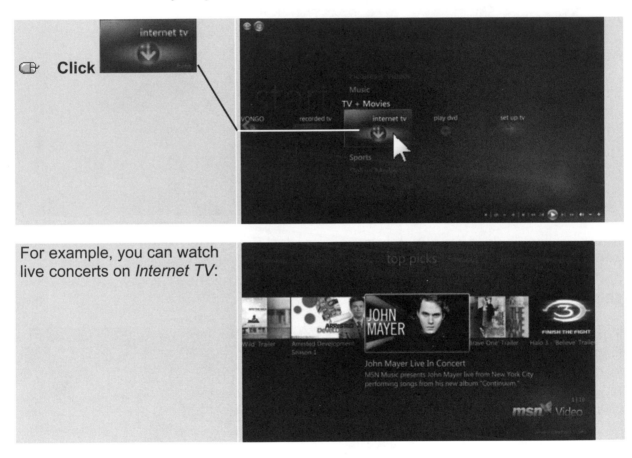

Take your time to discover what other options *Internet TV* has to offer. There is probably something there for you as well.

10.7 TV on Your PC

You can also use *Windows Media Center* to watch TV on your PC and record television shows. The connections you need to make depend on the type of TV signal you receive. There are four possibilities:

- an analog TV signal from an indoor or outdoor antenna;
- an analog cable TV signal **without** a set-top box or cable box;
- a digital TV signal from a cable box or satellite receiver;
- a digital cable TV signal with a digital cable tuner (US only).

When you watch TV using an analog TV signal from an antenna or a standard cable TV signal (without a set-top box) you need the following:

- a TV tuner (a separate box connected to your PC, or a built-in card);
- a standard F-connector coaxial cable;
- an F-connector cable splitter.

A TV tuner is a video card that is capable of receiving TV signals:

Often TV tuners are offered as a package together with a remote control to make using *Windows Media Center* even easier:

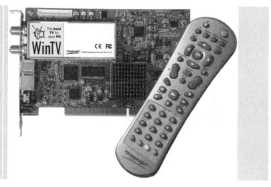

TV tuner card to build into a PC and a remote control

You can check the documentation you received with your computer to see if your PC has a built-in TV tuner.

You can use an F-connector cable splitter to divide the incoming TV signal. Using two coaxial cables and a splitter, you can transfer the TV signal to your TV as well as to your PC.

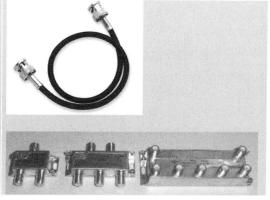

A coaxial cable with F-connectors

Two-way, four-way and six-way F-connector splitters

⇨ **Please note:**

When you buy a new TV tuner, make sure to check if it is compatible with *Windows Vista* and *Windows Media Center*. Not all TV tuners work smoothly with *Media Center*.

Also, please check with your hardware supplier which TV tuner card is most suitable for the TV signal (analog or digital) you receive. If you have no prior experience with the installation of TV tuner cards, it is a good idea to have that done by your supplier.

⇨ **Please note:**

If you would like to watch one channel and record another channel on your PC at the same time, you need a TV tuner card with two TV tuners. This is also called a *dual tuner*. With a dual tuner you can also record two TV programs at the same time. Both tuners need to be connected to the TV signal you receive from your cable television provider through your wall jack.

If you use an antenna to receive a TV signal, you can make the connection as follows:

☞ **Connect one end of the antenna cable to a signal splitter**

Then you can divide the TV signal between your television and your PC like this:

☞ **Connect one end of one standard coaxial cable to the cable splitter. Connect the other end of the cable to the TV IN jack of your TV.**

☞ **Connect one end of another standard coaxial cable to the cable splitter. Connect the other end of the cable to the TV IN jack of the TV tuner card in your computer.**

If you have a TV tuner card with two tuners (dual tuner), you can use a three-way cable splitter to divide the TV signal even further. Each tuner must have a TV signal connected to the TV IN jack.

⇨ **Please note:**

Most splitters weaken signals. Usually if a two, three, or four-way signal splitter is added, it will not weaken the signals enough to justify adding a distribution amplifier to the system. However, if there are more than four outlets in the house, a distribution amplifier will more than likely be needed.

If you use a standard cable TV signal, you can make the connection as follows:

Connect one end of the standard coaxial cable to the wall jack where you receive your TV signal.

If you want to connect the TV signal to your TV as well, you can use a cable splitter to divide the TV signal at the wall jack

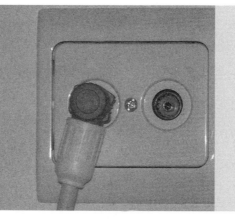

☞ **Connect the other end of the cable to the TV IN jack of the TV tuner card of your computer**

If you have a TV tuner card with two tuners (dual tuner) you can use a cable splitter to divide the TV signal. Each tuner must have a TV signal connected to the TV IN jack.

Digital television is a type of television in which the TV signal is broadcasted digitally. These days, cable companies offer both analog and digital television broadcasts.

Roughly, there are three types of digital television in the U.S.:

- Digital cable television: digital television delivered by way of the cable connection, offered by the cable television provider in your area. To be able to watch digital television you need a cable box (also called a set-top box). A set-top box is a decoder that transforms the digital TV signal to a signal that the TV is able to show.

- *DBS – Digital Broadcast Satellite*: digital television delivered by way of communication satellites. In the U.S., DISH Network and DirecTV are the main providers. You need a satellite receiver to transform the TV signal to a signal that the TV is able to display;

- *ATSC* digital broadcasts (U.S. only): over-the-air high-definition television. By February 17, 2009, this digital format will replace the analog NTSC television system. A digital cable tuner enables you to watch and record not only over-the-air high-definition TV (ATSC), but also standard and digital cable channels. In addition, a CableCARD inserted into the tuner enables you to watch premium digital cable channels (both standard and high-definition) which are available by subscription. If your cable provider supports CableCARD, you can obtain the CableCARD from your cable provider.

💡 Tip

Outside the U.S.? For countries other than the U.S., different options or systems may apply. Please refer to *Windows Help and Support* and the *Microsoft* website for specific information for your country.

When you watch digital cable television using a set-top box or digital satellite television using a satellite receiver, you need the following:

- a TV tuner (a separate box connected to your PC, or built in);
- two standard F-connector coaxial cables;
- if necessary, an F-connector cable splitter.

☞ **Connect one end of the first standard coaxial cable to the wall jack where you receive your TV signal**

☞ **Connect the other end of the cable to the cable input jack on the cable box or satellite receiver**

☞ **Connect one end of the second standard coaxial cable to cable output jack on the cable box or satellite receiver**

☞ **Connect the other end of the cable to the TV IN jack of the TV tuner card of your computer**

If you want to use a dual tuner in *Windows Media Center,* you must have two cable boxes or two satellite receivers. Each TV tuner requires its own TV signal input. If you want to receive the TV signal in your TV tuner and on your TV, you need two cable boxes or two satellite receivers as well.

If you have two cable boxes or two satellite receivers that you want to use with *Windows Media Center*, you can use a splitter to divide the TV signal from the wall jack to the boxes. Each cable box or satellite receiver must have a TV signal connected to the cable input jack.

Tip

Use only one set-top box
Using more than one set-top box is a costly option. There is a way around that. If you want to watch TV using *Windows Media Center*, the easiest and least expensive way to go is by using a splitter to divide the TV signal at the cable wall jack. Then you connect one cable to the set-top box, enabling you to receive the digital channels on your TV. As mentioned earlier, you will need to connect the second cable to the TV IN jack of the TV tuner card of your computer. This way you can receive all channels that are broadcasted on regular analog cable television on your computer.

When you watch ATSC digital broadcasts using a digital cable tuner, you need the following:

- a *Windows Media Center* computer that is marked Digital Cable Ready;
- a USB cable, type A/B;
- a standard F-connector coaxial cable;
- if necessary, an F-connector cable splitter.

☞ **Connect the digital cable tuner to a USB port of your PC, using the A/B USB cable**

A CableCARD inserted into the tuner enables you to watch premium digital cable channels (both standard and high-definition) which are available by subscription. If your cable provider supports CableCARD, you can obtain the CableCARD from your cable provider.

☞ **Insert the CableCARD (if you have one) into the Digital Cable tuner**

☞ **Connect one end of the standard coaxial cable to the cable source (wall jack)**

☞ **Connect the other end of the cable to the TV IN jack of the digital cable tuner**

If you want to use a dual tuner in *Windows Media Center,* you must have two digital cable tuners. Each TV tuner requires its own TV signal input.
If you want to receive the TV signal on your computer and on your TV, you need two digital cable tuners as well.

If you have two digital cable tuners, you can use a splitter to divide the TV signal from the wall jack to the tuners. Each tuner must have a TV signal connected to the TV IN jack on the tuner.

💡 Tip

Use only one digital cable tuner
Using more than one digital cable tuner is a costly option. There is a way around that. If you want to watch TV using *Windows Media Center*, the easiest and least expensive way to go is by using a splitter to divide the TV signal at the cable wall jack. Then you connect one cable to the digital cable tuner, enabling you to receive the digital channels on your TV. As described before in the section about regular analog cable television, you will need to connect the second cable to the TV IN jack of the TV tuner card of your computer. This allows you to receive all channels that are broadcasted on regular analog cable television on your computer.

💡 Tip

More information for Digital Cable Tuner users
If you use a digital cable tuner, either with or without a CableCARD, please refer to the PDF document **Digital Cable Tuner Users Guide** that can be found on the website of this book: **www.visualsteps.com/photovista**.
In this document, you can read about specific settings you need to make, for example when you use the digital cable tuner <u>without</u> a CableCARD.

💡 Tip

Would you like more information about the different connection options for your computer and the TV signal you receive at home in your country or region?
In *Windows Help and Support* you can find a lot of information:

☞ **Open *Windows Help and Support***

⌨ **Type in the *Search Box*:**
TV signal

A page containing articles on this subject appears:

☞ **Read the information that is applicable to your situation**

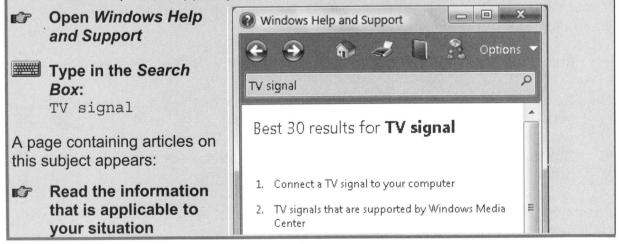

When the TV signal is connected to your TV tuner card (or the USB port of your computer if you have a digital cable tuner), you need to make a few adjustments to the settings of *Windows Media Center*. Begin with the option *settings*:

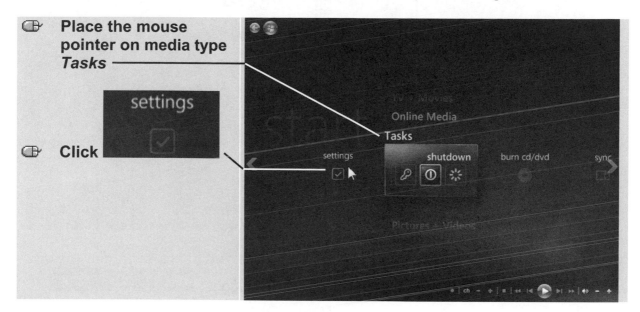

Place the mouse pointer on media type *Tasks*

Click

You are going to adjust the settings for TV.

Click Tv

General
TV
Pictures
Music
DVD
Extender
Library Setup

Click Set Up TV Signal

Recorder
Guide
Set Up TV Signal
Configure Your TV or Monitor
Audio
Subtitle

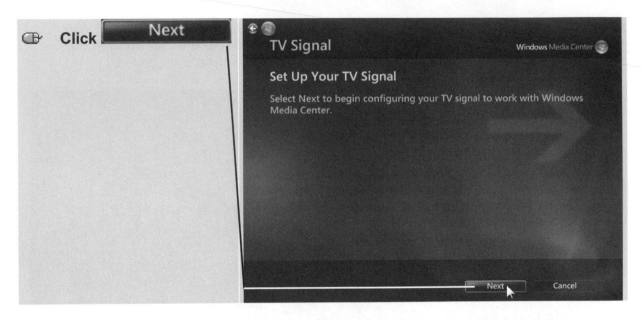

You need to confirm your region in order to receive the TV channels for your region correctly. In the U.S. for example, *Media Center* will suggest Region: United States .

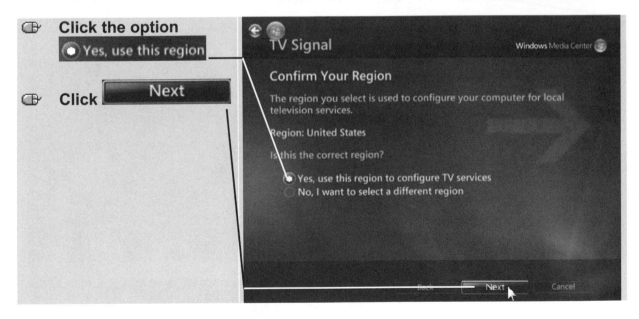

Windows Media Center gives you the option to automatically detect your TV signal. The TV signal can be configured manually, if you prefer.

☞ **Click the option**

☞ **Click** Next

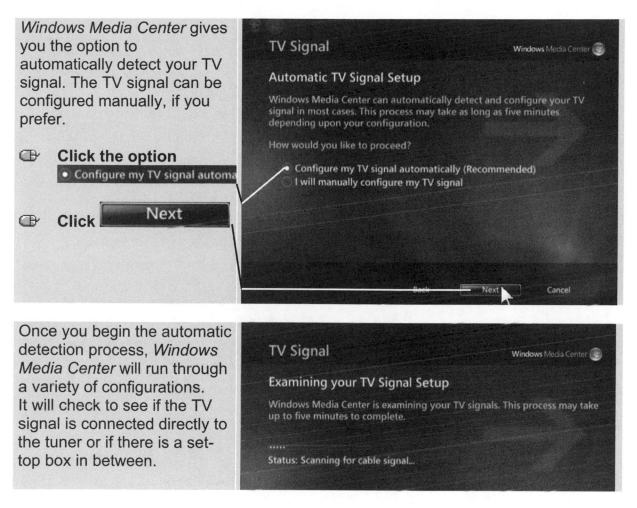

Once you begin the automatic detection process, *Windows Media Center* will run through a variety of configurations. It will check to see if the TV signal is connected directly to the tuner or if there is a set-top box in between.

In the example, a regular analog cable connection is found:

☞ **Click the option** Yes

☞ **Click** Next

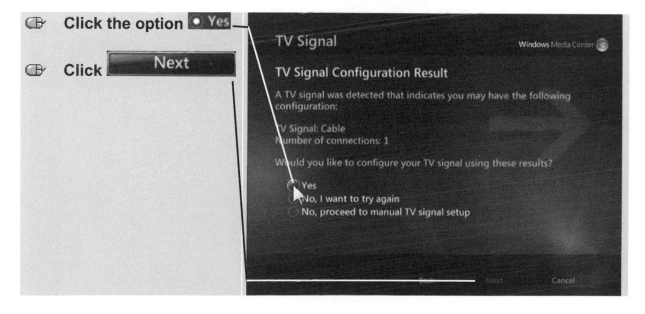

⇨ **Please note:**

If you use a digital cable tuner, make sure the TV signal is correctly identified as
TV Signal: Digital cable . If the signal is identified as cable using a set-top box, check the
cable and tuner connections and select ● No, I want to try again .
If you use a cable set-top box for your TV, but the TV signal is connected directly
from the wall jack to your computer, the signal should be identified as TV Signal: Cable
In that case, you receive the digital channels only on your TV, and the regular analog
cable channels on your computer.

The next step is to set up your *TV Program Guide*. The *Guide* is an electronic listing
of upcoming programs along with brief information about them.

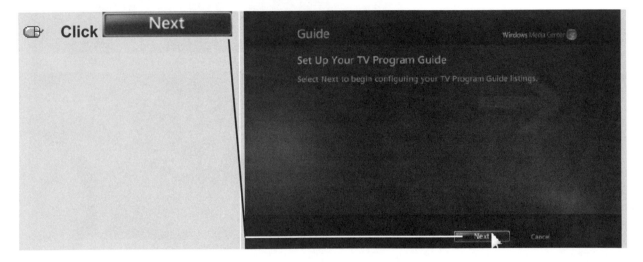

First, confirm that you want to use the *Guide*:

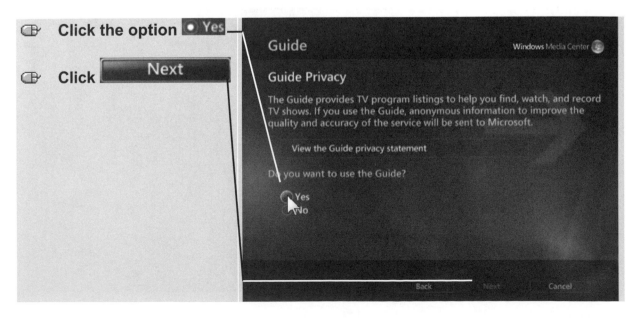

Before you can continue, you have to agree to the terms of service:

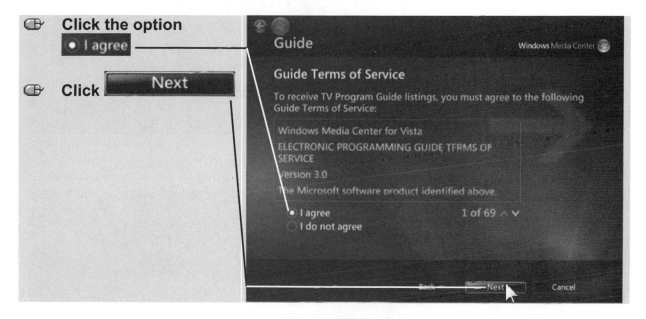

The *Guide* tailors program listings to your region and time zone, based on your ZIP code.

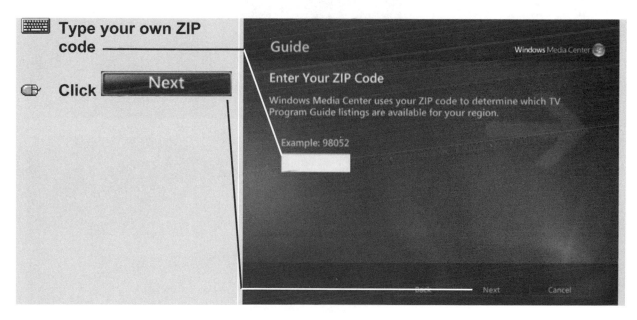

The *Guide* downloads a list of TV signal providers found in your area:

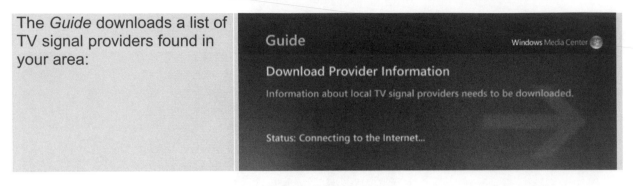

When the download is complete, you can select your own TV signal provider:

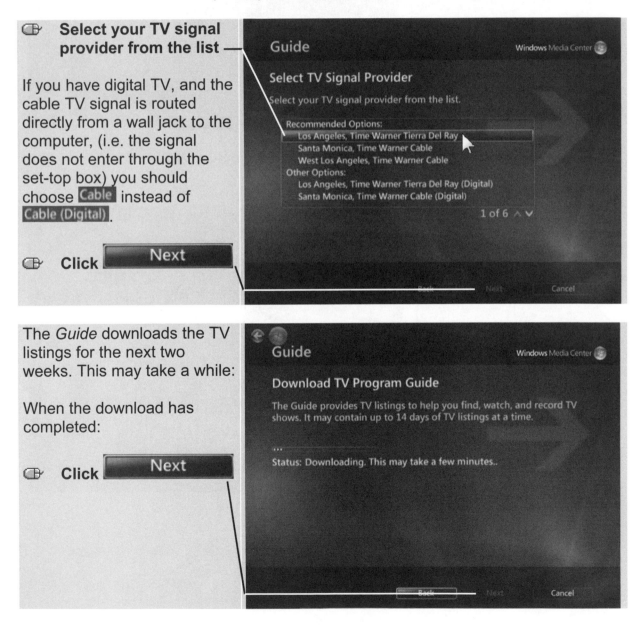

☞ **Select your TV signal provider from the list** —

If you have digital TV, and the cable TV signal is routed directly from a wall jack to the computer, (i.e. the signal does not enter through the set-top box) you should choose Cable instead of Cable (Digital).

☞ **Click** Next

The *Guide* downloads the TV listings for the next two weeks. This may take a while:

When the download has completed:

☞ **Click** Next

💡 Tip

Updating the Guide
In a Tip at the end of this chapter you can read how you can update the TV listings after the two weeks have elapsed.

Now you can return to the media menu:

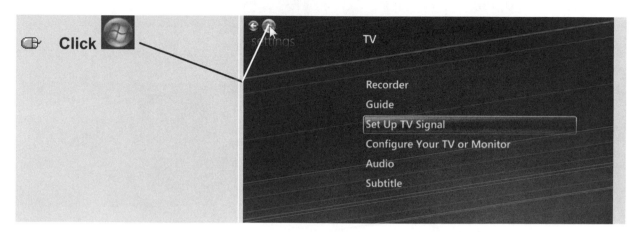

10.8 Watching Live Television

Now you can use *Windows Media Center* to watch live TV. You can do that like this:

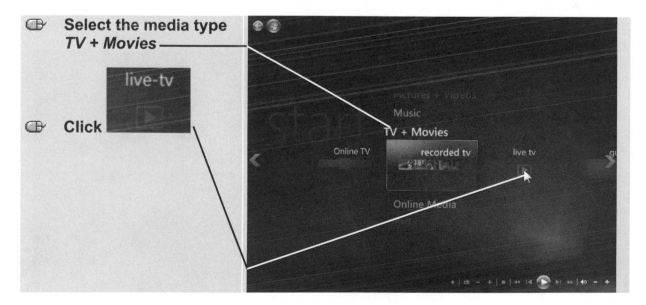

In this example, you see the current program on CNN. You can switch to the next channel like this:

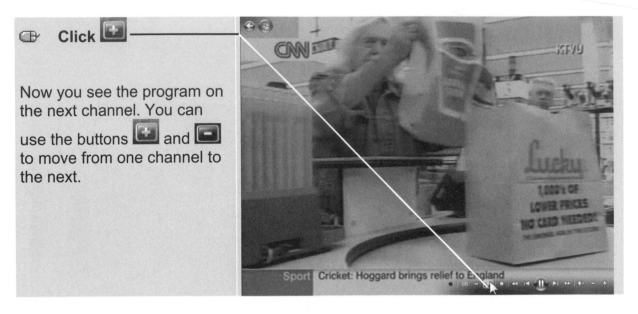

☞ **Click** ⊞

Now you see the program on the next channel. You can use the buttons ⊞ and ⊟ to move from one channel to the next.

Now you can return to the channel you watched before, in this example CNN:

☞ **Click** ⊟

A useful feature of *Windows Media Center* is the ability to pause a TV program. When you use this feature, you can get a drink from the fridge, or answer a phone call without having to miss part of your favorite show:

☞ **Click** ⏸

The picture freezes and the broadcast pauses. When you return, you can watch the program from the point when you clicked the pause button.

☞ **Click**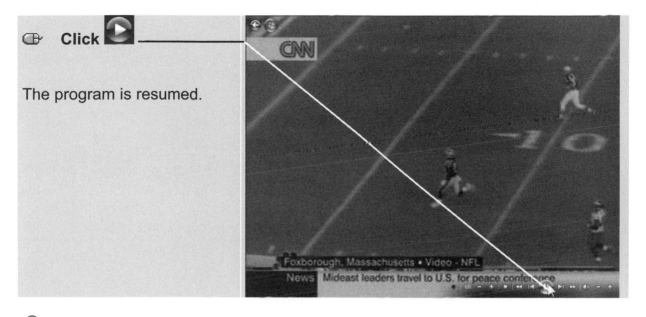

The program is resumed.

💡 **Tip**

Adjusting the volume
On the right side of the player, you can find three buttons to adjust the volume of the broadcast. Use 🔇 to mute the volume, use ➕ and ➖ to increase or decrease the volume.

Not only can you pause a TV program, you can also rewind a program, even when the program has not finished broadcasting! This is because the last half hour of the program you are watching is saved to a buffer on the hard disk of your computer.

You can rewind a maximum of thirty minutes of the live TV program you were watching. Like this:

☞ **Click**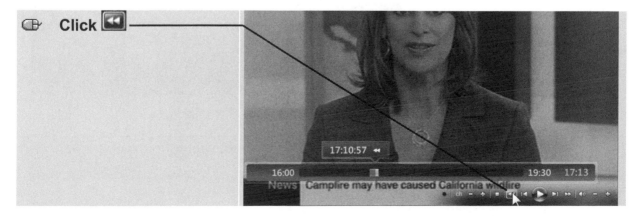

The broadcast is rewound. The next time you click 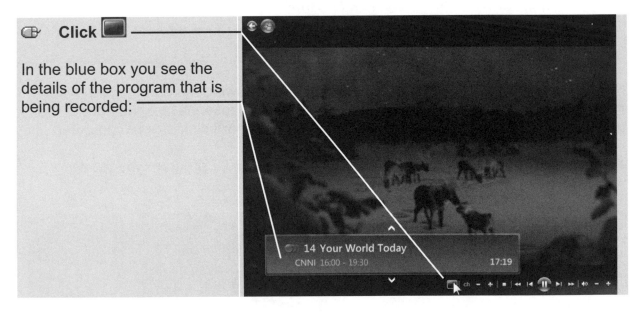, the rewinding will go faster. As soon as you have reached the point where you want to resume watching the program:

☞ **Click**

You see the TV program at a normal speed again.

✖ HELP! I rewound too much.

You can fast-forward the program as easily as rewinding. Use the button for that.

Please note: you cannot fast-forward the program beyond the point the broadcast has reached on TV.

10.9 Recording Live TV

If you decide during a broadcast that you would like to watch the program again later, you can record it. It takes just one mouse click:

☞ **Click**

In the blue box you see the details of the program that is being recorded:

14 Your World Today
CNNI 16:00 - 19:30   17:19

⇨ Please note:

If you use a TV tuner card with a single tuner, you cannot switch to another channel during recording.

You can also stop the recording in progress. To stop the current recording:

☞ **Right-click somewhere in the window**

☞ **Click** Stop Recording

You need to confirm this:

☞ **Click** Yes

10.10 Using the Guide

In the Electronic Program Guide, *Guide* in short, you can quickly see what will be on TV. The *Guide* is a timetable that contains the date and the time the program will be aired, and a brief description of programs and movies. The *Guide* is a free service. By using *Windows Media Center* you no longer need a paper TV guide or the TV listings from your newspaper.

You can start the *Guide* from the media menu of *Media Center*:

☞ **Click** 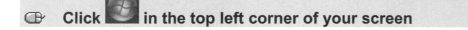 **in the top left corner of your screen**

As you can see, the TV
program is still visible in the
background. You also hear
the sound of the broadcast:

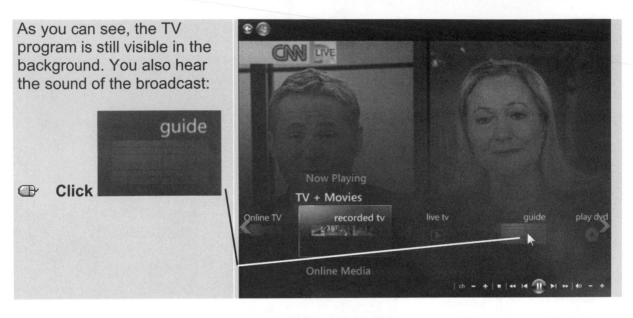

⬚ **Click**

You see the *Guide*:

The titles of the programs that
are on now are displayed in
white letters:

Programs that will be aired
later are displayed in blue
letters:

For example, take a look at
the current program on the
Discovery Channel:

⬚ **Click the title of the
program that is on
now**

You see the program that is being broadcasted on the Discovery Channel. Now you
can return to the *Guide* in one mouse click:

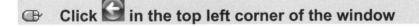

⬚ **Click** ⬅ **in the top left corner of the window**

You navigate through the *Guide* by using the arrow keys:

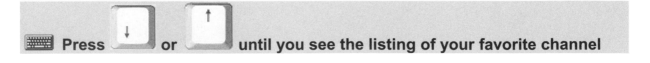

⌨ **Press** ⬇ **or** ⬆ **until you see the listing of your favorite channel**

💡 **Tip**

Navigating the Guide

Using the keys `Page Up` and `Page Down` you can scroll through the *Guide* while skipping several channels at once. If you already know the channel number of the channel you are looking for in the list, you can type that number to display the channel.

10.11 Planning a Recording in Advance

You can also record a TV program from the *Guide.* Try that with the TV program that is broadcasted tonight at 8:30 PM on your favorite channel.

⌨ **Press `→` until you see `8:30 PM` on top of the Guide**

🖱 **Click the program that is on at 8:30 PM**

Now you see the available information about this program:

With just one mouse click you can record this program:

🖱 **Click**

Record

World Business Today
14 CNNI-CNN International
11/29, 8:30 PM - 9:00 PM

The day's global business news which focuses on international business and market trends, economic developments, stock market trading and company takeover bids.

Original air date: 11/1/2000, Documentaire/Zaken, 30 minutes, English

You return to the *Guide* automatically:

A red dot has appeared next to the program you are going to record:

You can select the TV programs you want to record a maximum of two weeks in advance.

💡 **Tip**

Recording a TV series
Windows Media Center also gives you the possibility to record all episodes of a TV series automatically. In an extensive Tip at the end of this chapter, you can read how to do that.

10.12 Displaying Scheduled TV Recordings

When you have scheduled several recordings in advance, you do not need to browse the *Guide* to see which programs you are going to record. *Windows Media Center* keeps a convenient list for you. First, you return to the media menu:

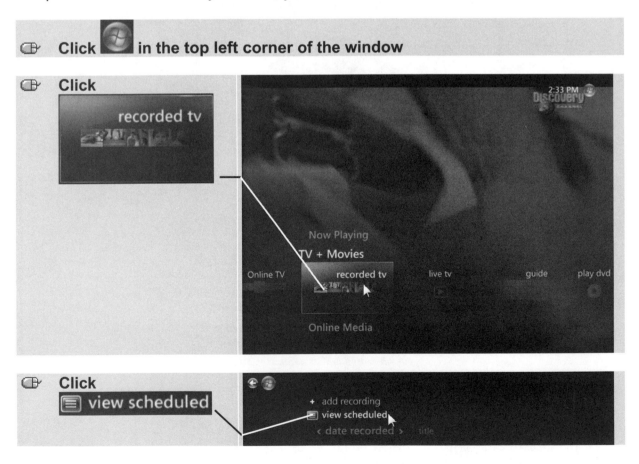

You see the recording you just added in the list of scheduled recordings:

⊕ **Click the program title**

If you do not want to record this program, you can cancel the recording here:

⊕ **Click**

Do Not Record

Now the recording has been cancelled.

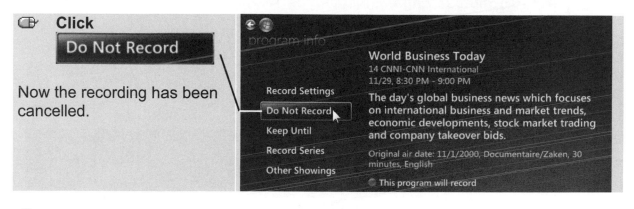

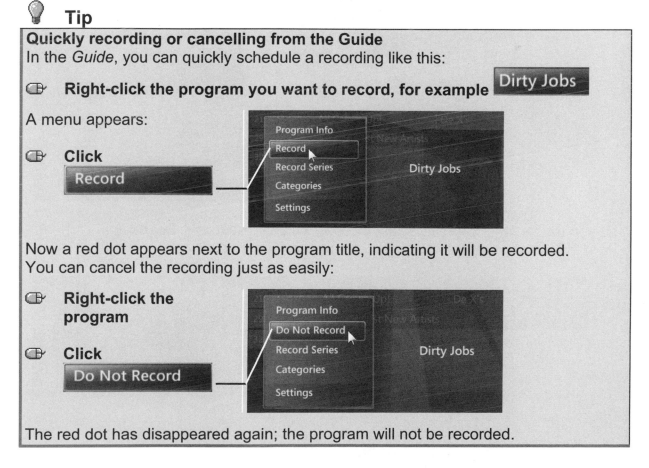

💡 Tip

Quickly recording or cancelling from the Guide
In the *Guide*, you can quickly schedule a recording like this:

⊕ **Right-click the program you want to record, for example** **Dirty Jobs**

A menu appears:

⊕ **Click**

Record

Now a red dot appears next to the program title, indicating it will be recorded. You can cancel the recording just as easily:

⊕ **Right-click the program**

⊕ **Click**

Do Not Record

The red dot has disappeared again; the program will not be recorded.

10.13 Adjusting the Recording Settings

You can adapt the way *Media Center* records programs to your own preferences. You return to the *Media* menu for that:

☞ **Open the *Media* menu** 𝒞𝒞101

☞ **Open the option *settings* at media type *Tasks*** 𝒞𝒞102

The settings for recording TV programs are part of the *TV* section:

☞ **Click** **TV**

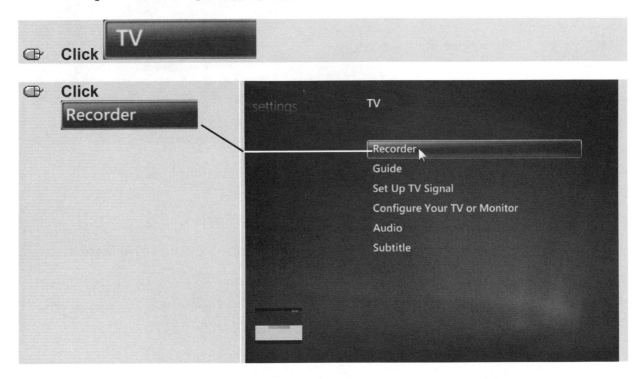

☞ **Click** **Recorder**

You see the settings you can adjust for recording TV programs. For example, check where the recorded programs are stored on your computer:

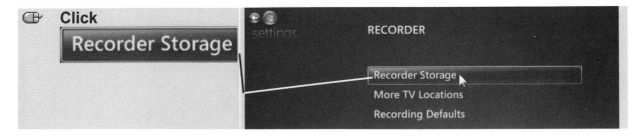

☞ **Click** **Recorder Storage**

At the top you see on which (partition of your) hard disk the recordings are stored.
In this example that is disk C which contains (59 GB) free space: ────────────

A maximum of 55 GB will be used for TV recordings:────────

Using the best possible recording quality, this is enough space for 7 ½ hours of recording: ────────────

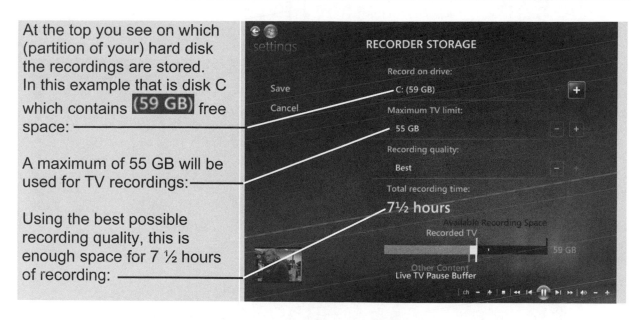

You can adjust these settings if you want to. You can select another (partition of your) hard disk, adjust the available space for recordings, or determine another recording quality. For example, here is how to select a different partition or hard disk:

Click **+** until you see the correct partition or hard disk ────────

The total recording time is adjusted to the new setting:

Did you change a setting?

Then click

Save

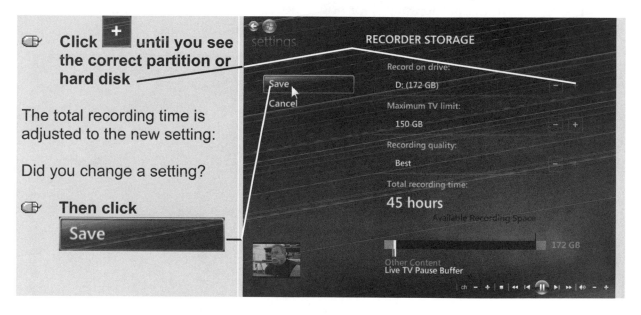

Did you leave the settings unchanged?

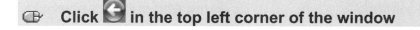

Click ⬅ in the top left corner of the window

Take a look at some of the other settings you can change:

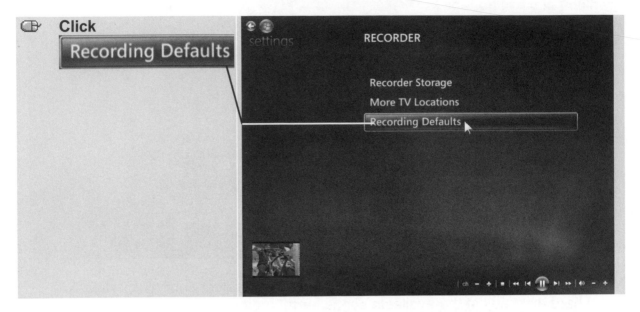

In the window *Recording Defaults* you can adjust a large number of settings. For example, you can adjust the setting for how long TV recordings are kept. If you want to keep the recordings until you delete them yourself manually:

☞ **Click** **+** **three times** at **Keep:**

Sometimes TV programs start a little early, or end a little bit later. You can have the recording start or end a maximum of four minutes before or after the programmed time: ———

The other settings apply to recording TV series. In a Tip at the end of this chapter you can read more about recording the episodes of a TV series.

☞ **Click**

💡 **Tip**

Adjusting the settings for each recording

The default recording settings apply to all recordings you start with one mouse click. If necessary, you can adjust the settings for an individual recording as well. Starting in the *Guide* you can do that like this:

☞ **Click the title of the program you want to record**

☞ **Click**

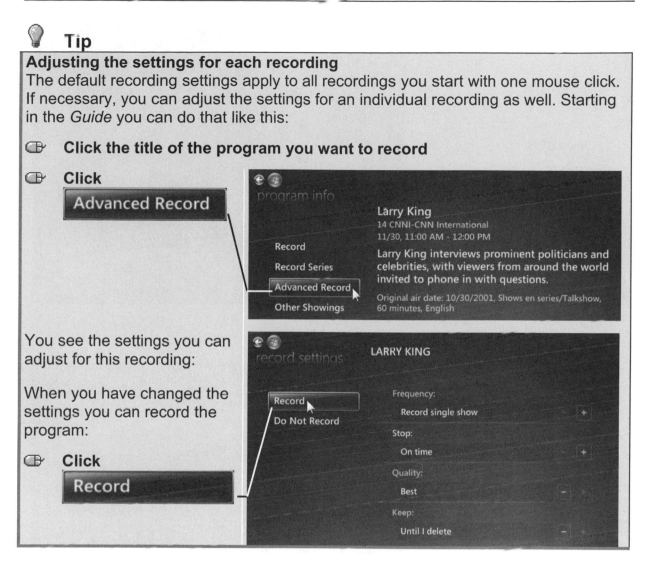

You see the settings you can adjust for this recording:

When you have changed the settings you can record the program:

☞ **Click**

10.14 Watching a TV Recording

Earlier in this chapter, you recorded a short part of a television program. You are going to look up that TV recording and watch it.

☞ **Open the *Media* menu** 𝓁𝓁**101**

☞ **Open the option *Recorded TV* at media type *TV + Movies*** 𝓁𝓁**103**

You see the TV clip you recorded. Next to it, you see some short sample clips from *Media Center*:

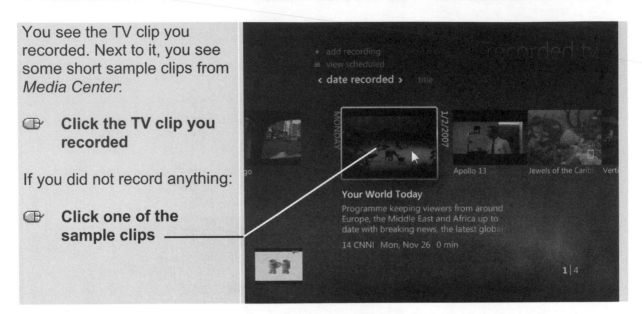

☞ **Click the TV clip you recorded**

If you did not record anything:

☞ **Click one of the sample clips**

You can play the clip now:

☞ **Click** **Play**

The recording is played. When it is finished:

☞ **Click** **Done**

10.15 SportsLounge

Windows Media Center also caters to sports fans: you can find the media type *Sports* in the *Media* menu (U.S. and Canada only). In addition to a TV tuner connected to a television source, you need a broadband Internet connection to be able to use the full potential of *SportsLounge*.

☞ **Click** [Windows logo] , [Sports]

Here you see the media type *Sports* with its options:

☞ **Click** [On Now thumbnail]

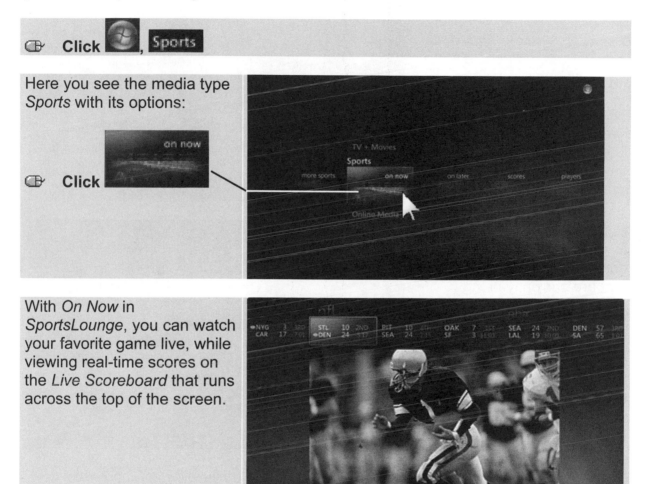

With *On Now* in *SportsLounge*, you can watch your favorite game live, while viewing real-time scores on the *Live Scoreboard* that runs across the top of the screen.

The displayed scores are shown for all the additional games on other channels that are available with your current antenna, cable, or satellite TV service, making it easier to track the action of all the other games that are on. You will not miss the action from games that are not broadcasted in your area either. FOXSports.com also provides sporting news updates along the bottom of the screen. If you see a story that you like, select it and you will be connected to FOXSports.com's new online sports portal experience.

If you want to quickly see what is happening with a different game on another available channel, just select the game from the *Live Scoreboard* and *Windows Media Center* will instantly tune to that channel. This means you do not have to navigate the *Guide*.

On Later finds all the games airing over a two-week period that are available from your television service. They are neatly arranged according to date and sport.

This means you no longer need to search the entire *Guide* to find out when the games you want to watch are coming on.

Use *Scores* in *SportsLounge*, to see the scores for all games in the U.S. or Canada that are currently being played.

The scores are arranged logically by sport, and FOX Sports constantly updates them, so you will always know who is in the lead.

You can even catch up on the games that you missed by viewing an entire week's worth of scores from your favorite league.

By clicking a game, *Scores* also provides you with more detailed information, such as what the last play was, or who scored last.

Another convenient *SportsLounge* option is *Players*:

With this feature, you can set up *Media Center* to track your favorite professional athlete. *Players* displays stats over the course of the season or the stats for a current or recently played game.

If you are using the *On Now* feature to watch one game, and your favorite player makes a huge play or is on deck to bat on another channel, you will be notified of that event. *SportsLounge* will give you the option to directly tune to that channel to watch the play.

10.16 Creating a Video DVD

You can write (burn) different kinds of media to CD and DVD with *Windows Media Center*:

☞ **Open the option** *Burn CD/DVD* **at media type** *Tasks* $\ell\ell^{105}$

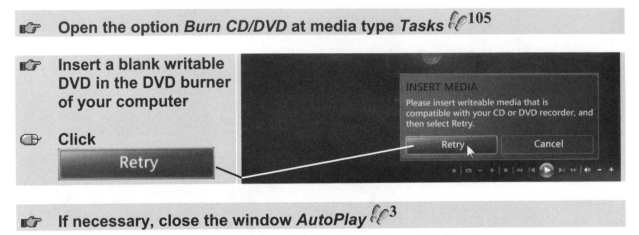

☞ **Insert a blank writable DVD in the DVD burner of your computer**

☞ **Click** Retry

☞ **If necessary, close the window** *AutoPlay* $\ell\ell^{3}$

Now you can choose the type of DVD you want to create. Select video DVD, that is the type of DVD you can play in the DVD player connected to your television.

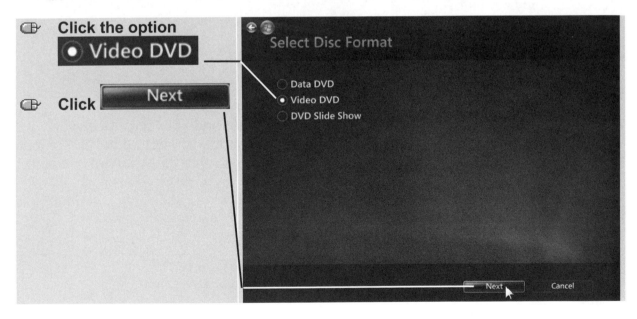

☞ **Click the option** ● Video DVD

☞ **Click** Next

You can enter a name for the DVD:

🖱 **Point to the box**

Untitled

⌨ **Type:**
Exercise

🖱 **Click** Next

A video DVD can contain up to 120 minutes of video. You can combine both recorded TV and video clips on one DVD.

Select the TV recordings you want to add:

🖱 **Click the option**
⦿ **Recorded TV**

🖱 **Click** Next

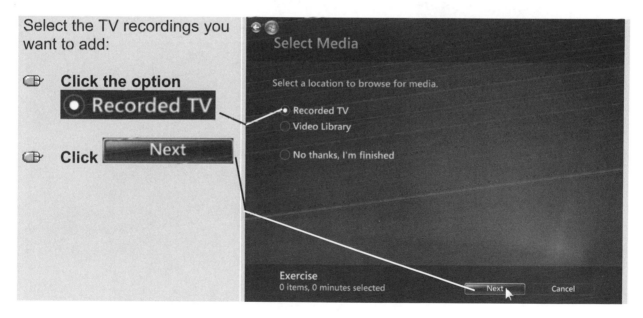

Now you can select the TV recordings:

☞ **Click to check mark the program you recorded**

It will take a few seconds before the check mark is added.

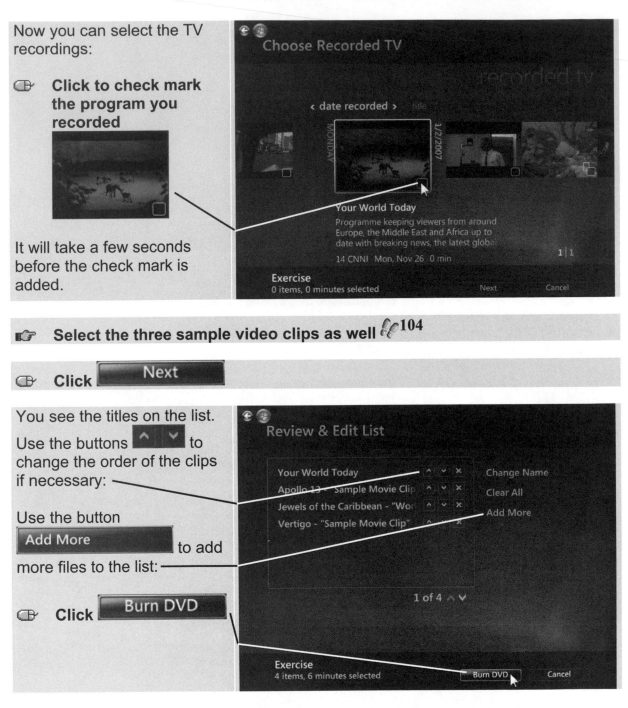

☞ **Select the three sample video clips as well** 🖑104

☞ **Click** Next

You see the titles on the list.
Use the buttons ∧ ∨ to change the order of the clips if necessary:

Use the button
Add More
to add more files to the list:

☞ **Click** Burn DVD

Media Center asks if you really want to write (burn) the files to the DVD:

☞ **Click** Yes

According to *Media Center*, burning the files to DVD may take several hours to complete. This is caused by the fact that the files are converted to a format that can be played in a regular DVD player. Since you only have a few short fragments on the list, burning the DVD in this example will not take that long.

You can make the window disappear:

☞ **Click**

OK

You see the *Media* menu again. As soon as the files are burned to the DVD, the drawer of the DVD burner opens.

☞ **Click**

Done

10.17 Playing a DVD in Windows Media Center

You can play the DVD in your regular DVD player, but also in *Windows Media Center* itself. Try doing that now.

☞ **Open the option** *Play DVD* **at media type** *TV + Movies* ℓℓ¹⁰⁶

☞ **Close the drawer of the DVD burner again**

☞ **Click**

OK

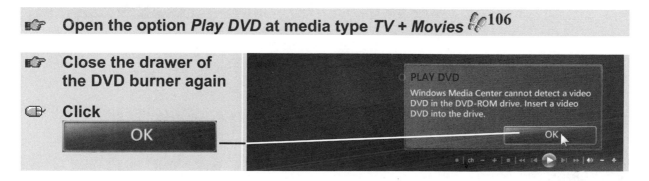

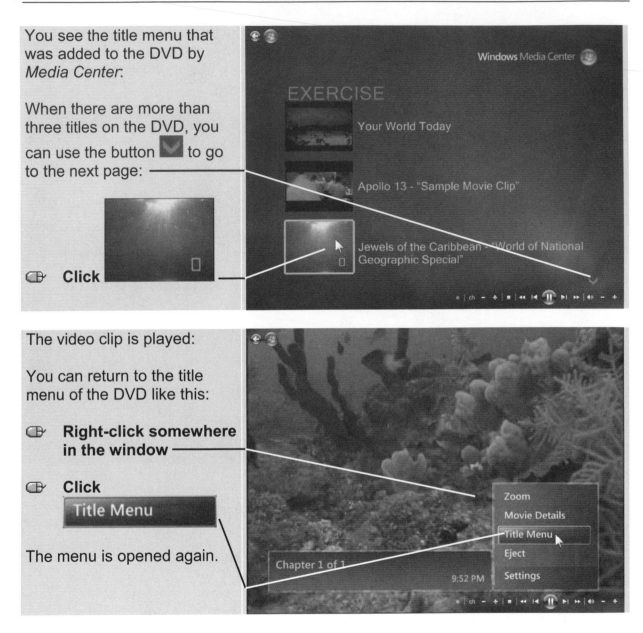

You see the title menu that was added to the DVD by *Media Center*:

When there are more than three titles on the DVD, you can use the button ⬇ to go to the next page:

☞ **Click**

The video clip is played:

You can return to the title menu of the DVD like this:

☞ **Right-click somewhere in the window**

☞ **Click**

  Title Menu

The menu is opened again.

10.18 Deleting a Recording from the Hard Disk

After you have viewed a recording or copied it to DVD, you can delete the original file from the hard disk of your computer.

☞ **Open the *Media* menu** 𝓁𝓁^101

☞ **Open the option *Recorded TV* at media type *TV + Movies*** 𝓁𝓁^103

👆 **Right-click the recording you want to delete**

👆 **Click**

   Delete

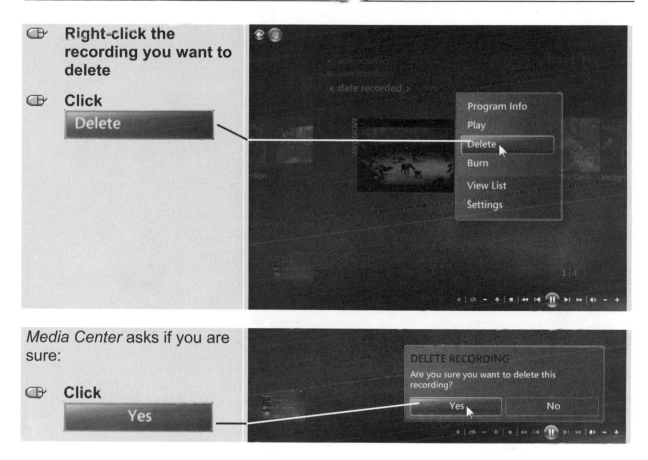

Media Center asks if you are sure:

👆 **Click**

   Yes

The recording has been removed from the hard disk of your computer.

☞ **Close *Windows Media Center*** 𝒶𝒶107

☞ **Remove the DVD from your DVD player**

In this chapter you have been introduced to *Windows Media Center*. You can practice working with this program using the exercises in the next section.

10.19 Exercises

Have you forgotten how to do something? Use the number beside the footsteps to look it up in appendix *How Do I Do That Again?*

Exercise: Playing a Slide Show

In this exercise you view a slide show in *Windows Media Center*.

✔ Open *Windows Media Center*. 108

✔ Open the option *Picture Library* in media type *Pictures + Videos*. 109

✔ Play the images in a slide show. 110

✔ Go back to the *Media* menu of *Windows Media Center*. 101

✔ Close *Windows Media Center*. 107

Exercise: Viewing Online Media

In this exercise you practice working with the *Online Media* in *Media Center*.

✔ Open *Windows Media Center*. 108

✔ Open the option *Explore* at media type *Online Media*. 111

✔ Open the start page of Discovery Channel. 112

✔ Watch a video preview of Animal Channel. 113

✔ Stop the preview and go back to the Discovery Channel start page. 114

✔ Close *Windows Media Center*. 107

Exercise: Viewing and Recording Live TV

In this exercise you are going to use *Media Center* to watch and record live television. **Please note:** you can only do this exercise if you have connected a TV tuner to your computer.

✔　Open *Windows Media Center*. 𝓁𝓁**108**

✔　Open the option *Guide* at media type *TV + Movies*. 𝓁𝓁**115**

✔　Watch the current program on CNN. 𝓁𝓁**116**

✔　Switch to National Geographic. 𝓁𝓁**117**

✔　Pause the program on National Geographic. 𝓁𝓁**118**

✔　Resume the program on National Geographic. 𝓁𝓁**119**

✔　Record about two minutes of the program on National Geographic. 𝓁𝓁**120**

✔　Stop recording the program. 𝓁𝓁**121**

✔　Go back to the *Media* menu of *Windows Media Center*. 𝓁𝓁**101**

✔　Close *Windows Media Center*. 𝓁𝓁**107**

Exercise: Viewing and Deleting a TV Recording

In this exercise you will view and delete the recording from the previous exercise.

✔　Open *Windows Media Center*. 𝓁𝓁**108**

✔　Open the option *TV Recordings* at media type *TV + Movies*. 𝓁𝓁**103**

✔　View the TV recording you created in the previous exercise. 𝓁𝓁**122**

✔　Return to the previous window. 𝓁𝓁**123**

✔　Delete the recording. 𝓁𝓁**124**

✔　Close *Windows Media Center*. 𝓁𝓁**107**

10.20 Background Information

Glossary	
Dual tuner	TV tuner card with two tuners. Using a dual tuner you can record two channels at the same time, or record one channel and watch another channel.
Guide	Electronic program listing of upcoming programs in the next two weeks, with brief information about these programs.
Media menu	The main menu of *Windows Media Center* that you can use to select the different media types and their options.
Media type	Group of connected options in the *Media* menu of *Windows Media Center*. The available media types are: *Pictures + Videos, Music, TV + Movies, Online Media, Tasks* and *Sports*.
Option	Task that belongs to a media type in the *Media* menu of *Windows Media Center*.
Set-top box	A decoder that transforms the digital TV signal to a signal that the TV is able to show.
Slide show	A series of still images displayed one after another with transition effects.
Splitter	A device used to divide the TV signal.
TV tuner card	Video card that is capable of receiving TV signals, for example from the analog cable connection or the set-top box of the digital television connection.
Video DVD	DVD you can play in a regular DVD player.
Windows Photo Gallery	Program you can use to view, manage, and edit digital photos in *Windows Vista*.
Windows Media Center	The center for all your digital entertainment in *Windows Vista*.

Source: Windows Help and Support

10.21 Tips

💡 Tip

Recording a TV series
Windows Media Center can record all episodes of a TV series automatically. This way you never have to miss an episode of your favorite series again!

☞ **Click a new episode of the TV series you want to record in the *Guide***

☞ **Click**

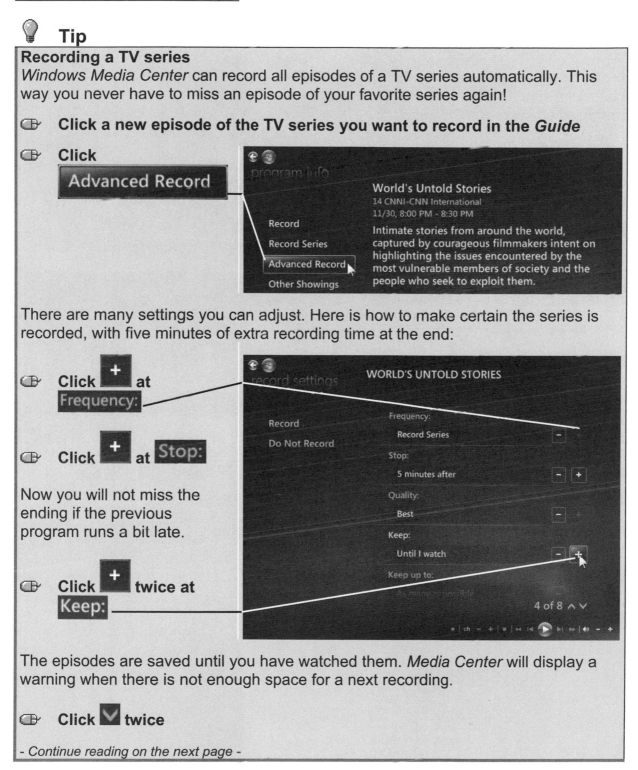

There are many settings you can adjust. Here is how to make certain the series is recorded, with five minutes of extra recording time at the end:

☞ **Click ➕ at Frequency:**

☞ **Click ➕ at Stop:**

Now you will not miss the ending if the previous program runs a bit late.

☞ **Click ➕ twice at Keep:**

The episodes are saved until you have watched them. *Media Center* will display a warning when there is not enough space for a next recording.

☞ **Click ▼ twice**

- Continue reading on the next page -

You can also choose how many episodes you want to keep:

When the series is broadcasted on several channels, select your preferred channel here:

When the broadcast time of the series varies, keep this setting on **Anytime**:

<img mouse> **Click** ☑

<img mouse> **Click** ⊟ **at** **Show type:**

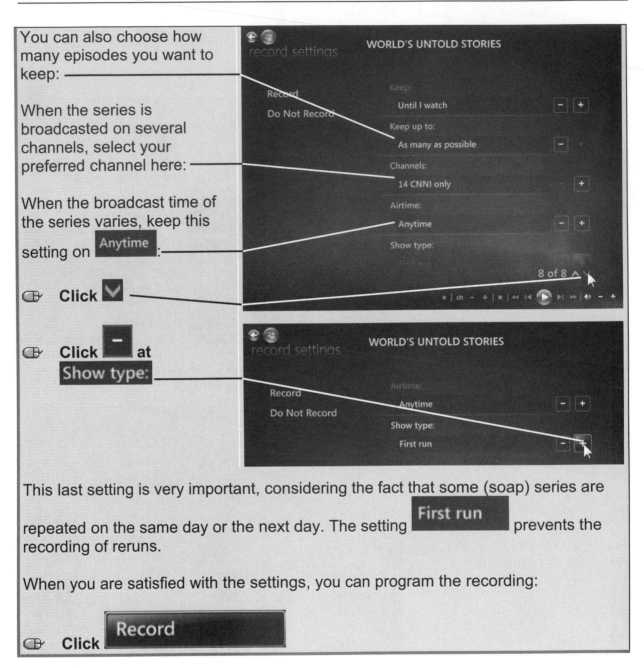

This last setting is very important, considering the fact that some (soap) series are repeated on the same day or the next day. The setting **First run** prevents the recording of reruns.

When you are satisfied with the settings, you can program the recording:

<img mouse> **Click** **Record**

💡 Tip

Cancel recording a TV series
You can quickly cancel recording a TV series like this:

☞ Click **≣ view scheduled**, **Series**

☞ **Right-click the title of the series**

☞ Click **Cancel Series**

Series Info
Cancel Series
Settings

1. World's Untold Storie

Media Center asks if you really want to cancel the recordings:

☞ Click **Yes**

The upcoming episodes of the TV series will no longer be recorded.

💡 Tip

Updating the Guide
You can download the updated program listings a maximum of two weeks in advance. Like this:

☞ **Open the *Media* menu** 👣^{101}

☞ **Open the option *Settings* at media type *Tasks*** 👣^{102}

☞ Click **TV**

☞ Click **Guide**

settings   TV

Recorder
Guide
Set Up TV Signal
Configure Your TV or Monitor

- Continue reading on the next page -

You see the *Guide* settings that you can adjust:

☞ **Click**

Get Latest Guide Listings

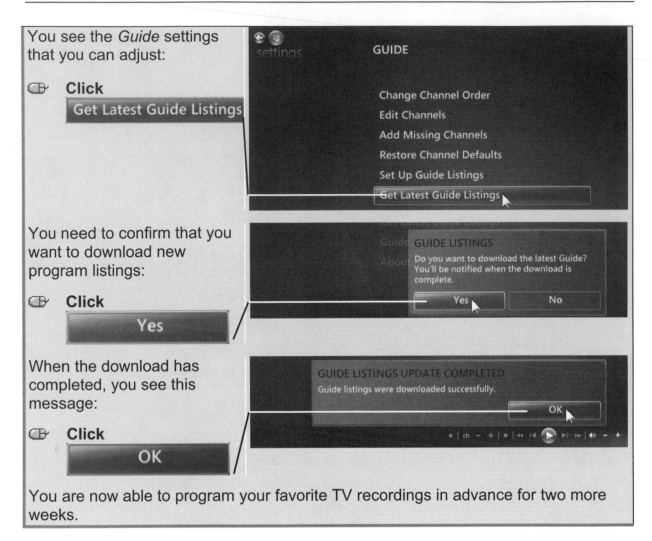

You need to confirm that you want to download new program listings:

☞ **Click**

Yes

When the download has completed, you see this message:

☞ **Click**

OK

You are now able to program your favorite TV recordings in advance for two more weeks.

Appendices

A. Copying the Practice Files to Your Computer

The CD-ROM disk included with this book contains practice files for you to use as you work through each chapter. You will need to copy the *Practice files* folder from the CD-ROM to the hard disk of your computer. It is easy to do and takes just a few minutes.

The CD-ROM is stored in a sleeve that is bound between the pages of the book. Carefully open the sleeve to take out the CD. Do **not** try to rip the sleeve out of the book, as this might damage it. When you are done working, you can store the CD-ROM in the sleeve again. This way you always have the CD-ROM at hand when you work with this book.

☞ **Insert the CD-ROM in the CD or DVD drive of your computer**

Make sure the printed side of the CD-ROM faces up.

In most cases, the following window appears automatically after a few moments:

☞ **Click**

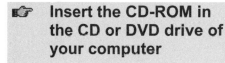

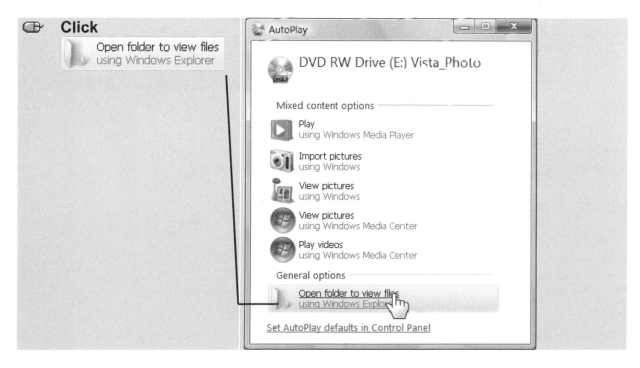

✖ HELP! I do not see that window.

If different *AutoPlay* settings have been made for CDs on your computer, it is possible that a different window appears or a program automatically opens. In that case do the following:

☞ **Close the (program)window** ℓℓ³

☞ **Click** , Computer

Now you see the *Computer* window:

You may have other drives and devices displayed on your computer than the ones shown here.

☞ **Double-click your CD or DVD drive**

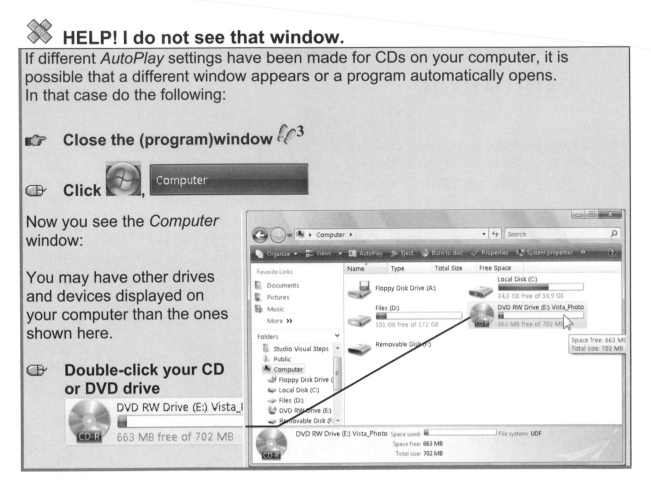

You see a *Folder window* that displays the contents of the CD-ROM on the right side:

The folders may be displayed differently on your computer. In that case look for the folder named:

Practice files
File Folder

☞ **Right-click**

Practice files
File Folder

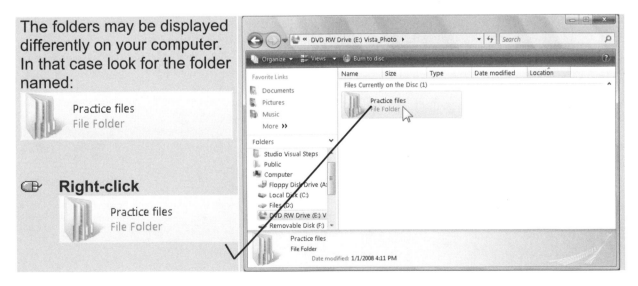

Now a menu appears:

Click Send To

Another menu appears:

Click Documents

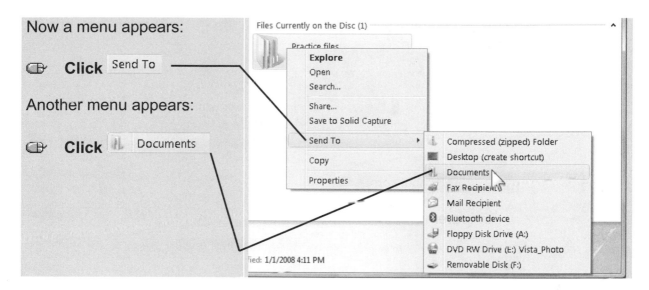

The *Practice files* folder is now copied to the *Documents* folder of your computer:

You can follow the progress in this window:

When all items have been copied, you can take a look at the contents of the *Documents* folder:

Click Documents

The *Documents* folder is opened:

Double-click

Practice files
File Folder

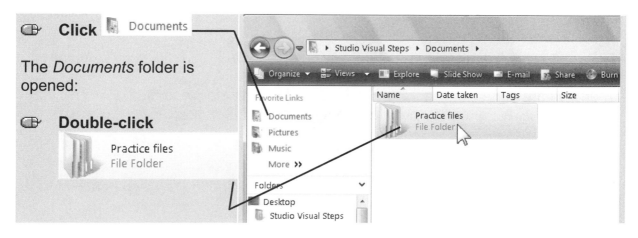

The *Practice files* folder contains three subfolders. You are going to move one of these folders to another location:

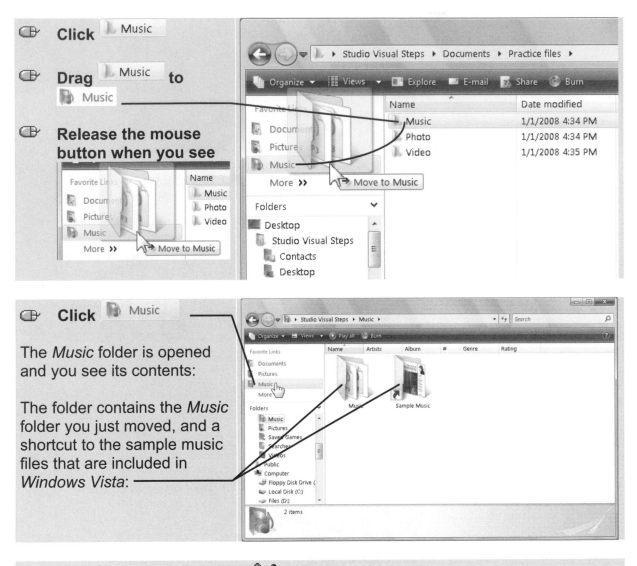

☞ **Close the *Folder window*** 3

When you are done working, return the CD-ROM to the sleeve in the book. This way you always have it at hand when you want to work with the book.

☞ **Store the CD-ROM in the sleeve in the book**

All of the files needed for practicing have now been copied to the *Documents* folder and the *Music* folder of your computer.

B. How Do I Do That Again?

In this book actions are marked with footsteps: 👣1
Find the corresponding number in the appendix below to see how to do something.

👣 1 **Play a CD or track**
- Click ▶

or:
- Click the track

- Click ▶

👣 2 **Stop playing**
- Click ■

👣 3 **Close a window**
- Click X in the top right corner of the window

👣 4 **Open the *Control Panel***
- Click 🪟

- Click Control Panel

👣 5 **Open *Windows Media Player***
- Click 🪟

- Point to ▶ All Programs

- Click ▶ Windows Media Player

or:
- Click ▶ in the *Quick Launch* toolbar

👣 6 **Open the *Options* window**
- Click ⬛⬛⬛ below Rip

- Click More Options...

👣 7 **Rate a track**
- Right-click the track

- Click Rate

- Click the number of stars you want to give the track

👣 8 **Open the *Library***
- Click Library

👣 9 **Change the way the *Library* is sorted**
- Click the preferred sorting method, for example ♪ Songs

👣 10 **Create a new playlist**
- Click ▣ Create Playlist

- Type the name of the playlist

- Press Enter ⏎

👣 11 **Add track to playlist**
- Click the track

- Drag the track to the *List Pane*

or:
- Right-click the track
- Click `Add to 'Practice playlist'`

12 Add album to playlist
- Right-click the album
- Click `Add to 'Practice playlist'`

13 Move tracks in playlist
- Click the track
- Drag the track to the preferred location

14 Delete tracks from playlist
- Click the track
- Click `Delete`

15 Delete playlist
- Right-click the playlist
- Click `Delete`
- Click `OK`

16 Name the *Burn list*
- Click `Burn List ▼`
- Click `Rename Playlist`
- Type the name
- Press `Enter ←`

17 Open *Burn list*
- Click `Burn`

18 Add album to *Burn list*
- Right-click the album
- Click `Add to 'Burn List'`

19 Add track to *Burn list*
- Click the track
- Drag the track to the *Burn list*

or:
- Right-click the track
- Click `Add to 'Burn List'`

20 Select audio CD for burning
- Click `▼` `Burn` below
- Click `Audio CD`

21 Burn the *Burn list* to CD-Recordable
- Click `Start Burn`

22 Set visualization
- Click `▼` below
- Click `Visualizations`
- Click the preferred group
- Click the preferred visualization

23 To skin mode
- Press and hold `Ctrl`
- Type: 2
- Release `Ctrl`

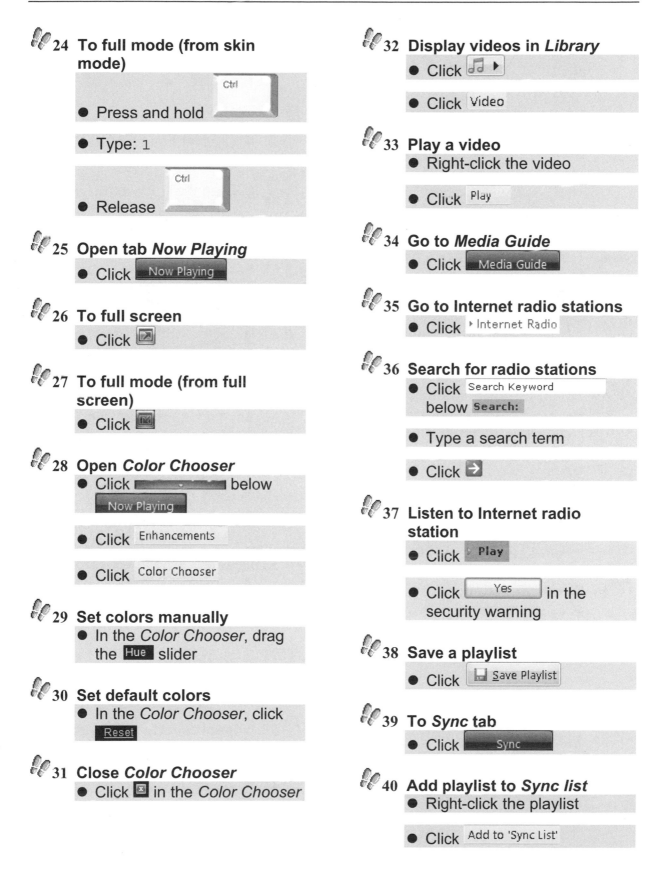

24 To full mode (from skin mode)
- Press and hold `Ctrl`
- Type: 1
- Release `Ctrl`

25 Open tab *Now Playing*
- Click `Now Playing`

26 To full screen
- Click

27 To full mode (from full screen)
- Click

28 Open *Color Chooser*
- Click `_____▼_____` below `Now Playing`
- Click `Enhancements`
- Click `Color Chooser`

29 Set colors manually
- In the *Color Chooser*, drag the `Hue` slider

30 Set default colors
- In the *Color Chooser*, click `Reset`

31 Close *Color Chooser*
- Click in the *Color Chooser*

32 Display videos in *Library*
- Click
- Click `Video`

33 Play a video
- Right-click the video
- Click `Play`

34 Go to *Media Guide*
- Click `Media Guide`

35 Go to Internet radio stations
- Click `▶ Internet Radio`

36 Search for radio stations
- Click `Search Keyword` below `Search:`
- Type a search term
- Click

37 Listen to Internet radio station
- Click `▶ Play`
- Click `Yes` in the security warning

38 Save a playlist
- Click `Save Playlist`

39 To *Sync* tab
- Click `Sync`

40 Add playlist to *Sync list*
- Right-click the playlist
- Click `Add to 'Sync List'`

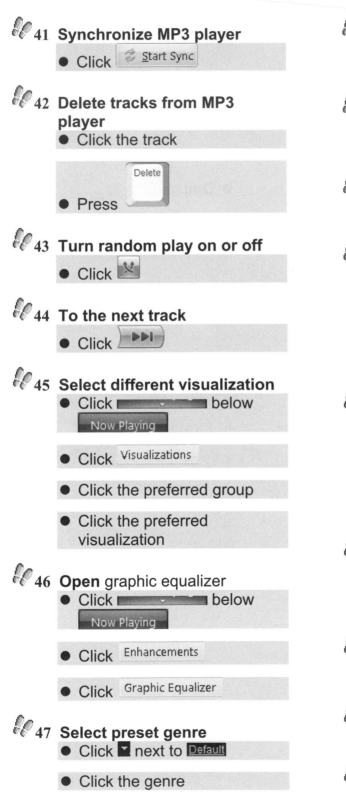

41 Synchronize MP3 player
- Click [⟳ Start Sync]

42 Delete tracks from MP3 player
- Click the track

- Press [Delete]

43 Turn random play on or off
- Click [icon]

44 To the next track
- Click [▶▶▶]

45 Select different visualization
- Click [◜ ▾] below [Now Playing]

- Click [Visualizations]

- Click the preferred group

- Click the preferred visualization

46 Open graphic equalizer
- Click [◜ ▾] below [Now Playing]

- Click [Enhancements]

- Click [Graphic Equalizer]

47 Select preset genre
- Click [▾] next to [Default]

- Click the genre

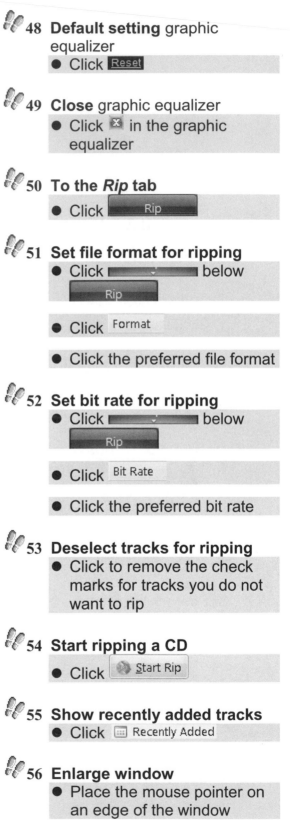

48 Default setting graphic equalizer
- Click [Reset]

49 Close graphic equalizer
- Click [✖] in the graphic equalizer

50 To the *Rip* tab
- Click [Rip]

51 Set file format for ripping
- Click [◜ ▾] below [Rip]

- Click [Format]

- Click the preferred file format

52 Set bit rate for ripping
- Click [◜ ▾] below [Rip]

- Click [Bit Rate]

- Click the preferred bit rate

53 Deselect tracks for ripping
- Click to remove the check marks for tracks you do not want to rip

54 Start ripping a CD
- Click [◉ Start Rip]

55 Show recently added tracks
- Click [▦ Recently Added]

56 Enlarge window
- Place the mouse pointer on an edge of the window

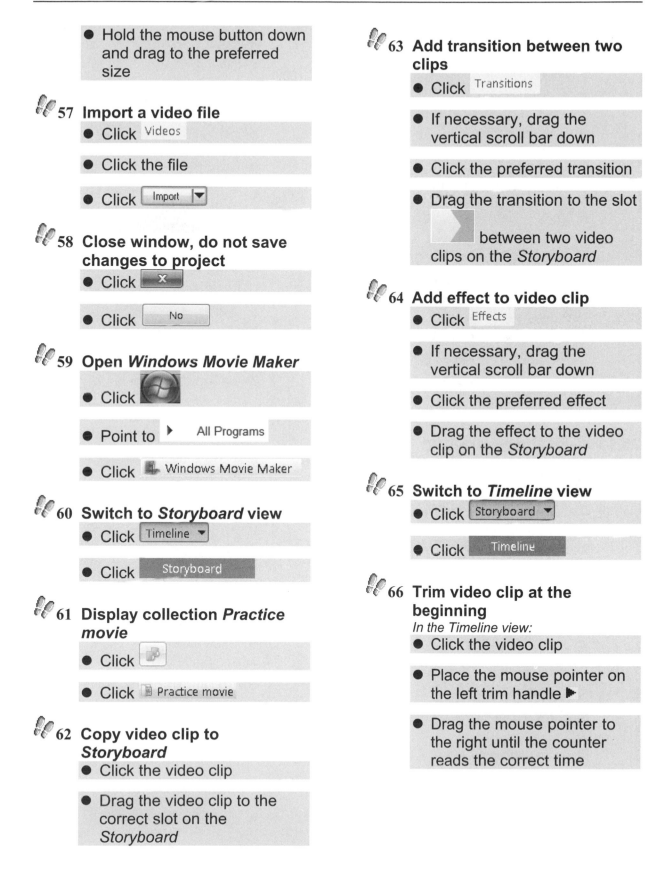

- Hold the mouse button down and drag to the preferred size

57 Import a video file
- Click Videos

- Click the file

- Click Import ▼

58 Close window, do not save changes to project
- Click X

- Click No

59 Open *Windows Movie Maker*
- Click

- Point to ▶ All Programs

- Click Windows Movie Maker

60 Switch to *Storyboard* view
- Click Timeline ▼

- Click Storyboard

61 Display collection *Practice movie*
- Click

- Click Practice movie

62 Copy video clip to *Storyboard*
- Click the video clip

- Drag the video clip to the correct slot on the *Storyboard*

63 Add transition between two clips
- Click Transitions

- If necessary, drag the vertical scroll bar down

- Click the preferred transition

- Drag the transition to the slot between two video clips on the *Storyboard*

64 Add effect to video clip
- Click Effects

- If necessary, drag the vertical scroll bar down

- Click the preferred effect

- Drag the effect to the video clip on the *Storyboard*

65 Switch to *Timeline* view
- Click Storyboard ▼

- Click Timeline

66 Trim video clip at the beginning
In the Timeline view:
- Click the video clip

- Place the mouse pointer on the left trim handle ▶

- Drag the mouse pointer to the right until the counter reads the correct time

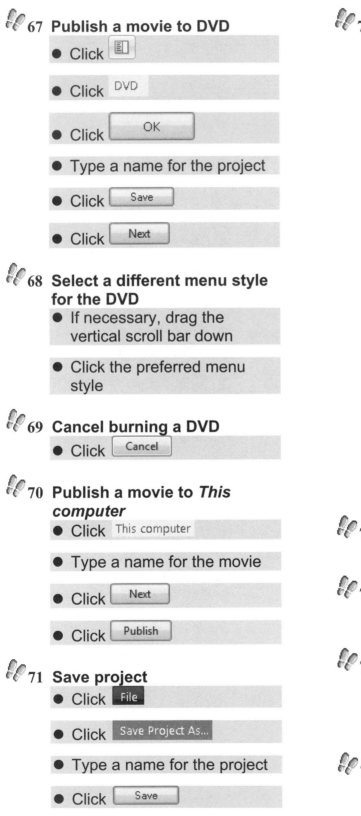

67 Publish a movie to DVD
- Click [⊞]
- Click DVD
- Click [OK]
- Type a name for the project
- Click [Save]
- Click [Next]

68 Select a different menu style for the DVD
- If necessary, drag the vertical scroll bar down
- Click the preferred menu style

69 Cancel burning a DVD
- Click [Cancel]

70 Publish a movie to *This computer*
- Click This computer
- Type a name for the movie
- Click [Next]
- Click [Publish]

71 Save project
- Click File
- Click Save Project As...
- Type a name for the project
- Click [Save]

72 Record narration
- Click [Tools]
- Click ✎ Narrate Timeline...
- Click Show options
- Drag the vertical scroll bar down
- Click to check mark
  ☑ Mute speakers
- Drag the vertical scroll bar up
- Click [Start Narration]
- Speak into the microphone while the movie is played
- Click [Stop Narration]
- Type a name for the audio file
- Click [Save]

73 Select photo
- Click the photo

74 Open *Edit Pane*
- Click [✉ Fix]

75 Undo all changes
- Click [▼] next to [↺ Undo]
- Click Undo All

76 Go back to *Gallery*
- Click [← Back To Gallery]

77 Select all images
- Click [File ▼]
- Click [Select All]

78 Open *Windows Photo Gallery*
- Click
- Click [▶   All Programs]
- Click [Windows Photo Gallery]

79 Display all images
In the Navigation Pane:
- Click [Pictures]

80 Group images by tag
- Click [ ] ▼
- Click [Group By]
- Click [Tag]

81 Add a tag to an image
- Click the image
- Drag the image to the preferred label in the *Navigation Pane*

82 Rate an image
- Click the image

In the Information Pane:
- Click the preferred star

83 Play slide show
- Click

84 Select a different theme for the slide show
- Click [Themes ▼]
- Click the preferred theme

85 Exit slide show
- Click [Exit]

86 Rotate a photo 45 degrees
- Click ↻ or ↺

87 Use *Auto Adjust*
- Click [Auto Adjust]

88 Adjust exposure
- Click [Belichting aanpassen]
- Drag the [Brightness] slider to the preferred location
- Drag the [Contrast] slider to the preferred location

89 Adjust color
- Click [Auto Adjust]
- Drag the [Color Temperature] slider to the preferred location
- Drag the [Tint] slider to the preferred location
- Drag the [Saturation] slider to the preferred location

90 Revert edited photo back to its original state
- Select the photo

- Click **Fix**

- Click **Revert**

- Click **Revert**

- Click **Back To Gallery**

91 Print photo
- Select the photo

- Click **Print ▾**

- Click **Print...**

- Select the preferred print size

- Select the correct number at Copies of each picture:

- Click **Print**

92 Compile video DVD
- Click **Burn ▾**

- Click **Video DVD...**

- Click **Next**

93 Select menu style for DVD
- Click the preferred menu style below

  Menu Styles ▾

94 Add music to the slide show
- Click **Slide show**
- Click **Add Music...**

- Double-click **Sample Music**

- Click the preferred track

- Click **Add ▾**

95 Adapt length of slide show to music
- Click to check mark
  ☑ Change slide show length to match music length

96 Apply changes to slide show
- Click **Change Slide Show**

97 Watch preview of video DVD
- Click **Preview**

- Click **Play**

- Click **OK**

98 Cancel burning video DVD, do not save the project
- Click **Cancel**

- Click **No**

99 Minimize a window
- Click **▢**

100 Open window from taskbar
- Click the taskbar button of the window, for example
  Windows Photo Gall...

101 Open *Media* menu
- Click in the top left corner

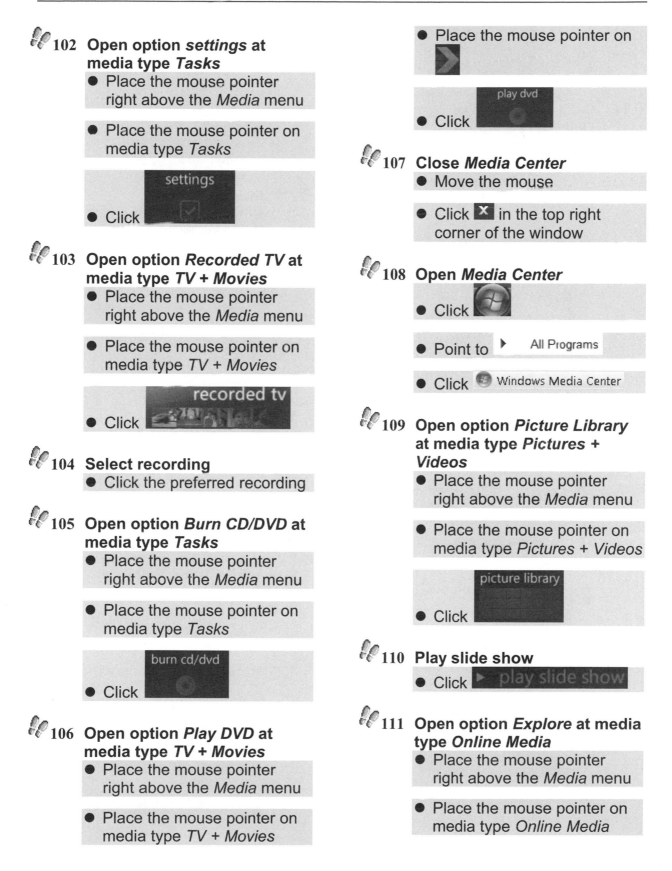

102 Open option *settings* at media type *Tasks*
- Place the mouse pointer right above the *Media* menu
- Place the mouse pointer on media type *Tasks*
- Click

103 Open option *Recorded TV* at media type *TV + Movies*
- Place the mouse pointer right above the *Media* menu
- Place the mouse pointer on media type *TV + Movies*
- Click

104 Select recording
- Click the preferred recording

105 Open option *Burn CD/DVD* at media type *Tasks*
- Place the mouse pointer right above the *Media* menu
- Place the mouse pointer on media type *Tasks*
- Click

106 Open option *Play DVD* at media type *TV + Movies*
- Place the mouse pointer right above the *Media* menu
- Place the mouse pointer on media type *TV + Movies*

- Place the mouse pointer on
- Click

107 Close *Media Center*
- Move the mouse
- Click ✖ in the top right corner of the window

108 Open *Media Center*
- Click
- Point to ▶ All Programs
- Click Windows Media Center

109 Open option *Picture Library* at media type *Pictures + Videos*
- Place the mouse pointer right above the *Media* menu
- Place the mouse pointer on media type *Pictures + Videos*
- Click

110 Play slide show
- Click ▶ play slide show

111 Open option *Explore* at media type *Online Media*
- Place the mouse pointer right above the *Media* menu
- Place the mouse pointer on media type *Online Media*

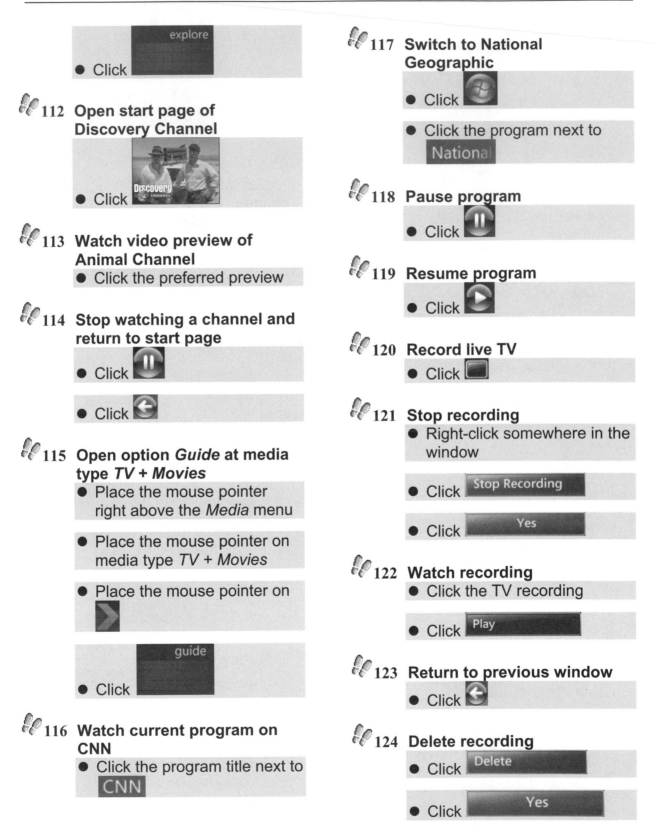

● Click **explore**

112 Open start page of Discovery Channel

● Click

113 Watch video preview of Animal Channel
● Click the preferred preview

114 Stop watching a channel and return to start page
● Click
● Click

115 Open option *Guide* at media type *TV + Movies*
● Place the mouse pointer right above the *Media* menu
● Place the mouse pointer on media type *TV + Movies*
● Place the mouse pointer on
● Click **guide**

116 Watch current program on CNN
● Click the program title next to **CNN**

117 Switch to National Geographic
● Click
● Click the program next to **National**

118 Pause program
● Click

119 Resume program
● Click

120 Record live TV
● Click

121 Stop recording
● Right-click somewhere in the window
● Click **Stop Recording**
● Click **Yes**

122 Watch recording
● Click the TV recording
● Click **Play**

123 Return to previous window
● Click

124 Delete recording
● Click **Delete**
● Click **Yes**

C. Index